EARLY AMERICAN CAR ADVERTISEMENTS

Selected by
Q. David Bowers

BONANZA BOOKS • **NEW YORK**

ACKNOWLEDGEMENTS AND CREDITS

Most of the material herein was taken from newspapers and magazines
of the 1900-1920 years.
Publications used include Motor World (the leading trade publication
at that time), Motordom, The Saturday Evening Post, Success Magazine,
Leslie's Weekly, Harper's, Munsey's Magazine and Popular Science as well
as catalogues and literature issued by the automobile manufacturers
themselves.
Special thanks go to Frank Chambers who furnished the author with
most of the source material from which this book was assembled.

— - - - - - - - - - - -

Other books by Q. David Bowers:

Coins and Collectors - The story of rare coin collecting in America
from the 1700's to the present day. Published 1964 by Windsor Re-
search Publications, Inc.

Put Another Nickel In - A comprehensive history of coin-operated
pianos and orchestrions (mechanical automatic orchestras). Published
1966 by The Vestal Press.

E A R L Y   A M E R I C A N   C A R   A D V E R T I S E M E N T S

selected by Q. David Bowers

Library of Congress Card Catalog number: 66-18277

Copyright © MCMLXVI by Q. David Bowers
Vestal, New York 13850

This edition published by Bonanza Books,
a division of Crown Publishers, Inc.,
by arrangement with the author
a   b   c   d   e   f   g   h

INTRODUCTION

From the turn of the century to the First World War the American automotive industry was in its formative stages. Unlike today, the marketplace was composed then of hundreds of small manufacturers and dozens of large ones. Today only a few of the old time names, Buick, Ford, Cadillac, Oldsmobile and Rambler for example, survive. Other once-familiar names such as Jordan, Pierce-Arrow, Cartercar and Apperson have long since disappeared from the American scene.

The years from 1910 to 1916 were especially active in the automobile industry. It was a transitional period of great historical importance. Many ideas were proposed. Some were accepted. Countless others never came to pass. Dr. Steinmetz, the great wizard of electricity, predicted that the electric car would become dominant, making the gasoline-powered car nothing more than a historical curiosity. In 1914 the Cadillac Company stated that it had no intention of marketing a six-cylinder car" and explained why four cylinders were the ideal number. The quaint Reeves Sextoauto had four rear wheels for better riding comfort, an innovation which was "bound to revolutionize automobile construction where comfort in riding is a consideration" the ad said.

In 1914 a Saxon car costing $395 traveled all the way from New York to San Francisco in just thirty days - a remarkable accomplishment. Firestone advertised that a motorist in Illinois went 3000 miles on his Firestone tires without any trouble. The elegant Moon car noted that it was "as carefully finished as a fine old grandfather's clock." The problem of punctures was solved by one manufacturer by making tires of solid rubber.

On the pages to follow the early cars tell their own stories. The advertisements and catalogue illustrations I selected emphasize the 1910-1916 years. The advertisements were selected for their historical interest and variety. The products of over two hundred different car, truck and accessory makers are represented. I hope that you'll enjoy looking through these nostalgic reminders of automobiling yesteryear as much as I did when I assembled the book.

--- Q. David Bowers

EASY FINDING LIST

This Easy Finding List will enable you to locate quickly any of the various products whose original advertisements are reproduced in this book.

GASOLINE AND ELECTRIC CARS; TRUCKS; CYCLES

COMPONENTS AND ACCESSORIES—MISC.

Four-Thirty—

Four cylinders; 32.4 H.P.; five passenger, fore-door body, with top, side curtains and slip cover, gas lamps and tank, windshield and speedometer - - **$2250.**

Same chassis, with open five passenger touring body; four passenger detachable tonneau; or three passenger runabout—$2000.

The question:—

Why did I buy an Apperson Jack Rabbit?

The answer:—

Direct result of an interview with an Apperson owner

THE INTERVIEW:

Pardon me, sir, but what car is that you are driving?

Apperson Jack Rabbit.

How long have you had it?

Just got it. Brand new 1911 model. Pretty car, isn't it? And it's the second Apperson for me.

How long did you drive its predecessor?

Let me see. Got it in the spring of 1905. Let it go last fall—neighbor of mine is driving it now—that's about five and one-half years, isn't it?

Cost you much for repairs?

No—had it overhauled and repainted in 1908 and it's O.K. now.

How far did you drive it?

Well, I didn't get a speedometer until about the middle of the first season, but the speedometer record up to the time I sold the car was 83,479 miles. I figure I drove that car fully 85,000 miles.

Gracious! That's more than three times around the world.

Yep! That's so, but it was a very powerful and strongly built car. I drove it summer and winter and it's good for another world circle and then some more besides. Ever hear of the Apperson brothers and the Apperson

factory? No? Well, I imagine you think of buying a car, and if so you should get acquainted with the Appersons and see their factory. You see, I used to drive a foreign car; fact is I bought it abroad and I've been in practically all of the best automobile plants in Europe, and this car—this Apperson Jack Rabbit—built right down here in Indiana at Kokomo by the Apperson brothers, comes from a factory that equals any I ever saw.

The Appersons are both mechanics—both expert automobile mechanics, and you will find them right in their factory personally superintending the work and testing and trying out every car. They know each car is right when it leaves their plant, and fit for the service which they likewise know it will be required to render to give its exacting owner absolute satisfaction.

The Appersons don't turn out a lot of cars each year, but every car that leaves their plant is a real car, built for long wear and hard work. Like all cars they get the hard work, but unlike many cars they stand up under it; and I have often said to my friends, "All I ever do to my car is to give her plenty of good oil, what gasoline she needs and she will go as far as I want her to go and a good deal faster than I ought to expect her to."

They must have a splendid factory.

Yes, and the finest lot of mechanics I have ever seen working together, many of them having been in the constant

employ of the Apperson brothers since they built their first car—which, by the way, was the first automobile, or horseless carriage, as it was then called, that was built in the United States. Speaking of that first car, I must tell you what Mr. Elmer Apperson, President of the Company, told me one day. Said he, "The general style of the first car was not greatly unlike the wonderful one hoss shay, and when we got it so that it would run we sent out of town to a carriage manufacturer and purchased the body for it—just a regular carriage or buggy body. When it came we were all much amused to discover that it was equipped with the usual whip socket." So you see that the first car equipment was simply a top and whip socket. Some different from this car, eh!

Are Apperson cars high-priced?

No. They build three models—one at $2,000, one at $3,000 and one at $4,200. You can't afford to risk a car at a lower price, and it's absolutely unnecessary to pay more. They will outlast, outrun and outlook half a dozen ordinary cars, and beautifully hold their own with the most expensive cars built.

Are Apperson cars what are called assembled cars?

Oh! No! The Appersons build everything that goes into their cars. They have separate departments for making all of

the important parts, each department under the supervision of a special foreman, and all parts passed upon by a special inspector, and in these various departments they build their own motors, transmissions, steering gears, axles, wheels, radiators, hoods and fenders and bodies; do their own upholstering and painting—really a lot of small factories all under one great head and all under the direction of the Apperson Brothers.

That all sounds fine to me. Does the car ride well?

Hop in and I'll give you a little ride. I'm as proud of the car as if I built it myself. Look it over—see that upholstering? The finest of leather. See how smoothly the motor runs? Notice how the springs eased us over that rough crossing? Just like sailing or flying, isn't it?

I wish to thank you for your kindness. You have certainly done me a great favor, as I must confess that the matter of selecting a car for my own use was very perplexing. I shall see an Apperson Jack Rabbit dealer at once and I shall soon be driving a car like yours.

Any Apperson agent or branch manager will tell you that nearly all of his sales can be traced back to enthusiastic Apperson owners who never miss an opportunity to advise friend or stranger to buy an Apperson Jack Rabbit car, and to tell them why they should do so.

APPERSON BROTHERS AUTOMOBILE CO.,   Dept. P,   KOKOMO, INDIANA

1911 Apperson Jack Rabbit ad featuring an owner "interview." Although not specifically billed as such this car was considered to be a sports car in its day.

From Any Point Of View

Model B, Five Passenger Touring Car, Standard
Equipment, $1500 F. O. B. Detroit.
Roadster, Standard Equipment, $1500 F. O. B. Detroit.
Fore-Door Demi-Tonneau (tonneau detachable), Standard
Equipment, $1650 F. O. B. Detroit.
Coupé, Standard Equipment, $2350 F. O. B. Detroit.

Abbott-Detroit

IS the most thoroughly developed automobile **value** of this season. It is the only medium-priced car that many people think costs $4000.

Up to this time we have not advertised this car extensively. We are advertising it broadcast **now** because we have spent two years in development. We have something to say that is not just the frame-up of an advertising shop.

First, last and all the time, the Abbott-Detroit is the only car selling at or anywhere near $1500 that has reached a perfect stage of standardization. By this we mean to say that, taking all that has been accomplished in motordom since the first automobile stood up, the Abbott-Detroit embodies, in every detail, the best that has been done. It is a composite revelation of perfections. Such mechanical excellence, such faithfulness to reproduce all the Blue Ribbon ideas cannot be found in any other car at this price.

Many features of the Abbott-Detroit are achievements of magnitude in themselves. Many of the fine points represent the best work of lifetimes, which were specialized on these details. The Abbott-Detroit looks like a $4000 car, runs like a $4000 car, endures like a $4000 car, can be bought for $1500.

The Abbott-Detroit has an enviable record. The significance of its victories in national and international speed and endurance events should not be lost to you. Run down the list hereon of a number of these successes.

In many respects the Abbott-Detroit has features like those in cars of a great deal higher price.

Abbott-Detroit painting and trimming specifications are parallel to those of any $4000 car on the market.

The Abbott-Detroit has Chrome Nickel Steel Construction in the transmission and rear axle with imported F. & S. Annular Bearings and Timken Roller Bearings.

The Abbott-Detroit has a complete electric light equipment of two electric head lights and combination electric and oil side and rear lamps and Bosch High Tension or Splitdorf dual ignition system.

From any point of view—coming or going—Abbott-Detroit 1911 is the strategic car. The car eminently feasible for your needs and economy. It's the car that will bring you home. Write for thoroughly descriptive literature. Let us help you to consider this car in your own home and let us give you an introduction to your local dealer so that you can see the Abbott-Detroit on exhibition.

Up-to-the-Minute Dealers Share Advantages. Certain territories are still open. If you want your district let us hear from you. If you had a car made to order to sell to your customers you'd make it as near like this one as you could. Write now.

Abbott Motor Co. 117 WATERLOO STREET Detroit, Mich.

1911 DISTRIBUTORS—Craig Auto Co., 465 Woodward Ave., Detroit, Mich.; M. M. Levy & Co., 2410 Strand, Galveston, Texas; H. J. Lindesmith & Co., Lima, Ohio; Royal Automobile Co., 517 Second Ave., Minneapolis, Minn.; Snyder Auto Co., 763 E. Long St., Columbus, Ohio; Whitten Motor Vehicle Co., 200 Meeting St., Providence, R. I.; Sullivan Auto Co., S. Charleston, Ohio; George L. Reiss, 1776 Broadway, New York City; J. H. Wright, 38 Market St., Auburn, N. Y.; D. A. Michael, Daytona, Fla.; Burdick & Hartwell, 231 River St., Troy, N. Y.; A. D. Motor Co. of New England, 9 Harcourt St., Boston, Mass.; J. S. Eby, W. Liberty, Iowa; Bison Motor Co., Main and Market Sts., Buffalo, N. Y.; T. J. Northway, 92 Exchange St., Rochester, N. Y.; A. D. Motor Co. of Pa., 211 N. Broad St., Philadelphia, Pa.; Centaur Motor Company, 1725 Michigan Ave., Chicago, Ill.; Van Vliet Fletcher Auto Co., Tenth and Walnut Sts., Des Moines, Iowa; John Deere Plow Co., Dallas, Texas; E. C. Thompson, Warren, Pa.; Jones Auto Exchange, Wichita, Kansas; Abbott-Detroit Motor Co., Los Angeles, Cal.

Rear view of
same car as above

ABBOTT-DETROIT VICTORIES
Prove Its Supremacy

An Abbott-Detroit never entered a contest until the last Vanderbilt Cup races. Since then the Abbott-Detroit has won a place in every contest entered.

Here's a very recent five weeks' record. No car in the world has made such a phenomenal showing in so short a space of time.

Until a few days before the Vanderbilt Cup Races—Massapequa Sweepstakes—the Abbott Motor Company had no idea of entering their cars in any contests. On the spur of the moment, the Abbott-Detroit was sent into the Vanderbilt Cup Races, winning second honors, maintaining an average speed of 53.1 miles per hour.

At the Fairmount Park Races, at Philadelphia, Abbott-Detroit car won first honors; in fact, was the only car in its class, running at the closing of the race. *The distance was run in record-breaking time without stops, tire trouble, ignition trouble, or any other mechanical trouble.*

In the recent Minneapolis Tribune Endurance Run of 1200 miles, an Abbott-Detroit secured a perfect score and shortly afterwards was driven through to Dallas, Texas, a distance of some 2500 miles. It is now on its way back to Detroit.

Another Abbott-Detroit stock car, "The Bull Dog," started from Denver, Colorado, and is making a 100,000-mile trip. By the time it reaches Detroit, it will have covered about 15,000 miles of its scheduled distance.

The Abbott-Detroit "Yellow Wasp," entered in the Desert Run from Los Angeles to Phoenix, made a trial trip over the course, which is over 400 miles long, in thirty-eight hours.

At the Atlanta Races of November 3, 4, and 5, the Abbott-Detroit established the official one-mile record of 55 6-10 seconds and broke the distance record for one hour by 3½ miles, and took second and third in the 10-mile stock chassis event for cars having 161 to 230 cubic inches piston displacement.

At the San Antonio, Tex., Races, November 10, the Abbott-Detroit "Blue Streak" was first in the 12-mile race; time 12.45, with the Abbott-Detroit "White Ghost" third. The Abbott-Detroit "Blue Streak" won the 9-mile race in 9.36 with the Abbott-Detroit "White Ghost" third. The "Blue Streak" won the one mile in 1.02, excellent time. This was a distinct clean-up for the day considering that all contests were "free for all" including cars from 30 to 50 H. P.

The Abbott-Detroit "looks like a $4000 car, runs like a $4000 car, endures like a $4000 car, can be bought for $1500," Note also the listing of racing triumphs.

14

A few interesting early ads from the 1909-1912 era. The Auto-Bug Runabout ad appeared in 1909. This vehicle was typical of many such machines, usually priced at less than $500.00, which were half automobile and half buggy.

THE BUICK CREED

A BUICK automobile must be so built that it will, at all times and under all circumstances, give the owner uninterrupted use of his investment. Every BUICK owner is entitled to, and will receive, prompt and efficient service, the kind that will insure him the motoring pleasure he expects.

BUICK reputation, so pre-eminently firm and fair, was not won by chance, but is due to the policy established with the production of the first BUICK car and so consistently adhered to ever since, that of giving the owner the maximum of service for the minimum of cost.

No matter what its price, a BUICK car must, and will, give the maximum of that service for which it was intended, and must bear its proportion of the responsibility of maintaining that high prestige which BUICK cars have attained.

The true significance of the slogan, "When Better Automobiles Are Built, BUICK Will Build Them," is manifested to its fullest possible extent in the 1914 line described in this book.

The Buick for Nineteen Fourteen

A Series of Six Models Embracing Both Four and Six Cylinder Types

BUICK motor cars for 1914 are still being built around the famous Overhead Valve Motor; differing somewhat in appearance from the handsome models of 1913, but identical in performance with the Buicks of the past. Changes have been few—but refinements have been made and details added for greater beauty and convenience, including the handier left-side drive and the simpler center control. But the fundamentals of Buick construction are unchanged—unchangeable. In addition—the Delco System of electric self-cranking and lighting is built into every motor as an integral part and is included without additional cost. A year ago, when untried, unproved self-starters were being bolted onto many an excellent car in any available place—a source of bitter disappointment in thousands of cases—the Buick management took a firm stand. It announced that no self-starter would be incorporated in any Buick car until a starter had been found as good as the Buick car itself. Such a starter is the Delco, and the Delco installation in the Buick is something you may rely upon as a fulfillment of the Buick ideals, which means "uninterrupted use of his investment" to every Buick owner.

All this at a cost which makes the self-starting, automatically-lighted Buick of 1914 the greatest motor car value offered this season. There is a reason for this super-value: Buick cars are built complete in the Buick plant, in such numbers that literally hundreds of economies are effected in the necessary operations of casting, forging, machining, testing, assembling, etc.; and when completed, Buick cars are trustworthy and reliable, for every operation is Buick's own and nothing is left to chance or outsiders.

The factory savings and service savings affected by this gigantic organization and the experience gathered from the 150,000 Buicks that have made good, render it possible today for the Buick Motor Company to offer for 1914 a line that challenges comparison. It has paid to build better cars.

The 1914 Models

This season's models of the Buick have been confined to three chassis and six styles of bodies, embracing both four and six cylinder types and are known as Models B24, B25, B36, B37, B38, B55. Each of these six styles is specifically described, and illustrated, on the following pages.

Models B24 and B25

Two favorite models, the most popular cars of their class ever produced—familiar sights on every thoroughfare in the world. They are unchanged in the essentials—refined here and there—housing the wonderful motor that has been the backbone of Buick success. The Roadster (B24) is the busy man's car par excellence; handsome in design, amply powered, easy riding, roomy. The touring car (B25) is, of its economical class, the ideal family vehicle—capacious, well upholstered, graceful in line and with a notable excellence of equipment and trimming.

In both B24 and B25 the Delco System of lighting, starting and ignition is installed, at no additional cost, for it is part of their regular equipment.

Models B36, B37 and B38

One word sums up the predominating merit of these three models. They are the cars for work, work and more work—anywhere, any time. Their predecessors were famous, yet these will even surpass that former record. More miles at less cost is guaranteed by the construction of these models.

The Roadster (B36) is generally accredited with being one of the most exquisite designs ever produced. In addition to the general excellencies of a car of this type in leg-room, speed and fuel capacity, it carries a wealth of special refinements and appointments.

The Touring Car (B37) is notable for the beauty of the lines of its body—handsome back, gracefully curved cowl, wide seats and full fenders. Every detail that stands for utility as well as beauty makes it surely "Buick's Best Buy," as it has often been called.

The Coupe (B38) is built on the same chassis. It affords like power with the luxury and weather proofness of the coupe body. Extraordinary pains have been taken in the design of this model. Every detail is complete—nothing is left to desire in any respect.

The New Buick Six—Model B55

The Buick Six is new in its design, but old in the experience of its makers. Throughout, it is founded upon the principles of sound construction that ten years have proved of unalterable worth.

It fulfills all that six-cylinder construction promises; it combines the valuable qualities of other cars of this type—while affording, in its Overhead valve motor, a feature that distinguishes it from any other Six whatsoever.

This Buick motor gives a compactness of design, a surplus of power and an economy of operation that make the Buick Six, in a way, revolutionary in six-cylinder construction.

The Buick Six Touring Car is a finished automobile, the sign and symbol of an owner of individuality. In body construction it is exceptional without being eccentric, combining comfortable equipment, extra deep cushions, wide seats, liberal tonneau space, ample leg-room, convenient driving position, long wheel base, noiseless operation—in fact, everything necessary to the complete equipment of an up-to-the-minute six-cylinder car.

NINETEEN FOURTEEN BUICK, MODEL B 24

The Story of the Overhead Valve Motor

Its Power Producing Superiority and its Marked Fuel Economy

THE motor is the most intricate and expensive single factor in the construction of an automobile, representing in round numbers one-quarter of the cost of the finished product. With an electric self-starter built in, it represents even more. So much for money-worth. In point of service possibilities and general satisfaction, the motor represents more nearly 75% of any automobile's value.

Intensely significant, therefore, is this big feature of Buick construction—the Overhead valve motor. Such an engine, not by theory but by the actual proof of over 150,000 Buicks now in use, develops from 15 to 20 per cent. more power than engines of any other type, of similar bore and stroke. The importance of this fact is worthy of a more detailed description.

An internal combustion motor operates by the conversion of a gas into energy through the medium of combustion. Unless every possible heat unit afforded by the act of combustion be conserved, the power stroke will suffer in direct ratio. Every possible chance for heat leakage must therefore be eliminated, if full power is to be obtained from a gas motor. A theoretically perfect engine would be one in which an extremely high temperature could be maintained in the metal cylinders. It is not practicable, however, to operate any mechanical device, especially a motor cylinder, when its surface is superheated; consequently some cooling device must be provided. In the case of an automobile motor, this is generally done by surrounding the cylinder walls with a hollow casing or jacket filled with water, which is kept in circulation and cools the cylinder walls uniformly. Yet in such cooling, many of the heat units are necessarily destroyed and wasted. The smaller the surface of cylinder walls which must be so cooled, the nearer a motor approaches the ideal.

The amount of cylinder surface in the three types of motor now in common use may be roughly shown by comparing them to the letter T, an inverted L and an I. The first is called the T head, the second the L Type and the third the Overhead or Valve-in-the-Head motor. In the last-mentioned type the cylinders have no arms or pockets; consequently they present the least surface to the cooling agent and lose, therefore, fewer heat units. On the other hand, in the "T" or "L" types, where side pockets are cast on the cylinders for inserting the inlet and exhaust valves, the combustion chamber is enlarged by the exact amount of extra surface in these pockets; and these surfaces must be as perfectly water-jacketed as the remainder of the cylinder wall. The result is a greater amount

Illustrations from the 1914 Buick catalogue appear on these facing pages. A wide assortment of models was offered.

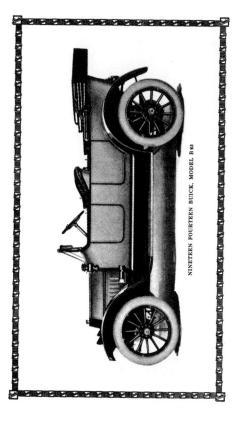

NINETEEN FOURTEEN BUICK, MODEL B 25

of cooling surface, which is continually giving up many heat units wastefully. The straight cylinder of the Overhead type avoids this, and consequently in the same size cylinder is able to develop greater power.

Apart from its saving of heat units, the Overhead valve type of motor has other superiorities. All motors must depend for their power upon the expansion of the compressed gas in the cylinders. This expansion is obtained by the firing or the burning of the gas under compression, and the rapidity with which this operation is performed and the greater its completeness, the more powerful will be the pressure developed against the head of the piston. It is this pressure of the exploding gas against the piston head that produces all the power of automobile motors.

A quick and complete explosion is therefore of prime importance. One of the first essentials to this is that all points in the combustion chamber be brought as nearly as possible to the point at which the flame is passed into the compressed gas; in other words, as nearly as possible to the points of the spark plug. This can be done only in a cylinder of the Buick type of construction. As a matter of fact, the distance from the points of the spark plug to the farthest point in the combustion chamber in the Buick motor is less than one-half that found in a "T" head motor of equal size; and some of the manufacturers of the latter type have even been forced to use two spark plugs, one at each end of the combustion chamber, in order to secure the same results Buick obtains with its Overhead and single plug. The disadvantages of doubling the number of spark plugs are too obvious to need further mention. In the "L" type, as ordinarily constructed, the spread

MANIFOLD SIDE VIEW OF A BUICK MOTOR

NINETEEN FOURTEEN BUICK, MODEL B 36

---

of flame must pass through the gas from the sparking points across the cylinder and around into the side pocket over the exhaust valve. This is necessarily a slower process of combustion, and there is a corresponding loss of power.

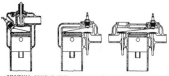

SHOWING COMPARATIVE DISTANCE FROM SPARK PLUG TO FURTHEST POINT IN CYLINDER

Therefore, as the gas expansion depends upon the rapidity of flame propagation, or, as commonly called, the explosion, it can be seen that the Overhead valve motor possesses an important advantage over both other types.

There are also additional advantages. Not only does the explosion in an Overhead valve motor prove more positive, but it cleans or scavenges the cylinders of burned gas more completely on the exhaust stroke of the piston. This is due to the fact that the exhaust stroke forces the burned gas straight out through the exhaust valve at the top of the cylinder, and not from the cylinder through a pocket and thence out. In the pocket type a certain part of the old gas remains after the exhaust valve closes. The dead gas that stays in the pocket of the motor cylinder is thus mixed with the fresh gas introduced through the inlet valve on the next charge, reducing it in amount and causing deterioration in quality. No such condition is possible with the Overhead valve. The fresh charge finds a perfectly clean cylinder. It fills it to the fullest capacity with clean gas, and this naturally produces a greater expansion and a correspondingly greater piston pressure when fired.

The absence of pockets or chambers in the straight walled cylinders of the Overhead type makes possible more accurate machining in their manufacture and insures a more symmetrical chamber for combustion. As this chamber is merely the upper part of the cylinder, it allows this full machining, whereas the pockets on other types, from the very nature of their construction, cannot possibly be reached with any tool, and therefore cannot be machined or smoothed out. From necessity there must be certain places in these pockets where there are small irregularities and where the wall is rough.

NINETEEN FOURTEEN BUICK, MODEL B 37

The smoother the surface, the less is the tendency to carbonization. It naturally follows that these rough places provide a greater opportunity for pre-ignition, due to the overheating of deposits or projections, especially when the motor is under heavy duty, or where full throttle or high speed is required.

The fully machined, smooth, straight cylinder of the Overhead assures an absolutely consistent motor, as all cylinder surfaces are exactly alike, and each cylinder will handle its charge in exactly the same way, under all driving conditions. No irregularity or roughness can exist in any part of it.

The conclusion that must therefore be reached, after a careful study of the shape of the combustion chambers of the three types of motors, is that the Overhead is the most reliable and most powerful motor, granting, of course, that the elements of carburetion and ignition are equal.

The purer the charge the more quickly it burns, as we have already seen. This explains the fuel economy of the Buick motor and its ability to handle a lower grade of fuel. If a charge of inferior fuel is drawn into a cylinder and there mixed with a quantity of already burned gas, it is thereby reduced in burning value until its power-developing possibilities are greatly impaired. This is especially true if the combustion is rendered slower because of the irregular or pocket construction in the cylinder walls, as is the case in the "T" Head or "L" type motor. But if the charge, though of inferior grade, be quickly fired and the dead gas be completely exhausted

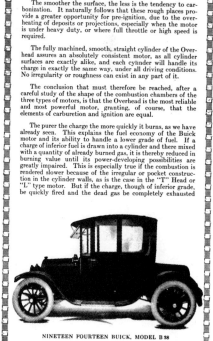

NINETEEN FOURTEEN BUICK, MODEL B 38

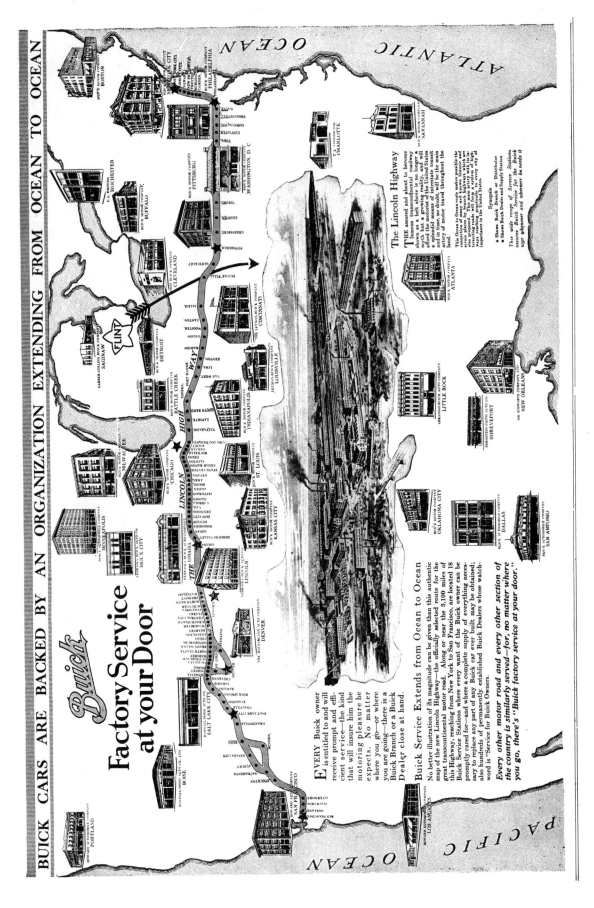

In its day the Lincoln Highway, extending from the Atlantic to the Pacific, was a sensation. One could buy plaques and pennants commemorating it. "The Lincoln Highway March" was composed to honor it. The above map showed the many Buick dealers located along this famous route. - From 1914 Buick sales literature.

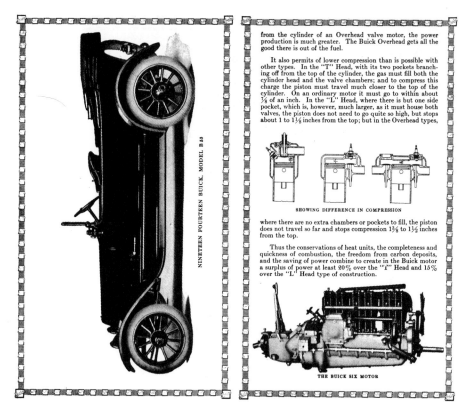

IGNITION SIDE VIEW OF A BUICK MOTOR

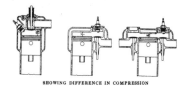

SHOWING DIFFERENCE IN COMPRESSION

THE BUICK SIX MOTOR

NINETEEN FOURTEEN BUICK, MODEL B.55

from the cylinder of an Overhead valve motor, the power production is much greater. The Buick Overhead gets all the good there is out of the fuel.

It also permits of lower compression than is possible with other types. In the "T" Head, with its two pockets branching off from the top of the cylinder, the gas must fill both the cylinder head and the valve chambers; and to compress this charge the piston must travel much closer to the top of the cylinder. On an ordinary motor it must go to within about $\frac{7}{8}$ of an inch. In the "L" Head, where there is but one side pocket, which is, however, much larger, as it must house both valves, the piston does not need to go quite so high, but stops about 1 to $1\frac{1}{8}$ inches from the top; but in the Overhead types, where there are no extra chambers or pockets to fill, the piston does not travel so far and stops compression $1\frac{3}{8}$ to $1\frac{1}{2}$ inches from the top.

Thus the conservations of heat units, the completeness and quickness of combustion, the freedom from carbon deposits, and the saving of power combine to create in the Buick motor a surplus of power at least 20% over the "T" Head and 15% over the "L" Head type of construction.

The Buick is a clean motor, and a clean motor is long-lived and extra efficient.

Cylinders are kept lubricated by oil which is splashed against the pistons and distributed by them along the walls. Some of this oil works its way past the piston rings and up into the combustion chamber at the top. This surplus is thrown out through the exhaust valve along with the burned gases. If it passes out as vapor, no harm is done and no opportunity to carbonize is given. But if the oil without vaporizing reaches hot surfaces, like the valve heads, the volatile parts are quickly thrown off leaving deposit or carbon. But Buick valves, being located in the top or head of the cylinders, are farthest from the piston and equidistant from the side walls. It is hard for oil to reach them. Herein they differ from the other types, which are set low in the combustion chambers, practically on a level with the top of the piston when at upper center, and wherein any surplus oil is thus easily thrown into the pockets and over onto the valves.

Furthermore, the arrangement of valves on the Buick permits a longer duration of opening on the intake. This insures a charge of clean gas to the fullest capacity. In the smooth, pocketless combustion chamber, this gas burns rapidly and delivers a full power stroke, after which the burned gases are quickly and completely discharged through an unobstructed exhaust. It is a cycle of conservation.

These are the reasons why the Buick motor, the backbone of the Buick success, gives the owner not alone "uninterrupted use of his investment" but the "maximum of service for the minimum of cost."

Three more pages from the 1914 Buick catalogue.

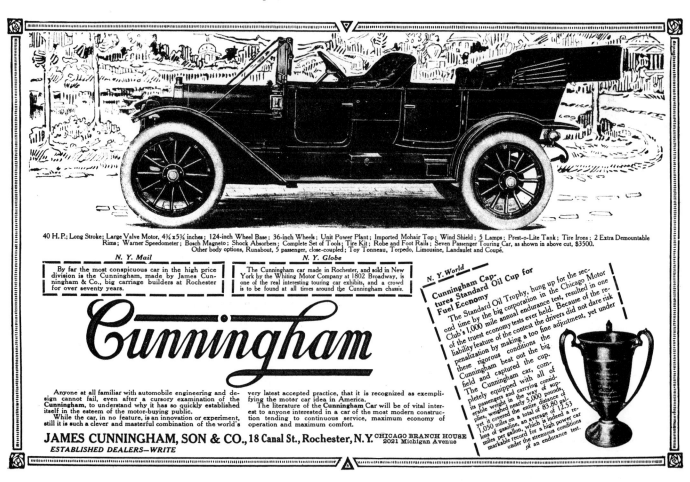
The Cunningham averaged 12.53 miles per gallon in the Chicago Motor Club's 1000 mile run and won the Standard Oil Trophy.

"On Behalf of My Associates and Myself I Want to Thank The Many Dealers—Old Friends and New—For Their Reception of Our Car and Our Company"—*Benj. Briscoe*

THE wonderful sales record of our car at the New York, Chicago and other shows, we believe, has never been surpassed in the history of the industry.

This surely indicates that the dealers have confidence in our product and in our company, and makes us happy indeed.

I want to thank the many dealers, old friends and new, on behalf of my associates and on my own account, for the splendid and spontaneous reception given to our car and to our company.

The very large demand for our car has caused us to make arrangements with our Manufacturing Department for an increased output, so that we will be able to execute contracts, based upon a larger production than we at first contemplated.

Inquiries from dealers in small cities and towns are especially welcome. We desire to deal direct with dealers wherever it is possible. We have one contract—the same for all.

I am very glad to be able to say that our manufacturing preparations are progressing most satisfactorily. We expect to begin

SHIPMENTS IN APRIL

We are "tooling up" in the best possible manner and our efforts are concerned only in such methods as will accomplish a uniformity in parts and the highest quality of workmanship. Chrome Vanadium steel is used practically throughout the car and all other parts are likewise of the highest quality.

Our rule of conduct—"Quality First, Last and All the Time"—is the guiding principle with us.

One of the *best* and *most gratifying* things connected with our reception by the industry, was the almost unanimous expression of good will on the part of the *older* automobile companies. Many of them are now regularly referring their dealers, who are seeking a smaller car, to ours as being *the* high grade medium sized car, and so a *fit* running mate for their higher priced, high grade productions.

WE ARE SATISFIED WITH SMALL PROFIT

We heard at the shows, the remark made many times—"You cannot do it at the price." We acknowledge that we are giving wonderful value, but we are satisfied with small profit. There are only five of us in this company, all active automobile men, and we are not desirous of getting rich too rapidly.

Our risks are negligible, because the car has been thoroughly developed and tested out, and we believe that this year's production of from five to seven thousand cars will surely mean a demand for from ten to fifteen thousand next.

The Briscoe car is *honestly* made and *thoroughly* good. Its appearance speaks for itself. Its action will be conclusive evidence of its goodness. Our customers will be our best salesmen.

Benj. Briscoe
President.

THE BRISCOE CAR

$750 $750

The New $750 Briscoe Car Designed by American Engineers; and "tailored" by Paris Artisans of Style Creation. Equipment: Electric lamps, horn, accumulator, demountable rims and tool equipment—$750. With above and electric lighting generator and electric self-starter, top and boot, windshield—$900.

BRISCOE MOTOR COMPANY
General Offices, Broadway and 59th Street, New York
Factories at Jackson, Michigan

The Briscoe appealed to the economy-minded car buyer. There were dozens of similar makes, mostly priced in the $500 to $1000 range on the market.

They Can't Convince Each Other On Technical Points and Argument Always Ends In Disagreement

But the <u>user</u> is the court of last resort and he <u>knows</u> that a car equipped with an Electric Starting and Lighting System <u>actually uses less gasoline</u> than one without.

Mr. Sidney Smith, of the Sheffield Simplex Motor Works, England, in the Automobile of December 25th, 1913, says the car driver secures an <u>extra two miles</u> per gallon of gasoline from the use of <u>electric starting and lighting</u>.

Add to the actual <u>saving</u>, the <u>efficiency, convenience</u> and <u>luxury</u> derived from electrical equipment and the arguments of the adherents to <u>old-fashioned</u> ideas fall to the ground.

STORAGE BATTERIES

have made possible the success of electric lighting and starting.

Ask ten of your friends what battery they use—eight of them (80%) will answer "the **LBA**"—that's the usual percentage.

LBA **WILLARD STORAGE BATTERY CO.,** **LBA**

New York Branch: 136 W. 52nd St.   **Cleveland, Ohio**   Detroit Branch: 736-740 Woodward Ave.
Chicago Branch: 2241 Michigan Ave.   San Francisco Branch: 243 Monadnock Bldg.
Indianapolis Branch: 438 and 439 Indiana Pythian Bldg.

SERVICE STATIONS IN ALL PRINCIPAL CITIES IN THE UNITED STATES, CANADA AND MEXICO

(93)

1914 Willard Storage Battery Company advertisement.

The Prospect's Timidity About the Dollar

Say "Fourteen Fifty," Not "Fourteen Hundred and Fifty Dollars," Advises Reilly—His Reasons Why.

By Ray W. Sherman

"Say! What about that Dr. Hayes car?"

Charley turned from the telephone on his desk, walked out to where Reilly was taking a morning saunter of exercise and inspection about the salesroom floor and shot the question at him.

"Whaddyuh mean, what about it?"

"SAY ONE THOUSAND, FOUR HUNDRED AND FIFTY DOLLARS, AND IT SOUNDS BIG. BUT SAY FOURTEEN FIFTY AND IT LOSES MUCH OF ITS BIGNESS"

"Is it all right to sell? What do we want for it? Is it in good condition?"

"Yes. Why?"

"I've got Dr. Morton on the 'phone and I think he may buy it. He's after a good used runabout."

Tommy Listens—Then Figures.

"Tell him it hasn't been overhauled and we'll sell it just as it stands for six hundred. Tell him it's been run about fifty-five days and is in good condition. Hayes turned it in to get a bigger car."

Charley, who was second man in Reilly's establishment, returned to the telephone. Tommy Trumbull, who was third—and last—man in the establishment, was busy at his desk laying out a day's work for himself.

Tommy never passed up a chance to listen to what was going on anywhere,

and he couldn't help hearing Charley's end of the conversation with the doctor-prospect on the other end of the telephone. While Charley talked, Tommy did a little figuring, which was thus:

"Fifty-five days. Seven's in fifty-five, in fifty-six—let's see—eight times. Eight weeks—two months. Car's been run about two months. What the ——'s he talking about? Fifty-five days?"

Charley led the doctor along, and when he hung up it was with the doctor's promise that he would drop in that afternoon to look at the car.

"What are you going to do? Change the calendar? Fifty-five days! What's the difference between fifty-five days and two months? You talk like a Dutchman; saying eight days and fourteen days and twenty-one days and such stuff!"

Making Two Months Into One.

"I don't know; maybe you'd better ask the boss. He said—— There he is now——" Reilly walked into the office. "Ask him yourself."

"What now?" smiled Reilly.

"Oh, nothing much," said Charley, with an answering smile, "except that Tommy

wants to know the difference between fifty-five days and two months."

"Yes; what is it?" demanded the youngest of the trio.

"About three or four weeks," replied Reilly, who nonchalantly turned to the mail that Nellie the typewriter chauffeur had put on his desk. Reilly indicated that the answer was sufficient and understandable and became very busy. Tommy puzzled a minute. He always had to think a minute to make sure he wasn't being kidded by his two older companions in the sale of Sennett cars.

The Effect Is Psychological.

"Three or four weeks!" he finally exclaimed.

"About that." Reilly kept on reading letters.

"I know I was poor in arithmetic when I went to school, but that's too deep for me. Must figure it out by logarithms, don't you?"

"It can't be figured. It's like the business depression that President Wilson talks about. He says it's psychological, you know."

"Yes?"

Reilly swung around in his chair. "Why do department stores mark their goods at ninety-eight cents, a dollar ninety-eight or two ninety-eight, instead of one dollar, two dollars or three dollars?"

Imitates the Department Store.

"Why," explained Tommy, "it sounds smaller."

"Well, there's your answer," replied Reilly. "It sounds smaller. The fifty-five days sounds, I should say, about half as much as it is."

"More of that funny stuff!"

"Not funny stuff at all!" retorted Reilly. "It's business! If the department store gets my money—or my wife's, which is the same thing—by advertising things at prices that sound small when they really are not more than a couple of cents smaller than a full, round price, why should not I get somebody else's money by the same plan?"

"No reason at all," admitted Tommy.

"Why do you say fourteen fifty instead

A few tips for the car salesman. From Motor World, June 24, 1914.

of fourteen hundred and fifty dollars?" demanded Charley.

"It sounds better," asserted Tommy.

"The way things sound, Tommy, means a whole lot," added Reilly. "You say one thousand, four hundred and fifty dollars, and it sounds big. Say fourteen hundred and fifty dollars and it still sounds pretty big. But say fourteen fifty and it loses much of its bigness.

"It all depends on what you want to emphasize. You certainly don't want to flaunt in the face of the prospect the fact that he has got to part with a lot of good money for a car. The things you want to emphasize are what the car can do and what it means to him. But the question of price must of necessity enter into the discussion, so why not make it as inconspicuous as possible?

"One Dollar" Has a Big Sound.

"When most men were kids they began accumulating pennies and nickels, and the first big mark was a dollar. 'One dollar' has a big, mouth-filling, ringing sound. If the man wasn't born with money one of his first marks was a thousand, and for several years a thousand dollars probably sounded to him like a whole lot of money—and it is. It may be that with the money he has to-day a thousand dollars doesn't mean as much to him as fifty cents did when he was a kid, but it still has a big sound.

"The man may be willing to spend his money; he may not be penurious or pinching and may be willing to spend a couple of thousand dollars if it is for something he wants. But a car in many cases comes almost within the luxury class, and if you hit a man just right you may set him to thinking that he is spending a lot of money for something he could just as well get along without. The things that may set him thinking are such as mentioning the price of your car as one thousand, four hundred and fifty dollars, or as any number of dollars.

May Give Him a Mental Start.

"Dollars represent the results of his life's labor, and the mere mention of the word is likely to give him a mental start that may upset all the good work you have done. It may cause him to decide that if he is going to buy a car he should get one that costs less money. And if he is that kind of man the mention of thousands may send him away on a dead run in a panic."

"I can see some of them going now," laughed Tommy.

"It's the same with this fifty-five day business. This may seem a bit far-fetched when compared to the fourteen fifty principle, but it has merit in it nevertheless. When you say 'one day' to the average man it means a very short time; if you say seven days it means a week. If you say thirty days it means a month, and if you say sixty days it means two months. Also, if you say four weeks or eight weeks it means a month or two months. But if you say fifty-five days it means just fifty-five days——"

Limitation to the Scheme.

"He can figure it out, can't he?"

"Yes, but he won't. If you say fifty-five days it means twenty-four hours multiplied by fifty-five. Let's see—fifty-five times twenty-four—thirteen hundred and—and—call it thirteen hundred. There are thirteen hundred hours in the fifty-five days. If you said the car had been used thirteen hundred hours it would would sound shorter yet, but it would be such an odd way of expressing it that it would lose its effect; the prospect would have to sit down and figure it out and it would detract attention from the sale. Fifty-five days isn't so odd or different as to cause any undue hitch in the mental working of the prospect.

"Furthermore, if you are talking to the prospect and say fifty-five days and keep right on talking, you have left him with the impression that the time the car has been used is short, and before he can stop to figure it out he has been carried on to another point; then, by the time he gets around to figuring it out he may be so favorably impressed with the car that he doesn't care if it has been used three months or six.

"If you're talking about gasolene economy you go strong on how far the car will go on a gallon. If the car will go fifteen miles on a gallon it means one thing, but if you tell the prospect the car will go from here to Midtown on a gallon that means something else. Fifteen miles is just fifteen miles, but the distance from here to Midtown is something he is very familiar with."

"Here's a scheme! How's this?" exclaimed Tommy, jumping up. "Have a half a dozen of our owners who are pretty handy with their cars start out from here and see how far they can drive on a gallon. One of them may get to Midtown, another may——"

Plans Gasolene Economy Tests.

"That's good! We'll do it!" Reilly slapped the desk.

Tommy had subsided and was snickering.

"What's the joke?" demanded Charley.

"Oh, nothing," replied Tommy. "I was thinking how I almost bought a raincoat the other day. I didn't really need it, but it looked good. The salesman said it was twenty-two fifty. I tried it on and was going to buy it, but when I took out my money and saw the big yellow-backed twenty I would have to part with I lost heart."

"What did you do?"

"Put the twenty back in my pocket. See it!" And Tommy fished out a beautiful sample of currency. "Lucky my money wasn't in fives that day."

CAR AND ACCESSORY DEALER BUILDS WEED CHAIN BRIDGE

THE SMITH MOTOR CAR CO., 921-23 CLINTON AVENUE, NEWARK, N. J., MADE MANY PEOPLE STOP AND LOOK AT THIS UNIQUE STRUCTURE WITH A MINIATURE MOTOR CAR ON THE CENTRAL SPAN

This Ajax advertisement gives an indication of the tire mileage one could expect in 1913.

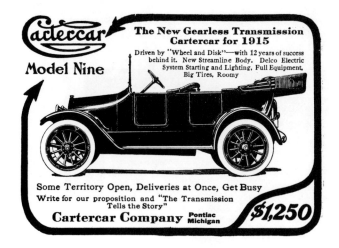

The New Gearless Transmission Cartercar for 1915

Driven by "Wheel and Disk"—with 12 years of success behind it. New Streamline Body. Delco Electric System Starting and Lighting, Full Equipment, Big Tires, Roomy

Model Nine

Some Territory Open, Deliveries at Once, Get Busy

Write for our proposition and "The Transmission Tells the Story"

Cartercar Company Pontiac Michigan

$1,250

GEARLESS

A big, strong, powerful car, having all those refinements and up-to-date features that make the Cartercar a continual source of pride and satisfaction to the owner.

The Cartercar Gearless Transmission insures the utmost ease in handling with no jerking or jarring clutch and clashing or stripping of gears.

Built in various body types $1250—$1700—$2000

CARTERCAR COMPANY, Pontiac, Michigan

THE CENTURY

A Car Embodying Advanced Ideas in Electric Car Construction

Of proper design, more room, more luxuriously furnished, graceful constructive lines, unit power plant. Motor has overload capacity of more than 300%. Two-passenger Century Roadster; five-passenger Century Brougham. In finish, lines and equipment either is ahead of the highest price cars money can buy. Get our proposition NOW.

CENTURY ELECTRIC MOTOR CAR CO.
1199 Woodward Avenue, Detroit, Mich.

"GO" $375.00 $450.00

2 to 25 miles per hour—30 miles on 1 gallon gasoline.

AS FAR AS YOU LIKE
—Up hill or through mud.
—At prices right to suit you for a

BLACK MOTOR RUNABOUT

Guaranteed every way—Safe—Dependable—Handsome finish—Most durable materials and workmanship. Engine 10 H.P., 2 cylinders, air cooled—Chain drive rear—Double brake. Also top motor Buggies and Surreys. Free Catalog No. 20¢ shows all—write.

BLACK MFG. CO., 124 East Ohio Street, Chicago, Ill.

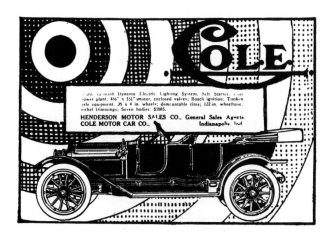

Standard Dynamo Electric Lighting System, Self Starter, unit power plant; 4½" x 5½" motor, enclosed valves; Bosch ignition; Timken axle equipment; 36 x 4 in. wheels; demountable rims; 122-in. wheelbase, nickel trimmings; Seven bodies; $1885.

HENDERSON MOTOR SALES CO., General Sales Agents
COLE MOTOR CAR CO., Indianapolis, Ind.

THIS *Cutting* **CAR**

Has more Horsepower and a longer Wheel Base than any other Four Cylinder Automobile in the World selling for this price **$1850**

Send for our Chart of Comparative Motor Car Values

Clarke-Carter Automobile Company Jackson, Mich.

Model T-55

Advertisements circa 1910-1915.

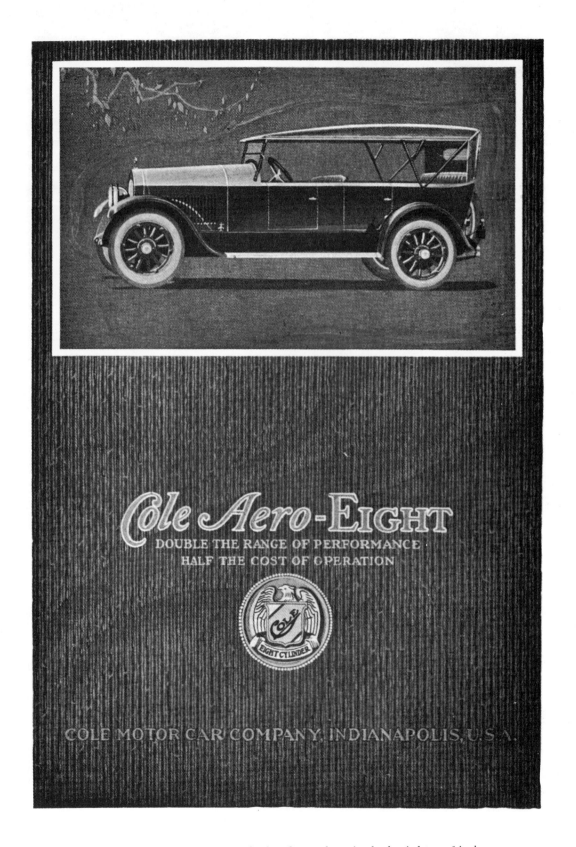

The Cole Aero-Eight stressed the fact that it had eight cylinders
at the time most cars had only six.

The Chandler was a popular car in the medium price range. The above listing offered models priced from $1795 to $3095. Unlike today it was common during early years for display ads in national magazines to have the prices of various car models listed. Today the list prices can be learned only by visiting the dealers' showrooms or by reading local newspaper ads.

THE STORY OF THE CADILLAC

This story not only describes the many superior features of the Cadillac car but it gives much information which the automobile buyer wants to know, and which will be of advantage to him no matter what car he may favor

IN THE FIELD OF MOTOR CARS, the Cadillac stands pre-eminent as representing the most advanced development along truly practical lines.

As it stands today it embodies principles and methods in construction which have proven their correctness in forty thousand Cadillacs which have preceded it.

Of these cars, some 2000 of them were made nine years ago and not one, so far as we are aware, has been discarded as worn out and unfit for further service. If there be any other car of which the same statement can truthfully be made, we do not know of it.

The Cadillac "Thirty" upon its introduction, in 1908, marked the beginning of a new era in motor car manufacture. It set aside all pre-existing standards of value. It established the new criterion by which motor values should thenceforth be judged.

This Cadillac represented the solution of the problem of producing the highest type of motor car, to be sold at a price which theretofore would purchase only mediocrity. It stayed the industry until it could adjust itself to the newly inaugurated condition. The Cadillac had many followers in its wake but its lead has never been lessened and after three years its position remains as clearly defined as at its inception. It was the first car to be offered at a so-called "moderate price" which was accepted as a serious competitor to cars selling at more than double its price. No better evidence can be offered of the correctness of this assertion than that the Cadillac finds a very material share of its purchasers among those discriminating motorists whose ideals had been realized only in cars for which they paid from $3000 to $5000 or possibly more.

NOONTIME AT THE MAIN PLANT

The success of the Cadillac has been pronounced remarkable. Yet, it is not remarkable—excepting by comparison. Its success is nothing more than what could be expected for a motor car such as it is. Its success is due to its deserving merit—to the thorough satisfaction and constancy of the service which it has rendered to its users.

The Cadillac embodies no untried principles in its make-up for the purchaser to try out at his own expense and annoyance. The fitness of every essential part and its ability to perform its functions has been proven in trying service.

Cadillac cars are manufactured almost in their entirety in the great Cadillac plants. These plants include foundries, both iron and brass. They include pattern shops, sheet metal shops, gear cutting shops and machine shops. They include body building, finishing, painting, enameling and trimming departments. In these plants are manufactured the motors, the transmissions, the radiators, the hoods and the fenders. There are also plants for the manufacture of even small parts—capscrews, bolts, nuts, etc.

The equipment of the Cadillac plant in the matter of fine machinery, fine tools, jigs and fixtures is not excelled in any other motor car factory in the world—a statement which will be verified by those who have had the opportunity of a personal inspection.

The unrivalled reputation enjoyed by the Cadillac product, the constant and enduring service rendered, the economy of operation and maintenance are not matters of mere chance. They are the logical outcome of Cadillac principles and Cadillac methods.

Of the many distinctive features characteristic of the Cadillac, that of thorough standardization has ever been one of the most pronounced. The advantages of standardization are manifold; a motor car cannot be what it ought to be without it. The disadvantages of its absence can scarcely be calculated.

Standardization means that every individual part is exactly like every other part of its kind, without even the one-thousandth of an inch variation where that degree of accuracy is essential. It means the absolute interchangeability of parts. It means that when for any reason it becomes necessary to replace a part that the part may be ordered from the factory and that it will fit without the slightest alteration.

In the Cadillac there are 167 parts and 237 operations which are not permitted to deviate to exceed one one-thousandth of an inch,—about one-third to one-half the thickness of a hair—from the prescribed limits of measurement. There are some parts in which the limit of variation permissible is cut down to the half of one one-thousandth.

So accurately is every piece made that thousands of pieces of a kind with thousands of pieces of other kinds are sent to the various assembling departments where they are all "put together" with the use of only wrenches and screwdrivers—not so much as the finest file or emery cloth being necessary.

Standardization means correct alignment and that the parts will work in perfect harmony. It precludes the possibility of ill fitting joints and bearings. Standardization decreases the great power absorbent—friction. It limits wear. Standardization reduces "automobile troubles" to a minimum. It brings operating and maintenance cost down to the lowest notch.

Standardization produces a quiet and smooth running car. In this respect the Cadillac is not surpassed even by cars selling at two to three times its price—and very few of those.

While standardization has reduced wear at friction points to the lowest possible limit, the car is provided wherever possible with adjustments for taking up any wear.

The Cadillac is a car manufactured practically under one roof instead of merely an assembly of motor, transmission, frame, axles, etc., obtained indiscriminately here, there and everywhere that they may be had at the lowest price, regardless of quality. This is a feature which no buyer can afford to overlook.

The Cadillac Company is prepared to replace any part of any car it ever built. No Cadillac user was ever obliged to discard his car because of inability to obtain some needed part. No Cadillac user was ever obliged to pay an exorbitant price to have such part made to special order because the maker had gone out of the business, had discontinued making parts for old models or had to depend upon some outside parts maker to supply them.

The Cadillac "Thirty" has repeatedly demonstrated its speed capabilities at from five to fifty miles an hour on high gear, and its superior hill climbing abilities are recognized the world over.

It is a sturdy and dependable car. Its motor is the most powerful of its dimensions ever designed. Its strong and substantial construction, the perfect fit and perfect alignment of its working parts enables the maximum of the motor's power to be delivered to the ground—in marked contrast with flimsily constructed cars in which material is skimped to save cost and in which the twisting and binding strains consume much of the power.

The Cadillac has demonstrated its right to the distinction of being the most carefully built car ever produced. It has demonstrated its right to the distinction of being the most economical multiple cylinder car, both in operation and maintenance. It has demonstrated its right to the distinction of being the most reliable and the most serviceable car. It has demonstrated its right to the distinction of being the greatest automobile value ever offered.

Motor

The Cadillac motor is entirely different from any other—and to its differences is attributable its superiority. The use of this type of motor in every four cylinder Cadillac ever made, covering a period of nearly seven years, has failed to develop a single deficiency. On the contrary, as the years go by and their numbers increase, the more pronounced is the conviction that for all the essentials that go to make a motor what it ought to be, the Cadillac motor occupies a position unique and alone.

It is constructed upon the "built-up" and "individual part" principle, a principle conducive to efficiency, power, simplicity, smoothness of action, long life and economy. Notwithstanding the advanced manufacturing methods employed in the Cadillac plant, this type of motor is the most expensive to produce. While that construction may necessitate a higher selling price for the complete car than would be required were we to build a motor in the ordinary way, the extra cost is compensated for many times over by the greatly increased service and satisfaction it will render and the lessened expense for operation and maintenance.

It is of the four cylinder, four cycle type, 4½" cylinder bore, by 4½" piston stroke. By the generally accepted method of calculation, it is rated at 32.4 horsepower. This method, however, which considers only the bore of the cylinders regardless of the general design of the motor, the accuracy of its workmanship or the fineness with which the multitude of small details are worked out, will be readily realized as totally inadequate for determining the power of a Cadillac motor, especially when compared with motors of ordinary construction.

CADILLAC "THIRTY" MOTOR

Each cylinder is cast by itself as are also the cylinder heads which contain the valve chambers. The heads are attached to the cylinders by right and left threaded nipples. The water jackets which surround the cylinders are of spun copper. By casting each cylinder by itself it enables us to make the walls of uniform thickness and by applying the copper jackets it leaves uniform space for water circulation resulting in even cooling of the entire cylinder with the resulting advantages.

CADILLAC CYLINDER AND COPPER WATER JACKET

Note the even thickness of cylinder wall and uniform space for water circulation.

We show here some of the advantages of our method of construction as against the ordinary practice of casting cylinders, valve chambers and water jackets together. In the illustration below is shown a cylinder with valve chamber and water jacket cast integral. This illustration is made from a photograph taken of a cylinder and water jacket cut in two horizontally. Note the varying thickness of the cylinder wall "A." With this condition existing it will be readily understood that it is impossible for the circulating water to cool the cylinder uniformly. The result is that the contraction and expansion of the metal will be so varying that the bore of the cylinder will not retain perfect roundness. In consequence it will bind the piston at certain points of its travel and fit so loosely at others that the lubrication is imperfect, that wear is uneven and disastrous and that there is a great waste of fuel with a corresponding loss of power.

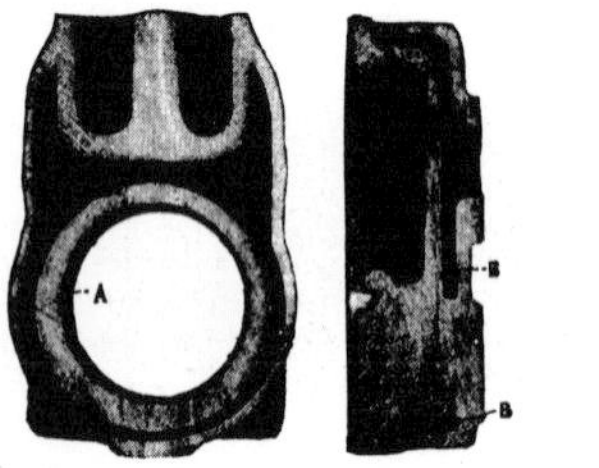

ORDINARY CASTING OF CYLINDER WITH WATER JACKETS INTEGRAL

Note varying thickness of cylinder walls and uneven water circulating space. Also webs which interfere with circulation.

In the smaller figure will be seen the webs "B" which are sometimes formed when the two parts of the core used in casting are not held firmly together. This web is sure to obstruct the circulation of the water, causing overheating of the cylinder with its undesirable consequences, and is something that is impossible to detect without destroying the cylinder.

We do not wish to be understood as saying that it is impossible to make such casting correctly, but it is a fact that many are not made correctly.

When cylinders, valve chambers and water jackets are made separately, as in the Cadillac, an injury to any one part calls for the replacement of only that particular part at but a moderate cost, while in the case of cylinder, valve chamber and water jacket cast together, and particularly when cast in pairs or all in one, an injury to any one part necessitates taking down the motor, replacing the entire combination casting and reassembling.

Our cylinders, pistons and piston rings are cast in our own foundry from special grades of metal made after our own formulas, the result of years of experience, experimenting and testing in our own laboratories. The superior qualities of Cadillac castings are so widely recognized and appreciated that for years we have made cylinder, piston and piston ring castings for a number of other automobile manufacturers making the highest priced cars in America.

The accompanying illustration shows the method of gauging Cadillac cylinders. Every cylinder after being ground must stand this final test. Two gauges are provided. One of them is marked "4.500 Go," meaning that it is exactly four and one-half inches in diameter. The cylinder must be large enough to permit this gauge to enter. The other gauge is marked "4.502 Not Go," meaning that its diameter is just

This double-spread ad gave salient Cadillac features.

THE STORY OF THE CADILLAC—*Continued*

two one-thousandths of an inch larger than four and a half inches, but the cylinder must not be so large that it will permit this gauge to enter. If a cylinder is too small to permit the "Go" gauge to enter, the inside is ground until it is the correct size. If the cylinder is large enough to permit the "Not Go" gauge to enter, it is discarded.

How CADILLAC Cylinders are Tested for Accuracy

When you realize that one gauge is less than a hair's breadth larger in diameter than the other; when you realize that one will enter the cylinder and the other will not; when you realize that there are 237 dimensions in the Cadillac car which are not permitted to vary more than the one one-thousandth part of an inch, which is about half the thickness of the average human hair, then can you form some conception of why Cadillacs are what they are, and why they render the constant service that they do.

Cadillac pistons are gauged to similar accuracy.

The result is that neither cylinders nor pistons can possibly vary in diameter even a hair's breadth. Consequently ANY piston will fit in ANY cylinder. They do not have to be "paired." If it ever becomes necessary to replace a piston, all the owner has to do is replace the piston. He is not necessarily obliged to replace the cylinder also, or possibly a pair of cylinders or the whole four as might be the case where they are cast in pairs or all together.

In finishing the cylinders and pistons, we do not stop at simply machining. Every one of them is ground to a polished surface resulting in practically perfect compression and consequently maximum power. The piston rings are finished with the same precision and are also made from our own special formula, differing from that of which the cylinders and pistons are cast. This metal possesses exceptional spring qualities not easily affected by the heat of the motor. Therefore, they retain their efficiency long after the ordinary ring would be rendered practically worthless.

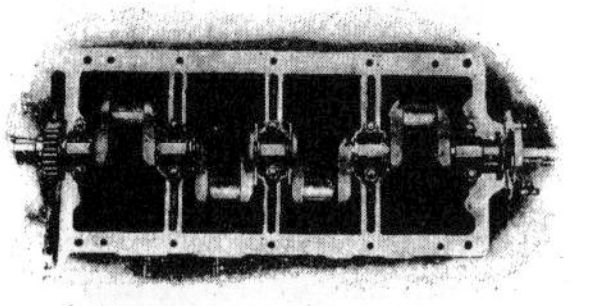

CADILLAC OIL PAN AND CRANK SHAFT

Note the five large substantial bearings
Also showing Oil Wells and Distributing Troughs

The crank shaft is substantially supported by five large bearings, insuring that firmness and rigidity essential to a smooth running, vibrationless and durable motor.

These bearings are of a large surface, made of Babbitt metal with bronze backing. Incidentally, we had occasion to examine the bearings of a car which had traveled 46,000 miles, yet the wear proved not to exceed the one one-thousandth of an inch. Each bearing is made in halves and, should occasion ever require, they may be removed, replaced or adjusted through the hand holes in the crank case without even disturbing the crank shaft.

The inlet and exhaust valves are all located on the right side of the motor and are operated by the single cam shaft. The valve lifting rods do not bear directly on the cams. The lower end of each rod is provided with a hardened steel roller and consequently the possibility of wear is reduced to an absolute minimum.

The cooling system used on the Cadillac is unexcelled in any other motor car at any price. The radiator is our own design, made in our own factory. It is composed of 150 seamless copper tubes passing vertically through 135 horizontal copper plates,—copper because it radiates or throws off heat better than other metals. In the method of manufacturing we have inaugurated a wide departure from the usual practice of dipping the entire radiator in molten solder after assembling, a practice which is followed to cover poor workmanship and poor material, and a practice which has a decided tendency to reduce the radiating efficiency. The Cadillac method is to confine the solder as closely as possible to the points where the tubes pass through the plates without covering the plates themselves. By this method we obtain the maximum radiating efficiency. All parts and passages with which the water comes in contact are made of either copper or brass—no iron or steel or other metal subject to rust. Before assembling, each individual tube is tested and the finished radiator is also tested by air and water pressure. The water circulation is promoted by a gear driven centrifugal pump. The air draft through the radiator is augmented by a ball bearing belt driven rotary fan. With our radiator construction, the copper jacketed cylinders and uniform water circulating space, we have a system that comes nearest perfection of any that has ever been devised.

The clutch is the leather faced cone type. It is of pressed steel, giving it great strength without needless weight. The ring with which the cone engages is split at eight points of its periphery and part of each section is sprung inward. This causes the clutch to take hold gradually so that in starting the car there is that noticeable absence of shock and jar characteristic of most cars.

This clutch is devoid of complications. It is extremely simple and requires the least attention of any motor car clutch ever designed. In the matter of efficiency, ease of operation, dependability and service, it is not even approached. It requires but a few minutes to remove it, if necessary.

The motor entire is mounted in the chassis frame by our three point suspension plan. By this method, any twisting strains to which the car may be subjected due to uneven road conditions do not materially affect the alignment of the motor and its working parts.

Ignition

In the very essential matter of Ignition the Cadillac is equipped with two separate and complete systems, each with its individual set of spark plugs. Either system is efficient for operating the car, entirely independent of the other.

For one system we use the Bosch high tension magneto.

As an auxiliary ignition, we have adopted the new Delco Distributor System.

We use this system not merely for starting but to afford Cadillac users a dependable reserve ignition that can be used for running any distance with satisfactory results.

Lubrication

In the important matter of lubrication, the Cadillac is provided with the most efficient, the most positive and the most economical system ever devised, the oil consumption averaging from 500 to 800 miles per gallon.

A quantity of oil is placed in the oil pan of the crank case. An oil reservoir is placed alongside the motor; in this reservoir is located a double acting force pump, the supply from which may be regulated to take care of the motor's requirements. By means of splashers at the end of each connecting rod which dip into the oil at each revolution of the crank, the oil is thrown completely over and upon all the inside working parts of the motor, including main bearings, cylinders, etc.

With the Cadillac system there is no possibility of the oil collecting in either end of the crank case as the sloping troughs on the sides distribute it from one compartment to the other, maintaining a uniform and constant level in each, regardless of road grades, up or down.

There is another prime advantage. There is not a multiplicity of feed pipes to watch that are liable to become clogged up and result in burned out bearings. On the contrary, there is but one and if the oil is shown by the sight feed to be feeding properly and the supply in the crank case adequately maintained, there is positive assurance that all bearings taken care of by this system are being perfectly lubricated.

SECTIONAL VIEW OF CADILLAC CRANK CASE AND CRANK SHAFT

Showing Oil Wells and Distributing Troughs

Transmission

The Cadillac transmission is as superior to the usual transmission as the Cadillac motor is superior to other motors. It is more substantial, more positive, and by operators of long experience it has been pronounced the most easily operated of any they have ever used. It is our own design, manufactured in our own factory. It is the selective type of sliding gear. There are three speeds forward and reverse, direct on high. The gears, also the transmission shaft and clutch shaft, are made of chrome nickel steel. The construction is Cadillac quality throughout. The utmost skill is exercised in cutting and finishing the gears and other parts according to the Cadillac system of limit gauges which insures hair's-breadth accuracy. These parts are then treated by a special process which gives them extreme strength, toughness and wear resisting qualities.

The gear teeth are "backed off" or beveled by machinery especially designed for the purpose. This facilitates the shifting of the gears without the crashing and grinding characteristic of some construction.

CADILLAC SELECTIVE TYPE SLIDING GEAR TRANSMISSION

The main transmission shaft, the jack shaft and the clutch revolve on five annular ball bearings.

Drive

The drive is direct by special heat treated high carbon steel shaft, fitted with two universal joints having hardened and ground bushings and pins. The joints are enclosed in spherical housings and run in oil baths. The forward joint, which is telescopic, is so constructed that it is self-centering, resulting practically in the elimination of friction and binding strains characteristic of ordinary construction. The drive shaft revolves on Timken bearings. The torsion member is "V" shaped, tubular. When the car is carrying a normal load the power is transmitted in practically a straight line from the motor to the rear axle, with the result that the maximum of the generated power is delivered to the ground.

The foregoing are some more of the reasons why the Cadillac shows more power than any other car having a motor of its size.

Steering Mechanism

Like most important features of the Cadillac the steering mechanism is different from any other type. It is of our own patented design and manufacture, of the worm and worm gear sector type. The parts are all accurately cut and hardened, and the worm gear is fitted with two ball thrust bearings. The teeth in the middle of the sector, being the ones which are in mesh when

CADILLAC STEERING GEAR

the car is driven straight ahead, naturally perform the greatest service and are therefore most susceptible to wear. To compensate for this the center teeth are cut on a slightly less pitch radius, so that any wear may be taken up without affecting the upper or lower teeth of the sector; consequently they do not bind when turning corners. We know of no other car equipped with a steering device capable of adjustment to the degree which characterizes our own.

A steering gear that is not provided with proper adjustments is apt to become worn to such an extent that the resulting back lash will make steering both uncertain and unsafe.

The adjustment provision of most gears is simply for original setting at the factories, so that when the parts become worn they must be replaced by new ones. In our mechanism the provision for adjustment is more adequate than will probably ever be required.

Springs

One has but to ride in the Cadillac to fully appreciate its superb riding qualities. It carries its own good road with it. Its spring suspension is generally conceded to be the most luxurious ever installed on a motor car.

The forward suspension consists of two semi-elliptical springs, 36 inches long by two inches wide.

CADILLAC REAR SPRING SUSPENSION

The rear suspension is of the three-quarter platform type, a type which is recognized as the most conducive to comfort, but which makers of cheaply constructed cars cannot afford to use and which few have sufficient knowledge of to apply correctly. Like most other features, this is one which the Cadillac Company has perfected to a marked degree.

Axles

The rear axle is the Timken full-floating type with Timken bearings throughout. This is a type of axle which outside of the Cadillac will be found only on higher priced cars. In this axle the load of the car is carried on the housing, the live axle shafts simply transmitting the power to the rear wheels.

The front axle is drop forged, I beam section with drop forged yokes, steering spindles, spring perches, and tie rod ends. The front wheels are fitted with Timken bearings.

Brakes

A thoroughly efficient and dependable brake system is one of the greatest essentials to the safety of the motorist.

The Cadillac is equipped with two pairs of powerful, double acting brakes which operate directly on the rear wheel hub drums, which are 14 inches in diameter by 2½ inches wide.

Brake and Control Levers

The Cadillac "Thirty" is equipped with the standard form of control. There are no confusing combinations on any one lever; each has its separate and distinct function.

Wheels

The wheels are the best obtainable and equal to those used on the highest priced cars.

Frame

The frame of the "Thirty" is strong and substantially braced. It is made of pressed steel, channel section. All cross members are hot riveted with pneumatic hammers, a process which prevents loosening of the rivets and parts.

Finish

No motor car is better finished than is the "Thirty." Cadillac finish is noted the world over for its excellence and durability. Inasmuch as this work is done in our own shops and not let out on contract, we are able to give it the same careful supervision and inspection which characterize all Cadillac workmanship.

The seats are luxuriously upholstered in selected full hides of hand buffed black leather, tufted over deep coil springs and fine quality genuine curled hair. The seat cushion springs are all Royal Arch construction, a type conducive to the highest degree of comfort, as it is practically impossible for the occupant to strike the base.

Styles

The Cadillac is furnished in several types of bodies at the following prices: Touring car, Demi-tonneau and Roadster, $1700; Foredoor touring car $1800; Limousine $3000. Prices F. O. B. Detroit including the following equipment: Bosch magneto and Delco ignition systems. Pair gas lamps and generator. Pair side oil lamps and tail lamp; horn and set of tools. Pump and repair kit for tires. 60-mile season and trip standard speedometer; robe rail; full foot rail in tonneau and half foot rail in front. Tire-holders.

Cadillac Motor Car Co., Detroit, Mich.

The Cadillac Company has no intention of marketing a six cylinder car

THE Cadillac Motor Car Company has always believed that there are so many good features in the Cadillac Car, that its advertising space could be best utilized exclusively in acquainting the public with those advantages.

We regret, however, that the occasion arises which makes it appear desirable for us to depart, temporarily, from that policy.

Inasmuch as it is not possible for us to control the "mouth to mouth" advertising with which we are favored, and inasmuch as that gratuitous publicity may sometimes contain elements of inaccuracy, unintentionally perhaps, on the part of the authors, we feel that we would not perform the duty which we owe to the public and the duty which we owe to ourselves, if we did not correct any misunderstandings or misconceptions which may exist concerning the methods, policies and plans of this company.

The pre-eminent position of the Cadillac Car as the "Standard of the World," its recognition as the criterion of excellence in practical construction, are not matters of mere chance.

For eleven years the Cadillac has been manufactured and marketed upon well defined principles. Adherence to those principles has been the dominant factor in Cadillac success.

The Cadillac has never aspired to ideals set by others; it makes its own ideals and raises them higher and higher.

The Cadillac has never striven after the achievements of other plants; it is a school and a model unto itself.

The Cadillac has never been obliged to make apologies for its product. It has never been obliged to smother its past, nor to discredit it by wiping the slate clean and beginning all over again.

The immaterial and the impractical, the fad and the fallacy, the delusion and the shallow "talking point" have no chapter in the "Story of the Cadillac."

The "Story of the Cadillac" is the story of that mechanical and commercial advancement which makes for permanency. The Cadillac product has been only that which its makers knew to be right; that which its makers know would satisfy and give to the purchaser "value received" in abundant measure.

The policy of the Cadillac Company has ever been to avoid exaggeration and overdrawn statements. Its policy has ever been to under-claim rather than to over-claim.

The Cadillac Company is gratified that the public feels secure in accepting Cadillac representations at their full worth. These representations are so accepted because the Cadillac Company has never misled and because the public could always expect and has always received more than was offered.

The Cadillac Car of today has behind it the experience gleaned in the successful production of the seventy-five thousand Cadillacs which have preceded it—by far the greatest number of high grade motor cars produced by any one manufacturer in the world.

The Cadillac Company is ever alert—its ear is ever to the ground; it feels the throb of the public pulse. Yet never has it yielded to clamor by giving endorsement to principles which would take advantage of the uninitiated or the uninformed, even though temporary benefits might accrue.

The experimental division of the Cadillac Company is not excelled in the motor car industry. We do no believe it is even equalled.

Every design, every appliance, every idea, every principle offered which has a semblance of merit, is subjected to the most gruelling tests.

For every idea or feature adopted or considered worthy of the Cadillac seal of approval, scores are discarded.

One reason why most of the new ideas of inventors and manufacturers are first offered to the Cadillac Company is because these inventors and manufacturers realize that with the Cadillac seal of approval their future is practically certain.

As an example, take the electrical system of automatic cranking, lighting and ignition, first introduced by the Cadillac Company and now used almost universally.

Take also the two-speed axle introduced into the present Cadillac, and which engineering authorities on both sides of the Atlantic are predicting will soon come into general use.

Witness this from "The Automobile Engineer," published in London, England. In commenting upon Cadillac engineering progress and Cadillac initiative, it says:—

"Already there is a very decided movement among other makers to try and provide some type of two-speed rear axle similar to the Cadillac, for 1914 or 1915."

In our experimental division we have built automobile engines of almost every conceivable type and size and have tested scores which we did not make ourselves.

We have built them with one, with two, with three, with four and with six cylinders. We have never tried five.

We have cast them en bloc, we have cast them in pairs and we have cast them singly. We have made them with water jackets cast integral and with copper water jackets. We found the latter method most expensive, but the most efficient—hence we use it.

We built cars with one cylinder engines, more than 15,000 of them, and they were good ones. "One-lungers" they were called, and they are practically all going yet, after eight to eleven years of service, hundreds of them having passed the 100,000 mile mark.

We built a few cars with two cylinder engines and they were as good as that type could possibly be made. But we never marketed any of them although the rumor was current that we intended doing so.

Yes, and we built cars with three cylinder engines, as good of that type as could be made. Probably few readers ever heard of such a car. Some people thought they wanted that kind and they

bought them. But not from us. Rumor had it, however, that we intended to market them.

Cars with four cylinder engines! We have built and distributed more than sixty thousand (60,000) of them. That was something more substantial than a rumor.

Cars with six cylinder engines! We have built a number of them in the last four years. We have tested them to the utmost, and they proved to be good ones—by comparison. In fact, by comparing them point for point with a number of the most highly regarded "sixes," which we bought for the purpose of making comparisons for our own enlightenment, we failed to find a single car which, in our opinion, outpointed our own, and our own outpointed most of them.

These experiments may have given rise to the rumor that the Cadillac Company contemplates marketing a six cylinder car. But,—as in the cases of the two and three cylinder cars—such rumor is entirely without foundation. This Company has no such intention.

And we made other comparisons as well; in fact nothing worth while was overlooked or omitted.

Our tests, investigations, experiments and comparisons demonstrated conclusively to us, that a four cylinder engine, designed with the skill and executed with the precision which characterizes the Cadillac engine—and scientifically balanced, affords the highest degree of all 'round efficiency possible to obtain.

These tests further demonstrated that with such an engine, in conjunction with a properly designed two-speed axle, there is obtained an extraordinary range of operating flexibility, an extraordinary reduction of friction, an extraordinary degree of operation and maintenance economy, an extraordinary degree of luxurious riding qualities, and a reduction of vibration, particularly at high speeds, almost to the vanishing point.

We have cited the foregoing facts because we believe that the public is entitled to know them, because we believe that we owe it to the public to make the facts known and because we want the public to know that the Cadillac Company leaves no stone unturned, that it spares no expense in its efforts to discover and to provide that which it knows to be right, that which it knows will satisfy and that which will give to the buyer "value received" in abundant measure.

And above all, the Cadillac Company has no intention of departing from that policy.

There can be no better evidence of the appreciation of the Cadillac policy than the fact that there have already been manufactured and distributed, more than 9000 of the 1914 Model Cadillacs, amounting in selling value to more than eighteen millions ($18,000,000) of dollars—a volume of cars which nearly equals, if it does not exceed, that of all other 1914 high grade American cars combined, selling at or more than the Cadillac price, regardless of their number of cylinders.

CADILLAC MOTOR CAR CO.
Detroit, Michigan.

This statement of policy published by Cadillac in 1914 notes that the firm had tested engines with various numbers of cylinders and found that four cylinders were best.

Cadillac
Standard of the World

SEVEN-PASSENGER CAR
Price, $2080.

TWO-PASSENGER ROADSTER
Price, $2080.

FOUR-PASSENGER VICTORIA (CONVERTIBLE) (Open)
Price, $2550.

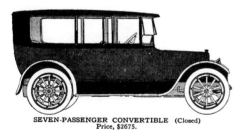

SEVEN-PASSENGER CONVERTIBLE (Closed)
Price, $2675.

FIVE-PASSENGER BROUGHAM
Price, $2950.

SEVEN-PASSENGER LANDAULET
Price, $3750.

CADILLAC ENGI-neers have pro-vided a mechanism of matchless performance.

CADILLAC COACH builders have evolved body types of exquisite beauty.

NO MATTER WHAT your taste or your pref-erence, it would be diffi-cult for you to suggest to yourself a type or style of motor equipage which has not been anticipated in the Cadillac offerings.

CADILLAC MOTOR
CAR CO.
DETROIT, MICH.

Prices include standard equipment, F. O. B. Detroit.
Prices are subject to advance without notice.

FOUR-PASSENGER PHAETON
Price, $2080.

FOUR-PASSENGER CLUB ROADSTER
Price, $2080.

FOUR-PASSENGER COUPÉ
Price, $2800.

SEVEN-PASSENGER CONVERTIBLE (Open)
Price, $2675.

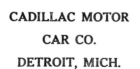

SEVEN-PASSENGER LIMOUSINE
Price, $3600.

SEVEN-PASSENGER IMPERIAL
Price, $3750.

The Cadillac line - models are priced from $2080 to $3750.

1915 - ANNOUNCEMENT - 1915

JUDGING by the unprecedented interest created, when we announced the first CHELSEA Speedster for the 1914 season, and considering the boundless enthusiasm, shown alike by the veteran automobile dealer of the large cities and the garageman or implement dealer of the farming districts—we began preparations for the 1915 season, firmly determined to continue our original and from the start well defined policy and make each CHELSEA car represent to its purchaser the highest attainable DOLLAR FOR DOLLAR **VALUE**.

VALUE

We believe that to the dealer and the consumer alike "Value" is the first and chief consideration, and that is what we offer in each CHELSEA car: VALUE—unconditionally—absolute and proven Value.

When the consumer purchases a CHELSEA car he positively gets a Dollar's value for each Dollar paid.

THE DEALER that sells the CHELSEA car can rest content in this knowledge, and besides will find at the end of the season, that each CHELSEA customer is a CHELSEA BOOSTER. There are NO "come-backs"—NO "knockers"—NO "profits paid out for free repairs" items on his books. A CHELSEA agency knocks the "Loss" out of the "Profit and Loss" account of the wide-awake dealer.

DEALERS—ACT NOW!

REMEMBER, we offer three models, of the kind and at the price that will make them SELL. They are WHAT the public wants, at the price they WILL PAY.

We don't want to sell you any of our capital stock—we don't expect you to put up large sums of deposit money—we will not ask you to contract for more cars than we expect to deliver to you.

IF YOU WANT a good clean selling proposition—a car that will MAKE GOOD—a manufacturer that will help you by treating you right—a contract that will mean PROFITS, CLEAN and HONEST PROFITS to you, do not hesitate one moment. Waste no time.

Write or Wire Us Today

WE shall immediately mail you our literature and write you regarding our sales plan. IT'S ENTIRELY UP TO YOU.

Chelsea Manufacturing Company
5-7-9 Webster Street, NEWARK, N. J.

READ!   READ!
DETAIL SPECIFICATIONS

MOTOR—4 cylinder, water-cooled by Thermo-Syphon System. Bore 2¾-inch, stroke 4-inch, developing full 18 H. P. Large valves. Positive hill proof oiling system. Valves enclosed.

CLUTCH—High grade cone clutch, leather faced, having pickup springs under the leather. Ball-Bearing Thrust.

TRANSMISSION—Selective sliding gear type, providing 3 speeds forward and reverse. Gears of large proportion, and made of highest quality steel, double heat treated and oil hardened.

IGNITION—High Tension Magneto. No batteries. No coils

CARBURETOR—Float Feed.—Very simple adjustment.

FRONT AXLE—Tubular.—Extra heavy. Ball-Bearings in wheels.

REAR AXLE—Special-Floating-Roller Bearing.—Extra heavy throughout.

DRIVE—Enclosed shaft drive, running on Roller Bearing.

UNIVERSAL JOINT—The famous Spicer Universal Joint.

SPRINGS—CHELSEA Special Cantilever type. Extra long. Wonderful riding quality. Made of highest grade Manganese Steel.

FRAME—High Grade Channel Steel, 3-inch by 1¼-inch. Pressed to form.

RADIATOR—Extra large capacity. Horizontal Finn type.

WHEELS—High Grade Wire Wheels. Heavy Spokes. Triple-baked black enamel.

WHEEL BASE—102 inches.

TREAD—Standard 56-inch Tread.

TIRES—Standard 28-inch by 3-inch. Corrugated Tread.

BODY—Latest type perfect Torpedo Stream-line body. Large and roomy. 21-inch wide doors. 40-inch wide seating. 54 inches of Leg room. Tool compartment under seat. Large compartment for baggage, suit case, etc., under rear deck. Deep and comfortable cushions and upholstery.

COLOR—Hood, Fenders, Running Gear in rich black. Body in "CHELSEA Special" dark blue. Hub caps CHELSEA RED.

EQUIPMENT—2 Electric Head Lights, Electric Tail Light, Horn, Tools, Pump.

PRICES

Chelsea Speedster $390
Chelsea 600-lb. Panel Body
   Delivery 425
Chelsea Touring Car, fully
   equipped 485
All Prices F. O. B. Newark, N. J.

1915 Chelsea ad featuring its low-priced $390.00 model.

Receiver's Sale Automobile Factory

THE property of the Amplex Motor Car Company of Mishawaka, Indiana, may now be bought at private sale, subject to the approval of the Judge of the St. Joseph County Circuit Court; or, in the event of no sale being made prior to January 20, 1914, the property will be offered at public sale—as a whole, or in such parts as may be deemed expedient and not detrimental to a reasonable sale of the remainder.

Location . . . . On L. S. & M. S. Main Line at Mishawaka, Indiana, with private switch to property.

Size of Land . . . . (Valued by Company at $15,000.00) — 15 acres. Railroad frontage 1305 feet, depth 550 feet. All city improvements, except pavement.

Buildings . . . . (Cost of Buildings $63,704.00) — Sixty thousand square feet of floor space. Brick-mill construction, except test sheds, boiler room, etc. Main buildings 385 ft. by 80 ft. and 250 ft. by 80 ft.

Equipment . . . . (Cost of Equipment $22,250.00) — Fully equipped with Automatic Fire Protection, Electric Power, Heating, Lighting, Compressed Air, Sewer and all underground service, Shafting Equipment, Etc., and Office Equipment.

Machinery and Tools . . . . (Cost of Tools, Etc., $75,350.00) — Best available for Automobile Engine service, or for any medium machine shop production.

Merchandise, Stock, Etc . . . . . . (Inventory on basis of Company's Cost and Records, $123,750.00) — Finished and partly finished for Amplex Cars; raw supplies are standard; over 500 Amplex Cars are in use. Parts are available to complete about 15 cars, with other parts available for a number of standard type Four Cycle Cars.

This factory made the great "Valveless Amplex," admittedly the best *all-around-car* on the market for Cross Country and hard driving—a chassis that is not surpassed by any car of its class—equally available for Four Cycle Engines.

Please understand this: The difficulties of the Amplex Motor Car Company were not due to the failure of the two-cycle engine principle. It stands as a successful demonstration of a two-cycle Valveless Engine, and it only needs a practical business management to make the business a trade success for pleasure or utility cars.

Old owners are more enthusiastic over the **Amplex** Car as the years go by, because they withstand the most severe road grief.

This plant is exceedingly well located for the manufacture and distribution of Automobile Trucks, Gas Engines, Auto Motors, Machinery, (except that requiring crane service, etc.).

This is an exceptional opportunity to acquire a plant convenient to the great and growing manufacturing section of the Central West, situated 90 miles from Chicago, and in the heart of the St. Joseph Valley—an industrial center without an equal.

Negotiations may be started at once as it is my intention to recommend an early sale as soon as a satisfactory bid is received. The plant may be inspected at any time.

Everything is in first-class shape and ready for immediate operation.

There is a bargain here for somebody, or some firm. Address:

M. W. MIX, Receiver
AMPLEX MOTOR CAR COMPANY
1 Byrkit Avenue
MISHAWAKA, INDIANA

This receiver's sale notice is representative of many such notices which appeared in automobile trade publications in the 1910-1920 years. At this time there were hundreds of companies in the automobile business; and many failed to achieve success.

ELECTRIC   GASOLENE

MARK XII COLUMBIA RUNABOUT

Columbia Improved 1901 Models for Quick Delivery

AUTOMOBILES

40 Miles ON ONE CHARGE OF BATTERIES

Reliability in Service
Simplicity in Operation
Readiness in Action
Cleanliness in Handling

To obtain the Leading Type of Vehicle at Moderate Cost it will pay you to
Write for 1901 Illustrated Catalogue or Call at
ELECTRIC VEHICLE COMPANY, 100 Broadway, NEW YORK

Chalmers Talk Number One

This monogram on the radiator stands for all you can ask in a motor car.

AN automobile is not an extravagance. It is an economy. It increases your efficiency. It makes "two minutes grow for you—where only one grew before." Some extravagant people buy automobiles, but not very many. Only a few really extravagant people ever can afford to buy them. They spend their money for less useful things. Think that over.

The automobile industry is now the third in the country in point of volume and is still growing. The everyday, sensible, careful-buying business man has made this volume possible. If the motor car was an extravagance he would soon find it out—and quit buying. But he goes on buying. He sees that the motor car is a necessity.

Each year the Chalmers Motor Company has had more orders than it could fill. We have, already this season, shipped to customers more than 60 per cent. of our 1911 output. The remainder is going fast. We take these conditions to mean that we have succeeded in building cars that appeal to the careful business buyers of the country as unusual value at their prices. "30"—$1,500. "Forty"—$2,750. All types. Dealers in all leading cities.

"Forty" $2750

Chalmers Motor Company
(Licensed under Selden Patent)
Detroit, Michigan

Above: This 1901 Columbia was battery-operated. Note that the vehicle was steered by a tiller rather than by a steering wheel.

Left: This 1911 Chalmers ad states that the automobile is not an extravagance but is an economy.

Below: The 1909 Buffalo Automobile School ad reproduced below is one of many such ads which extolled the money to be made with automobiles.

A LARGE SALARY FOR YOU

If you will let us prepare you to become an expert automobilist. This is one of the highest paid professions. Our students attain *Success* in a few weeks time through our

HOME STUDY COURSE

Simply by giving a few hours of their spare evenings time to a subject more interesting to them than the best novel published. Cost of course is low and you pay us only half while learning—balance when you secure a satisfactory position. Either cash or installment plan. Small Payment Starts You. You keep your present job until graduated. Write for our Free prospectus.

BUFFALO AUTOMOBILE SCHOOL, 43 Franklin St., Buffalo, N. Y.

The Columbia Silent Knight, "one of THREE BEST cars built," this ad notes.

The United States Motor Company and its divisions.

DURYEA IMPROVES HIS "ELECTA"

Veteran Manufacturer Further Simplifies His Already Simple Vehicle—Wherein He Found it Possible.

Having moved bag and baggage from Reading, Pa., to Saginaw, Mich., and having become settled in new quarters, Charles E. Duryea once more has started in earnest to produce Buggyauts, runabouts, motor accessories and novelties, this time under the firm name of the C. E. Duryea Co., successor to Chas. E. Duryea of the Pennsylvania city, and his latest product, which is styled the "Electa," though much like its immediate predecessor, is of even simpler construction. It already was very nearly the simplest vehicle of its kind extant, but despite that fact room for improvement has been found in several minor details, and by reason of several additions and alterations, its attractiveness has been considerably increased.

By way of permitting the greatest possible flexibility and the fullest benefit from the springs being obtained without danger of body distortion being transmitted to the mechanism of the vehicle, a triangular chassis frame has been adopted in place of the rectangular frame which heretofore has been used. The frame is attached to the front of the body by means of a ball and socket joint, and in addition to permitting a virtual three-point suspension of the body, allows lower suspension and thus increases the stability of the vehicle. As the front of the frame is carried by the body, which is supported by the springs, the motor and transmission gear is relieved from much of the shock incident to the passage of the vehicle over rough roads. Incidentally, the new arrangement furthers accessibility by permitting the body to be removed quite easily and quickly by the loosening of a few bolts.

The engine remains the same as it always has been, i. e., two air-cooled cylinders with the flywheel located between them, and the crankshaft serving also as the drive axle. The arrangement, which has always been a distinctive feature of Duryea cars and probably always will be, is shown quite clearly in the accompanying picture of the chassis. One of the new features is the incorporation of what is styled an easy starting device. In consists of a miniature pump by means of which the cylinders may be primed with gasolene, which, it is explained by the inventor, "makes an explosive mixture and also cuts the heavy cylinder oil, and makes the engine turn as freely on a cold day as when warm." Another slight change which has been made embraces the use of lighter inlet valves.

The transmission elements remain unchanged, the roller drive, which provides two speeds forward and reverse, being re-

tained intact except that the method of attaching the rings to the wheels has been improved by the substitution of forged instead of partly cast fastenings. As heretofore, control and brake levers are placed in the center of the footboard, so that the vehicle may be operated from either side. In order to facilitate control, steering is

DURYEA'S LATEST—THE "ELECTA"

effected by means of a lever, which is hinged at the top, so that it may be swung over to either side. Practically the only other alteration which has been deemed advisable concerns the muffler, which has been enlarged in size and provided with

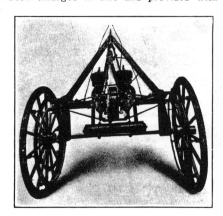

DURYEA'S "ELECTA" CHASSIS

a greater number of expansion chambers the better to silence the exhaust.

Hyatt Publishes a "Plant Book."

An unusually handsome piece of press work is the "plant book" published by the Hyatt Roller Bearing Co., of Newark, N. J., and Detroit, Mich.—so called because it is devoted to descriptions and illustrations of the plant at Newark, where the Hyatt roller bearings are made. The book—it really is more than a pamphlet—is of large size with an embossed, gold-lettered cover, and contains 52 pages. Beginning with a view of the complete plant, the various departments are illustrated by fine engravings, each occupying half of one of the large pages, with the descriptive matter printed below. The handsome offices and reception room, engineering offices, analytical and physical laboratories, testing depart-

ment, power plant, stock room, the numerous machining departments and finishing rooms, tempering furnaces—all these and more are illustrated and described in a way that is highly creditable to the compilers. The "plant book" not only is interesting to read and look at, but it is well worth keeping. The Newark plant is the only factory of the Hyatt company, the Detroit offices being devoted to sales work and the arrangement of engineering matters in connection with the use of Hyatt bearings in motor cars.

"Peroxide Discovery" Is Exploded.

The British chemist who discovered that the addition of two ounces of "20-volume" peroxide of hydrogen to each pint of water used in an acetylene generator would increase the illuminating powers of the gas generated by about 50 per cent., has been "undone" and his theory being that the oxygen liberated from the peroxide materially aided combustion and hence the greater luminosity of the gas has been flouted. That there is absolutely no benefit derived from the practice has been demonstrated in a series of photometric tests conducted by Professor Vivian B. Lewes, chief superintending gas examiner of the City of London. Professor Lewes' tests were conducted in a very systematic manner, under varying conditions as to the types of generators used and the design of the burners and the pressure of the gas. Apart from the fact that the practice does not add light, Professor Norton declares that it is positively dangerous, as the mixture of oxygen and acetylene is very explosive.

Miller's Catalog a Near-Encyclopedia.

Attractive covers always have been features of the catalogs issued by Charles E. Miller, of 97-103 Reade street, New York, and the 1912 catalog, which just has been issued, is no exception to the rule. With a motor car in the foreground, flanked by a motorcycle and a motor boat and a couple of aeroplanes in the background, done in colors, the contents are vividly suggested. As usual, the Miller catalog is practically an encyclopedia of motor supplies; its 256 pages list an enormous variety of the things that pertain to motoring on land and water and in the air, from complete motors down to the smallest parts. Big as the catalog is, there is no difficulty in finding any particular article, a good index, which also is a Miller feature, making this easy.

Battery Gas That is Inflammable.

It not infrequently is denied that the fumes from a storage battery on charge are inflammable, but such is the case, and it is by no means safe to bring a naked flame near a cell that is "gasing" freely. Battery repair shops and charging stations usually are careful in this respect, knowing by practical experience that the gas can be ignited.

Page from a 1912 issue of Motor World...the Duryea "Electa" and other news items.

DORT

Service, the Criterion of Our Owners

The Dort, in making good with its owners, has automatically made good with its dealers.

Its low cost of maintenance and remarkable economy have strengthened the feeling of co-operation between owner and dealer.

Time Has Proved This

Those dealers who last year were skeptical are now convinced by their own balance sheets that there is an extra margin of profit in handling the Dort; because of the continuous motoring satisfaction the Dort gives under every condition of service—and this with a minimum of service expense to the dealer.

Those who visited the New York Show witnessed an exchange of experiences between Dort owners and dealers that was veritably illuminating—experiences that conclusively prove that the Dort makes good every time—all the time.

Don't miss the Dort. At the Chicago Automobile Show, the Dort exhibit will be located in the Greer Building.

DORT MOTOR CAR CO.
FLINT, MICHIGAN

$650
COMPLETE
F.O.B. Flint, Mich.

Electric Starting
Electric Lighting
Demountable Rims

SPECIFICATIONS
Model 5 Touring Car

Five-passenger; left-hand drive; center control; 4-cylinder motor cast en bloc; circulating splash lubricating system; thermo-syphon cooling system; Connecticut ignition; gravity feed gasoline system in cowl; selective type transmission; 3 speeds forward and reverse; three-quarter floating rear axle; internal expanding and external contracting brakes; DEMOUNTABLE RIMS, 30x3½ in. tires; GOODYEAR ALL-WEATHER TREAD on rear; 50 in. full cantilever springs in rear; front semi-elliptic; stream line with ample leg room in both compartments; 105-inch wheelbase; standard equipment including WESTINGHOUSE ELECTRIC STARTER, electric generator, electric lights throughout, one-man top, speedometer, gasoline gauge, electric horn and complete tool equipment.

This ad beseeched automobile dealers to handle the Dort line.

The Haynes Car

There are two guarantees of quality in a timepiece for your motor-car. One is the name "Waltham" on the dial. The other is the names of the cars which use the Waltham for standard equipment.

The Waltham Automobile Clock

is the *only* timepiece satisfactorily adapted to the exacting conditions of motoring. In accuracy, appearance, durability it is worthy of its ancestry and your car.

Waltham clocks are included as regular equipment on the following makes of cars:

Brewster	Marmon
Cadillac	Owen Magnetic
Cole	Packard
Crane	Pierce-Arrow
Detroit	Rauch & Lang
Franklin	Rolls-Royce
Haynes	Russell-Knight
Jeffery	Simplex
Locomobile	Stearns
Lozier	Winton

WALTHAM
WATCH COMPANY
WALTHAM
MASS.

The Waltham Watch Company, a famous maker of watches, broadened its market by making automobile clocks.

"The Car of the Hour"

5-Passenger Touring **$985** **Elgin Six** 4-Passenger Roadster **$985**

Distinction and Comfort

The Elgin Six is the only car in its price class having the fashionable center cowl of the high-priced European models. Its beautiful yacht line design was established by a famous artist and gives the Elgin Six a style and distinction that set it apart from the monotonous design of the average car.

Elgin engineers have perfected an improved rear spring suspension, found only in the Elgin Six, which sets a new standard of motoring ease and comfort at high speeds, reducing shock and vibration to a point not surpassed in any car at any price.

The special construction of the Elgin velvet-acting clutch enables the Elgin Six to be started at high gear, under ordinary conditions, eliminating to a large degree the necessity of gear shifting, *thus removing the last barrier to the safe and easy handling of a motor car by women.*

Endurance and Economy

The Elgin Six, now in its second triumphant year, has stood "The Acid Test" by winning perfect scores and highest honors in some of the most gruelling endurance and economy runs of the past year.

Three Elgin Sixes, on a hard two-days' run under the auspices of the Chicago Motor Club, made perfect scores and averaged 25.6 miles to the gallon of gasoline.

The Elgin Six has just established a new record of 1,626 car-racking, stamina-testing miles, in 67½ hours, between Chicago and Miami, Fla.

Thirteen hours of this time was driven in a heavy rainstorm that made the roads slippery and dangerous, and in some places so deep and heavy with mud that the average car could not negotiate them at all.

The route included the steep, rocky mountain grades of Kentucky and Tennessee, the heavy sands of Georgia, and the slimy, treacherous swamp roads of Florida.

An Elgin Six touring car won a race against a fast express train through the wilds of Minnesota and Dakota, over roads that in some places were little better than a mere rocky trail, covering 552 miles without mechanical adjustment and without a single stop of the motor.

Many other remarkable Elgin performances have firmly established the Elgin as *a mechanical masterpiece,* and the champion for long sustained speed, endurance and economy.

IMPORTANT TO DEALERS—The completion of our big, modern, daylight Plant No. 2 has so increased our production that we are now entering new territory. Yours may be open. Better wire us for application blank and full particulars of 1917 best money-making proposition for dealers.

Elgin Motor Car Corporation, Chicago, U. S. A.

The 1917 Elgin Six offered a "velvet-acting clutch" which removed "the last barrier to the safe and easy handling of a motor car by women."

The 1911 (this page) and 1910 (facing page) Enger ads point out features of the Enger line. Note the testimonial on the facing page by a Norristown, Pa. gentleman whose $2000 Enger outraced a $5000 car on a steep hill.

41

How Can You Blind Yourself to the Advantages of The Elmore Valveless High Duty Motor?

Elmore

VALVELESS
Two-Cycle

Five-Passenger Touring Model 36-B, 50 H.P., $1,750

The average broad minded American, no matter how it may upset his plans, is quick to discard the old for the new—the wrong for the right—when he is confronted by incontrovertible facts.

There is an invincible logic about the Elmore Valveless *High Duty Motor* which no right reasoning motorist can escape.

Assuming you to be of that class which is seeking the highest efficiency, and the highest form of motor car enjoyment, we venture to confront you with certain advantages enjoyed only by an owner of an Elmore, with its *High Duty Motor.*

High duty literally means a higher range of power than can be secured from any other engine extant.

In a preliminary sense this is due to the fact that the four cylinders of the High Duty Motor, unlike any other in existence, act as a single power unit—not as four separate cylinders.

This in turn is rendered possible by the principle of the patented gas distributor found in the Elmore and no other.

By means of this distributor the gas is "timed," so that by admitting it early or late, the Elmore owner may select that degree of power desired.

The Elmore owner thus has, within a range unknown to other motors, a low power for easy work or a high power for difficult going, with an engine that is ideally economical and efficient at every point.

The Elmore owner never needs to regrind his valves—never, mark you—The High Duty Motor has no valves.

The Elmore owner has a motor which does not carbonize, while the ordinary motor must be taken down at frequent intervals in order that the carbon may be scraped and chipped out.

The Elmore Valveless High Duty Motor has no small outer parts, while ordinary motors have twenty or more on each cylinder; must have them to operate its valves.

The Elmore Valveless High Duty Motor has twice the power impulses per crank shaft revolution of an engine with valves—more nearly continuous power than is possible with any four-cycle motor yet built or likely to be built.

The four related Elmore cylinders have as many power impulses as could be secured by an eight cylinder four cycle, could such a motor be made practical.

This brings home to you the opening words of this announcement. Are you open minded?

Do you want to find the best? Will you profit by the facts when you learn them?

Ask us today for the 1911 Elmore book, as your first step in answering these important questions.

Write today for the 1911 Elmore literature

Roadster Model 25, 30 H. P., $1,200   Touring Model 25, 30 H. P., $1,250

**Demi-Tonneau (Detachable) Four-Passenger Touring Model 36-B,
50 H. P., $1,750**

Elmore Manufacturing Company, 704 Amanda St., Clyde, Ohio

1911 Elmore ad. Elmore later became a part of the General Motors complex.

In 1916 only 5 minutes were needed to change a Firestone tire.

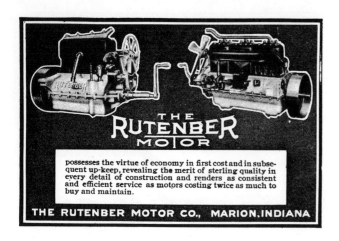
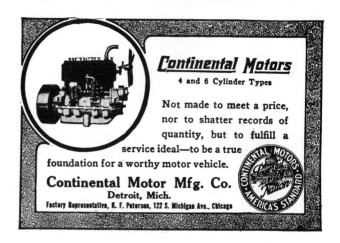

Automobile accessory ads circa 1912-1917.

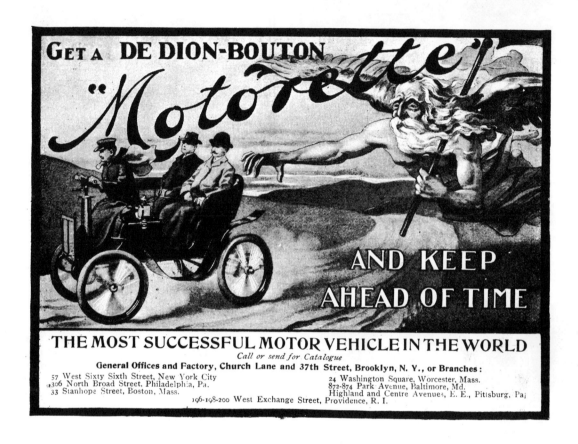

Early ads by Fiat, De Dion-Bouton, Detroiter and Empire. De Dion-Bouton was a French firm which began experimenting with various self-powered vehicles in the 1880's. By the early 1900's it was one of Europe's leading manufacturers.

45

The Five-Passenger Fore-Door EVERITT

Price $1400

Any Member of Your Family Can Be Safely Trusted with the Simple, Reliable EVERITT

Anyone who can drive at all, can be safely trusted with the EVERITT. There is nothing complicated about it. Start the motor, and there is nothing to do but steer.

The EVERITT'S unique simplicity is strikingly apparent. Every useless detail has been eliminated. The motor alone contains 156 less parts than usual; its utter simplicity is apparent in the picture below.

The whole body is big and roomy; the tonneau seats give unusual width. The doors are wide and easily entered. All levers are inside, close to the driver's hand. There are no outside brake-rods or other attachments to get caught in. The exterior presents a smooth, unbroken surface of clean-cut simplicity.

THE EVERITT 30

Of the four cars in the EVERITT'S class, but one other is manufactured in a single factory. Only one other has equal power,—and it is a thousand pounds heavier and costs 20 per cent more. Only one sells within a hundred dollars of its price,—and the necessary magneto for this one costs $80 extra. No other car has equal tire-equipment, weight considered; or equal ratio of power-to-weight. All these are catalog figures; easily verified.

In the EVERITT you get far more for your money than you can buy elsewhere. You get a thoroughly modern, Fore-Doored automobile of rare mechanical excellence and certain performance. You get a completely manufactured car. You get an unusually comfortable and easy-riding car. And the cost—*fully equipped*—is only $1500; or from $190 to $350 *less* than any other in its class.

A nearby dealer is waiting to show you the EVERITT and what it can do. Write us for his address and our latest catalog.

METZGER MOTOR CAR CO.

Detroit, Michigan

The Motor— An Instance of EVERITT Simplicity

Model K2
Price $75
Other Models
$50 to $145

WARNER AUTO-METER

"The Aristocrat of Speed Indicators"

THE man who takes pride in his car is the one who appreciates the Warner most. He would never disgrace it with anything cheap, inferior and unreliable.

WARNER INSTRUMENT CO., 1197 Wheeler Ave., Beloit, Wis.

Branches at

Atlanta	Chicago	Denver	Kansas City	Philadelphia	San Francisco
Boston	Cincinnati	Detroit	Los Angeles	Pittsburgh	Seattle
Buffalo	Cleveland	Indianapolis	New York	Portland, Ore.	St. Louis

---

Above left: This Everitt ad stressed simplicity and ease of operation.
Above: One of many speedometer models made by Warner.
Below left: The Utility car heater.
Below: 1916 ad of Akron's Swinehart Tire & Rubber Company.

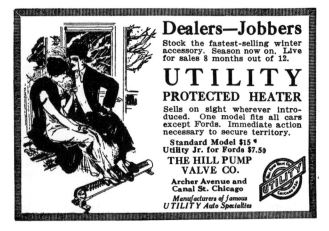

Dealers—Jobbers

Stock the fastest-selling winter accessory. Season now on. Live for sales 8 months out of 12.

UTILITY PROTECTED HEATER

Sells on sight wherever introduced. One model fits all cars except Fords. Immediate action necessary to secure territory.

Standard Model $15
Utility Jr. for Fords $7.50

THE HILL PUMP VALVE CO.

Archer Avenue and Canal St. Chicago

Manufacturers of famous UTILITY Auto Specialties

Swinehart

The established reputation of SWINEHART TIRES is responsible for their demand which will not be affected by the pleas or promises made for other tires.

Write for our agency proposition

SWINEHART TIRE & RUBBER CO.
AKRON, OHIO

Tires

Keston Type

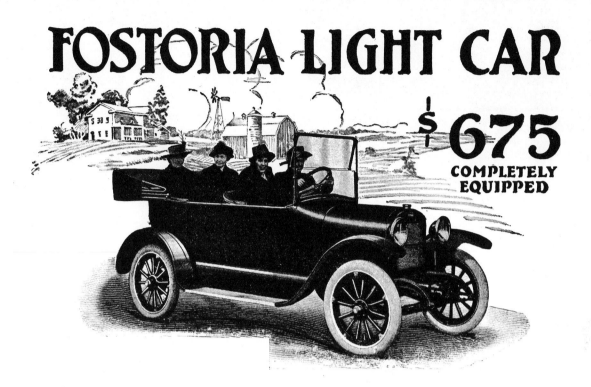

FOSTORIA LIGHT CAR

$675 COMPLETELY EQUIPPED

Announcing—
The Surprise Car of 1916

READ THESE SPECIFICATIONS

MOTOR — Sterling 4 cylinder valve-in-head; 3x4½; full 26 h. p.

TRANSMISSION—3 speeds forward and reverse, in unit with motor; dry disc clutch.

WHEELBASE—108 inches.

SPRINGS — Semi-elliptic front; CANTILEVER rear—same type as used in latest $2000 to $3000 cars.

FUEL FEED—Stewart Vacuum system with 15-gal. tank—same system found on high priced cars.

ELECTRICAL SYSTEM—Full electric starting and lighting system.

CARBURETOR—Zenith.

IGNITION — Atwater Kent, Unisparker, automatic.

STEERING GEAR—Worm and sector type, with Neville folding More-Room wheel, permitting easy access from either side.

COOLING SYSTEM—Thermo-syphon with large cellular radiator.

WEIGHT—1910 pounds with full equipment.

TIRES & RIMS—30x3½ tires, non-skid rear; demountable rims.

EQUIPMENT—Complete, of Standard quality.

—a full-size, powerful, handsome, **standardized car**, completely equipped, selling at the price of under-sized cars;

—in power, wheelbase and appearance equal to or greater than well known cars that sell for $1000 and upwards;

—possessing advanced features in accessibility, easy riding and freedom-from-friction not yet found in **any other cars**—except a limited few of the highest priced.

Dealers:

The Fostoria Line is Complete with Touring Car, Roadster, Coupe, Speedster and two styles of Delivery Car; prices range from $495 to $825. No lost prospects—a style for every service requirement.

Wire, Write or Call for Open Territory

THE FOSTORIA LIGHT CAR CO.,   **Montana Ave., Fostoria, Ohio**

The Fostoria Light Car priced at $495 to $825 furnished inexpensive transportation in 1916.

THE FRANKLIN CAR

FIND a man who has experienced the luxury of a Franklin Enclosed Car for *summer use*.

Ask him what he thinks of the Enclosed Car idea for summer.

He will tell you that he has made a *discovery* in motoring: that he will never use any other type of car: that all the objections you can think of are not true or do not apply to the Franklin.

He will tell you that the lightness and resilience of the Franklin make it practical for *any kind of driving*, on any sort of road, any time, anywhere.

That he gets all the *free-blowing air* there is—as much or as little as he wants.

That he can *regulate* the amount of ventilation. That he can instantly adjust the windows for any sort of weather—shut out dust or rain; drive for fifty miles on a hot summer afternoon and step out of the car *clean* and *cool*.

Then he will tell you what it means to his wife and family. The comfort of wearing what they please *en tour;* the freedom from grimy, parched skins and enveloping veils; the joy of stepping onto a hotel veranda without looking like the rescued survivors of a wrecked Cook's Tour.

Then he will come back to the specific features of Franklin construction—its *flexibility*, the *lightness* of its unsprung weight. He will tell you of *easy riding* over rough roads, its *liveliness* on the hills, its *maximum speed* from place to place, its economy in gasoline, its remarkable tire mileage.

Features that apply *equally* to Enclosed or Open models—the features that make the Franklin so definitely an *all-around efficient car*.

Touring Car	2280 lbs.	$1950.00	Cabriolet	2485 lbs.	$2750.00	Town Car	2610 lbs.	$3100.00
Runabout	2160 lbs.	1900.00	Sedan	2610 lbs.	2850.00	Limousine	2620 lbs.	3100.00
Four-passenger Roadster	2280 lbs.	1950.00	Brougham	2575 lbs.	2800.00	*All Prices F. O. B. Syracuse*		

FRANKLIN AUTOMOBILE COMPANY
SYRACUSE, N. Y. U. S. A.

FRANKLIN G TOURING

The seventh year for this model—the same high grade material and workmanship as the larger Franklin models.

BETTER THAN EVER BEFORE

Horse power with the G touring has been increased from eighteen to twenty-five.

Wheel base is 103 inches. The car turns around easily in a narrow street.

Tire equipment is 32″ x 4″ front and rear.

Franklin quality throughout, it is a high grade small car.

Body is of aluminum and will not rust, check or crack.

Full equipment included.

FRANKLIN AUTOMOBILE COMPANY Syracuse N´Y

The Franklin is the automobile with the air-cooled motor.

It is the highest development in motor car design, the automobile that thinking people everywhere are turning to more and more.

Every automobile is air-cooled, either directly or indirectly. Franklin air cooling is direct, positive and efficient. It does its work perfectly and entirely without complication. It has no moving parts.

Separate currents of fresh, cool air, equal in volume, are drawn by a suction-fan fly wheel down over vertical steel cooling flanges set in the walls of each cylinder.

The motor is evenly cooled and properly cooled under every possible condition of driving.

Franklin air cooling eliminates all the weight of water cooling. This, together with Franklin light-weight construction, lessens the load on the tires.

Tire service on the Franklin is from two to four times greater than on other cars. The tires are never overloaded. Road shocks are minimized by full-elliptic springs. Blowouts are avoided.

Let us send you our booklet "Hiram Percy Maxim, Air-Cooled Convert". It relates one of the most interesting changes of mind ever made by an engineer of recognized authority. We will be glad to mail to you a Franklin catalogue upon receipt of your address.

FRANKLIN AUTOMOBILE COMPANY Syracuse N Y

Left page, above and right: The Franklin Automobile Company of Syracuse produced one of America's most popular cars. The copy at the left stresses the advantages of a closed car, as opposed to the open type in which the passengers are exposed to the elements arriving "looking like the rescued survivors of a wrecked Cook's Tour." Note also the emphasis on light-weight construction and air cooling.

Below: The Wayne gasoline pump stood 11 feet high and pumped over 20 gallons per minute.

To deliver 20 gallons a minute is easy and 30 gallons are possible on the

Wayne Monarch Curb Pump

Fastest Gasoline Pump in existence—and the most accurate

Only pump that requires no backward strokes

Its BIGNESS commands
Its BEAUTY attracts
Its SPEED and "HONESTY" win and hold trade

The Wayne Monarch Pump—11 feet high and massive all over—makes all other pumps in the neighborhood look cheap and insignificant.

It automatically **takes command** of the gas situation wherever and whenever it is set up.

Its advertising and trade-bringing value make it a fabulous dividend-payer.

It fairly shouts to every passer-by—"THIS IS HEADQUARTERS!"

It also makes money because it stops leakage-losses, evaporation-losses, stealage-losses, excess-measure losses and its SPEED enables you to serve nearly twice as many patrons in a given time.

See the large CLOCK DIAL! It tells the customer exactly what he's getting—and every motorist likes **that**.

They also like the CLEAN GASOLINE delivered through the Wayne FILTER.

And customers like the QUICK SERVICE—5 gallons for 12 forward strokes and the plunger is returned by three more forward strokes—only pump on the market that requires no backward strokes!

You'll pump 5 gallons and return the plunger in 10—12—or 15 seconds, depending upon how fast you turn the crank. That means 20 to 30 gallons a minute!

And you can set the machine to pump any part of 5 gallons, by pints, quarts or gallons.

From **every** standpoint the Wayne Monarch is the pump **you** want.

Send for our descriptive circular.

WAYNE OIL TANK & PUMP COMPANY 9 CANAL STREET FT. WAYNE, IND.

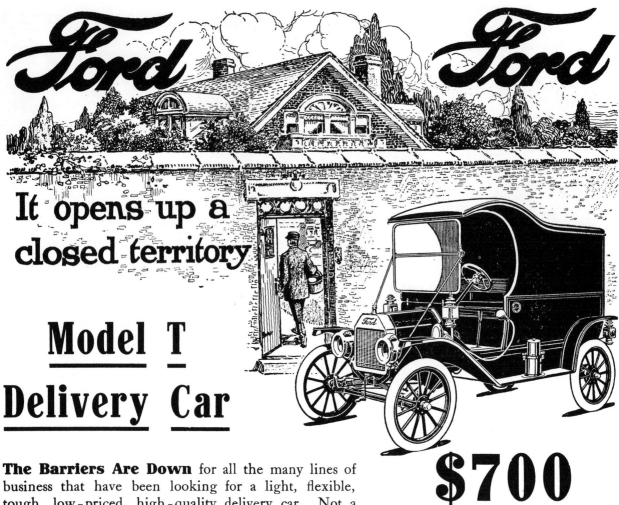

It opens up a closed territory

Model T Delivery Car

The Barriers Are Down for all the many lines of business that have been looking for a light, flexible, tough, low-priced, high-quality delivery car. Not a truck nor a van, but a CAR—that can cover the ground, open up new territory, bring in new customers, advertise its owner, extend the business, outwork a team of horses and cut the maintenance bill. **That car is this FORD Model T Delivery.**

THERE IS NO CLOSED TERRITORY to the wholesaler, the retailer, the power or light company that uses the Ford Model T Delivery Car. It eats up space and annihilates time. It makes relics of more than a million old style delivery vehicles in the United States. It is the feature of 1912 in commercial automobiles. It advertises its dealers and booms its buyers.

TWO YEARS OF HARD PRACTICAL TEST lie behind this statement of fact. The Wanamaker stores of New York and Philadelphia, and the Bell Telephone Company all over the Country, have taken these Ford Model T Delivery Cars and driven them now for over two years, winter and summer, uphill and down. No factory test here, but the actual grind of work. Result—not a change. The **guarantee of Accomplishment** stands on this car.

Light: weighs 1200 pounds—low tire expense—less fuel, multiplies the actual horsepower—carries 750 pounds of merchandise—carries it anywhere, any time.

$700

This price includes full equipment—Automatic Brass Windshield, Speedometer, Ford Magneto built into the motor, two six-inch Gas Lamps and Generator, three Oil Lamps, Horn and Tools. No Ford cars sold unequipped.
Capacity, 750 pounds of Merchandise.

Flexible: turns in a circle of 28 feet—accommodates itself to owner's and customers' space.

Tough: the same strong chassis of all Ford Model T cars—same simplicity of operation, same Ford magneto built into the motor, same Vanadium steel throughout (40 locomotives of vanadium at twice the cost of carbon steel are now being considered by the Secretary of War for use at Panama).

Low-priced: completely equipped—$700—no more than a team and wagon.

High-quality: stands side by side with the other productions of Ford genius—with more than 100,000 drivers vouching for them.

Your competition is active. Think hardest and FIRST. Send for our descriptive booklet. Ford branches and dealers everywhere.

Good dealers in unoccupied territory are requested to write us.

Ford Motor Company

Detroit, Michigan, U. S. A.

50

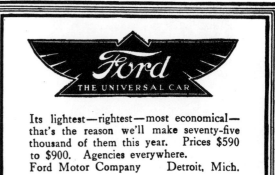
Ford, of course, produced THE American car. The Model T (of which over 15 million were made in the two decades after 1908) became renowned...and was the subject of countless songs, stories and anecdotes. A large business in supplying accessories for Fords sprung up. Some of the many gadgets offered to Ford owners are shown on this and the next five pages. Henry Ford billed the model T as "The Universal Car." At one point the list price of the Model T dropped to only $290.00.

SMALL TOURING MACHINE CAN BE CLOSED CAR, TOO

Town Car Body Offered and Limousine, Too, by Different Makers —Both Detachable, Light and Easily Applied.

Small cars have increased and multiplied with such rapidity that it is by no means surprising that, among the multitudes of users, there should be many

REISS'S HUPMOBILE DETACHABLE TOWN CAR BODY

who want to use their machines in all kinds of weather and in all seasons. It is for these year-round users that several styles of detachable or convertible bodies have been designed, one of which was illustrated and described in Motor World for January 15. The accompanying illustrations show two more, which, as may easily be seen, differ considerably from each other and from the one already referred to.

The Mandel "limosette," which is built by the Mandel Limousine Co., of 1457 W. Congress street, Chicago, is designed especially for Ford cars and is a separate unit that is put on the regular Ford touring body and will fit all cars of the 1912, 1913 and 1914 models. It is of composite construction, of steel and wood, with brass trimmings, mahogany ceiling and window framing, and broadcloth upholstery. The windows can be opened and the doors connect with the permanent doors so that both open together. Of the forward doors only one, that on the driver's right, is made to open. A windshield is incorporated with the structure, and over it the hood projects in an overhang that not only adds much to the appearance, but also serves as an additional protection in inclement

weather. Where the front of the body joins the dashboard there is a rounded steel cowl that makes an extremely neat finish. In fact, the appearance of the "limosette" leaves little to be desired, and the makers state that it is absolutely weatherproof and also extremely durable.

The body can be attached to a Ford car without other preparation than the removal of the standard top and windshield. No tools are required except an ordinary monkey-wrench and the only assistance needed is for the lifting on

MANDEL "LIMOSETTE" DESIGNED FOR FORD CARS

and the balancing of the body—which, incidentally, weighs but 150 pounds. The price is $150. A smaller tiype is made to fit Ford roadsters and costs $100. The general construction is the same in both cases.

Of quite a different type is the body designed by Charles E. Reiss, who is

president of the Chas. E. Reiss & Co., Inc., of 1690 Broadway, New York, Hupmobile distributers. It is built for Hupmobiles and differs from the Mandel body chiefly in the fact that it is designed along town car lines, only the rear part of the machine being housed in.

Overhead protection for the chauffeur is provided by an extensible canopy which fastens to the top of the windshield. The door of the attachable body fits the permanent door and opens with it. The design is worked out with such skill that there is little or nothing in the appearance of a car, with the attachment in place, to show that it is not a permanent, built-in body. The construction is metal and the lining of whipcord. It takes about 20 minutes to change a Hupmobile from an open car to a closed town car, and the addition of the housing does not in any way necessitate the marring of the permanent body.

Exploiting American Motors Abroad.

While it has been the fashion, even in many parts of America, to imagine that most of the truly good automobile engines come from abroad, the Continental Motor Mfg. Co., of Detroit, is upsetting these notions by making an active bid for European trade. Its enormous facilities afford advantages in the way of

both protection and price that even foreign manufacturers cannot overlook and the big company is making the most of its position by instituting an active campaign through a branch office which will be established in Paris. It will be in charge of R. A. Rothermel, who is already on the ground.

Detachable bodies for Ford cars - motoring news in the Feb.12,1914 Motor World.

Other Ford accessories.

The Lewkowicz Convertible Body

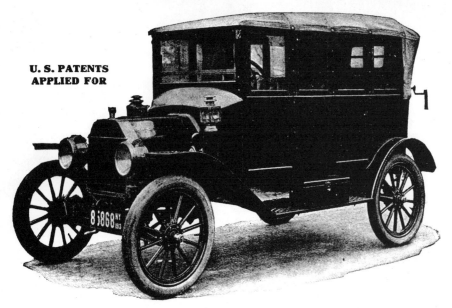
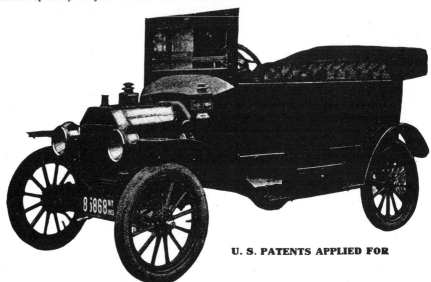
The Lewkowicz Convertible Body was designed to fit the Model T Ford.

ELECTRIFY YOUR FORD
FROM HEAD LAMPS TO TAIL LAMP IN TWO HOURS

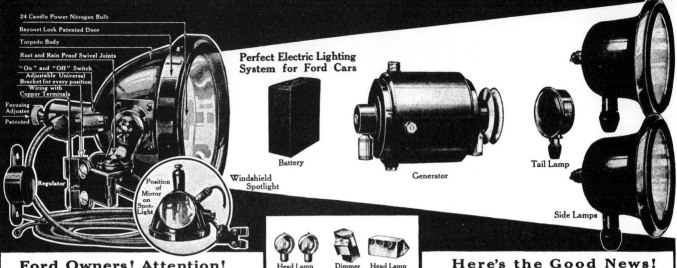

24 Candle Power Nitrogen Bulb
Bayonet Lock Patented Door
Torpedo Body
Rust and Rain Proof Swivel Joints
"On" and "Off" Switch
Adjustable Universal Bracket for every position
Wiring with Copper Terminals
Focusing Adjuster
Patented
Regulator
Position of Mirror on Spot-Light

Perfect Electric Lighting System for Ford Cars

Battery

Generator

Windshield Spotlight

Tail Lamp

Side Lamps

Head Lamp Bulbs   Dimmer Switch   Head Lamp Control

Ford Owners! Attention!

No more Headlight worry—no more glare—no more uncontrollable run-away light—no more oil side lamps—no more oil tail lamp— no more fumbling in the dark, the wind and the rain with matches. But now—all annoyance and inconvenience swept away by the push of the button. Convenient headlight control from the switch mounted on the steering post. Headlights brightened or dimmed at will for pleasure and safety.

Also two beautiful electric side lamps and a high grade electric tail lamp to switch on and off instantly. No cost but the low first cost. No machine work. No need of an expert mechanic. This necessary Electric Lighting System can be installed upon your great little car complete in two hours.

Here's the Good News!

And there's beauty, good looks for you. Safety, pleasure and night-driving comfort as long as your car exists.

The improved Genolite is an achievement for Ford Owner satisfaction, comparable only to the service and the quality performance of the car Ford Owners are proud to own.

Genolite Type "C" $29.85

An improved and complete Electric Lighting System that gives you a brilliant light from a storage battery in both side and tail lamps irrespective whether motor is running or idle.

Genolite also furnishes you with two powerful Nitrogen headlight bulbs (to replace your present ones), lighted through our patented regulating device which governs the flow of electric current from the magneto, resulting in a more constant light, which is sufficient for touring even at low speeds and a most satisfactory light at all speeds.

And this can be instantly accomplished at the will of the driver from a control switch conveniently located on the steering post.

Genolite [Type C] also includes a generator, and a storage battery which it charges without cost. With the beautiful electric side lamps and tail lamp, also bulbs, wiring and all attachments complete as described and ready for application (no extras needed) Genolite is an efficient and complete Lighting System for five electric lamps for Ford Cars.

Genolite Type "D" $31.85

In the unique Genolite [Type D] equipment Ford Owners are given an exclusive combination Electric Lighting System that includes a powerful windshield Spotlight with many patented features.

This spotlight that throws a brilliant ray of light ten feet or a thousand ahead, behind, at left or right, which can be diffused or concentrated at the will of the driver, offers together with the Genolite Electric Side Lamps and Tail Lamp, generator, storage battery, bulbs, wiring and all necessary attachments, a complete Electric Lighting System that any Ford Owner may well be proud of.

Sum up the unusual advantages obtained in Genolite Type D.

A brilliant and continuous light in side lamps and tail lamp without regard to the motor whether running or idle.

One operation of the switch conveniently located in the spotlight throws on a brilliant light and thereby automatically dims the two headlights.

This spotlight is the first and only practical windshield light ever designed exclusively for Ford cars.

This beautiful and powerful spotlight is complete with mirrorscope for day driving convenience.

It includes a patented hand focusing device to meet State lighting laws. It has a universal bracket that will not rust in the joints and fits all Ford cars ever made. It possesses many other exclusive and patented features.

It gives almost full candle power at very low car speeds and maximum candle power at nine miles or more— maintaining this maximum lighting capacity at any speed.

This is accomplished by a patented regulator which automatically delivers current at the proper voltage to the spotlight at all speeds.

Genolite Type C at $29.85, or Type D at $31.85, comprise respectively perfect systems of Automatic Electric Lighting for Ford Cars. Their only cost is the low first cost. Their installation is simple and their service and convenience lasting. After you have equipped your car with Genolite you will wonder how you ever did without it.

Genolite will be a revelation to you of Economy and Service. To every Ford Owner, whether living in city, town or country, Genolite Type C or Type D will light the way for pleasure, pride and safety.

To insure prompt delivery send your order now.

Fill out the coupon. If your dealer should be unable to immediately supply you, send his name with your remittance and we will send you Genolite either Type C or Type D as ordered with full instructions to save you delay and to provide you at once the pleasure, convenience and enjoyment this perfect Electric Lighting System will give you.

P-R-24

DETROIT STARTER CO.
Detroit, Mich.
Enclosed please find remittance for $_____
CHECK IN SQUARE
☐ Express me Genolite Electric Lighting System Type C $29.85 f.o.b. Det.
☐ Express me Genolite Electric Lighting System Type D $31.85 f.o.b. Detroit.

Name_____
Street_____
City_____ State_____
Your Dealer's Name_____

Dealers! Tremendous volume of orders already received at our factory prove that every Ford Owner has been waiting for a dependable Electric Lighting System. *You know our reputation as manufacturers.* There are large, immediate and assured sales of Genolite Type C and Type D in your locality. Wire or write us at once.

The Detroit Starter Company, Detroit, U. S. A.
Our Reputation is Your Guarantee.

"Electrify Your Ford" with these gadgets from the Detroit Starter Company.

More Ford accessories are shown at the top and lower left of this page. Below, right is a Gulf Refining Company ad of about 1916. The various gasoline, oil and tire companies advertised heavily then - as they do now.

Garford MOTOR CARS

The large number of influential people who own Garford cars signifies, probably better than anything else, the calibre of this machine. For instance, the list of bankers forms a very interesting group of prominent individuals—men that control some of the most powerful banking institutions in America.

¶ H. P. Davison, of the Morgan house, owns a Garford. So do A. P. Hepburn, President of the First National Bank, S. G. Bayne, President of the Seaboard National Bank, William H. Porter, President of the Chemical National Bank, and F. B. Schenck, President of the Liberty National Bank—all of New York City. J. B. and R. D. Forgan, the big Chicago bankers, both own Garfords. And there are many others. For nine years the Garford has been the choice of those who are accustomed to the best. Back in 1902 it was—as it is today—the most advanced car made. Its fine and unquestioned mechanical perfection, thorough construction, and superb finish are seldom equaled in any other car.

¶ The model, illustrated here, is our "Forty" Town car, priced at $4800—a very practical and unusually comfortable car for this time of the year.

¶ In addition to the well known Garford "Forty" we now have the "Four-Thirty" and "Six-Fifty." Made in all styles of open and closed bodies. We will be glad to send you a Garford book which fully describes the complete line.

The Willys-Garford Sales Company, Toledo, Ohio

We make a complete line of commercial cars

The $4800 Garford was a car for the wealthy...as the above ad illustrates.

The "GRANT"

The Standard Small Car

There is nothing freakish or experimental in the whole car. Every part is standard, the 56-inch tread—4 cylinder motor—cone clutch—sliding gear transmission—shaft drive—floating rear axle—full elliptic springs—every unit has been tried out and proven by two years actual testing—not only in the hands of our engineers but in the hands of inexperienced drivers.

The Grant has a decided foreign appearance that gives it an air of distinction and commands attention immediately. The bull nosed radiator—stream line roomy body with moulded turtle back—wire wheels—close to the ground effect—in fact every detail shows the "last word" in high priced construction.

The Grant is the most economical automobile built—an average of 30 miles to the gallon of gasoline and 100 miles to a pint of lubricating—the wire wheels give a greatly increased tire mileage—this means a low cost of upkeep—as well as a low initial cost.

The equipment of the Grant is unusually find and complete—in fact it is equal to the equipment on cars costing three times as much as the Grant—and all furnished for $495.

Dealers:
Here is an opportunity to close your territory for the first high grade fully equipped automobile to sell under $500 that has ever been produced.

A car that embodies the qualities of the highest priced motor cars at the price of the cheapest.

We are BUILDING and DELIVERING 125 of these CARS THIS MONTH—250 in February—400 in March, etc.

You can see for yourself, the kind of dealers we are getting. Let us hear from you at once.

Interesting literature sent on request.

"GRANT" SPECIFICATIONS---Compare these specifications with any car you think of, irrespective of price

MOTOR—4 cylinder, 4 cycle, 2¾ x 4 in. Cylinders and crank case cast en bloc. Inlet and exhaust passages cast integral. Valves enclosed, three point suspension. Develops full 21 H. P. Large valves and drop forged shafts of special alloy steel. The Grant Motor can not be made to knock, advance the spark and throttle levers from the lowest to the highest point at any speed you elect, the motor jumps forward like a race horse.

IGNITION—Swiss High Tension, the accepted standard ignition of the world, superceding in all cars of character, the obsolete battery systems of earlier days.

LUBRICATION—Constant level vacuum feed, integral with motor, overcoming absolutely lack of lubrication at varying speeds.

CARBURETOR—Mayer, specially constructed for Grant Motor, dash adjustment.

TRANSMISSION—Sliding gear, progressive type, two speeds forward, one reverse, integral with rear axle, a compact assembly carried on ball and Hyatt Quiet Roller Bearings, not plain bearings.

CLUTCH—The reliable, leather faced, cone clutch, generally regarded as the most serviceable and reliable type of clutch construction.

STEERING GEAR—Pinion and gear fully adjustable.

FRONT AXLE—I beam, drop forged, large knuckles and spindles.

DRIVE—Propeller shaft with ball joint at end of torque tube.

REAR AXLE—Three-quarter floating. Load carried on housing, not on live axle. The live axle and driving shaft of superlative high grade steel, heat treated. The outer ends of live axles carried on Hyatt Quiet roller bearings. Differential of the two pinion type.

BRAKES—Foot brake, external contracting, emergency brake, internal expanding; both brakes on rear wheels. Extra large braking surfaces with asbestos linings.

FRAME—Pressed channel steel U section of unusual strength and rigidity.

SPRINGS—Front, full elliptic. Rear transverse, shackled back of rear axle, the best quality of springs obtainable in the American market, infinitely superior to the abbreviated cyclecar cantilever type. The Grant is the easiest riding car in the world, irrespective of name or price.

RADIATOR—Bull Nose English type providing maximum water capacity and radiating surface. Thermo Syphon circulation with fan.

CONTROL—Center shift lever, spark and throttle advance under wheel. Foot brake and clutch operated with one pedal.

SPARK and throttle control — under steering wheel (no fixed spark) where the best practice and usage indicates it should be. Advancing the spark at the discretion of the driver will not injure the Grant Motor.

GUARDS—Full sized guards of extra heavy gauge steel, graceful in outline. Complete running boards and mud splashers, admittedly the only type of construction satisfactory to the owner.

WHEELS—28 x 3 wire, English type.

TIRES—28 x 3 Bailey tread, clincher.

WEIGHT—1075 pounds, fully equipped for the road.

BRAKES—Two, both on rear wheels, generous in size, positive in action.

WHEEL BASE—90 inches.

ROAD CLEARANCE—Ten inches.

BODY — Pure stream line, double doors 18½ in. wide, 32 in. leg room between seat and dash.

COLOR—Body, black; chassis, rich red.

EQUIPMENT — Grant equipment is complete. Top and top slip of real mohair, not oil cloth, heavy automobile bows, not buggy bows. Windshield—folding, non-rattling, one-piece, plate glass, not cheap coach glass.

SPEEDOMETER—Stewart sixty mile instrument. Lamps, five. Acetylene head lights, with generator, oil side and tail lamps. Horn, jack, tire kit, full set of tools. Accessories finished in black enamel and nickel.

EXTRA EQUIPMENT—Full electric starting and lighting with electric horn at reasonable price.

PRICE—$495.00, with complete equipment, F. O. B. Findlay, Ohio.

The "GRANT" With Full Equipment---$495

Address Dept. "C" Grant Motor Company, Findlay, Ohio

This 1914 Grant ad gives many specifications and points of technical information.

6 Cylinder $2375
Fully Equipped
Moore Multiple Exhaust

Howard

130 inch wheel base

There is a great similarity between men and motor cars

Here's the man-side

Each possesses characteristics that make them fit or unfit for service.

When you set out to find a man to work for you, you don't hire the most flashily dressed man you meet; neither do you hire the fellow who talks the most.

You look rather to what that man has to offer you for the money you plan to lay down for his salary.

If you choose such a man, because of his good appearance and then find nothing to back it up: what do you do?

And if you are impressed by his conversation and discover that his entire brain is in his mouth; chances are ten to one you stop his pay check.

4 Cylinder *Lexington* $1335
Fully Equipped

114 inch wheel base

Dealers!

Don't be satisfied with merely reading this announcement. Write today and ask us to tell you just wherein the value of the Lexington-Howard organization lies. We will show you very quickly that there are a great many reasons why you should sell the Lexington "Four" and the Howard "Six" in your city.

Here's the car-side

Many a car has found favor through its paint job; in fact a good finishing department is the salvation of poor construction; for a time.

Many an advertising man has gained a dealer's confidence by his assumed sincerity in the product he was selling.

But as with men, motor cars must deserve such trust in order to hold the ground thus gained.

There is a law in human affairs that rewards the fit against the unfit; that sends the deserving up the success ladder with exactly the same speed as it tumbles the unworthy down.

Now the points behind all this is that you, as a motor car dealer must be very sure of your ground before you enter into a binding contract with anybody.

We want to put before you in very simple terms, the high character of the Lexington-Howard organization; its methods; its value to you. Then we want you to judge us, our sincerity, our responsibility; solely upon your own knowledge of human nature.

First of all the Lexington-Howard is an organization of specialists; men who have spent their lives in perfecting themselves in their individual lines. These men have proved their experience in profit paying plants before they entered ours.

We don't want you to take our word for this; we want you to make us prove it.

What you are most concerned with is our method of manufacture and the provision we have made for our permanency in the automobile business. The Lexington-Howard plant has been most carefully and profitably departmentized.

Each part of the car represents a unit of manufacture; each unit is working every day at a profit. The fact that we have made so liberal a provision for our dealers is only good business.

Unless you as a dealer receive the proper share of profits you will not remain in business; and it is upon you and you alone that our future as motor car manufacturers must rest. Then if you will ask us for our sales proposition you will receive another very pleasant surprise; because it's your interest that's at the bottom of this whole affair. We have laid our plans along lines that mean your success and ours; which, of course, means your profit and ours.

THE LEXINGTON-HOWARD COMPANY
126 Main Street, Connersville, Indiana

The Lexington and Howard automobiles (1914).

Hupmobile

"32" Touring Car or Roadster $1050 f. o. b Detroit

In Canada, $1230 f. o. b. Windsor Factory

EQUIPMENT—Electric horn; rain vision, ventilating windshield; mohair top with envelope; inside quick adjustable curtains; speedometer; cocoa mat in tonneau; gas headlights; oil side lamps; trimmings, black and nickel.

With regular equipment and additional equipment of two-unit electric generator and starter; electric lights; oversize tires, 33 x 4 inches; demountable rims, extra rim and tire carrier at rear. $1200 f. o. b. Detroit.

In Canada, $1380 f. o. b. Windsor Factory

A Composite of the Best Engineering Authority

One of the things you noticed at the Show was the preponderance of the new style bodies, aptly christened the "Stream Line."

We were not clever enough to invent the name—we wish we were.

But our engineers were advanced enough to develop this type of body two years ago; and at the Chicago Show of 1912, the Hupmobile was the only car fitted with the stream line type.

Naturally it pleases us to see so many of our costlier and more luxurious brothers falling into line and advocating this style.

A feature, too, that probably impressed you was the almost unanimous tendency toward motors of the long-stroke type.

The Hupmobile vindicated the superior pulling qualities of that type of motor two years ago, and at the Chicago Show of the same date was the only car that exhibited the long-stroke design — with the exception of one or two makes that have since passed out of the market.

When you looked over starting and lighting equipments, you found the Hupmobile, as usual, in high class company.

Of the seventeen makes that you will see equipped with the same starting and lighting system as the Hupmobile, four of them belong to the costliest types; and every one of the others thus equipped is higher priced than the Hupmobile.

At the recent Paris and London Shows, six of the best known and most expensive cars manufactured in Europe were equipped with this same make of electrical equipment that the Hupmobile is using.

We mention these things as a convincing illustration of our claim that in every department of mechanical excellence, quality is considered first, regardless of price.

As a careful dealer who wants to give his customers the worth of their money, we feel sure that you will give every thoughtful consideration to the Hupmobile.

Hupp Motor Car Company
1254 Milwaukee Avenue, Detroit, Michigan

The car of The American Family

The Hupmobile was inexpensive and achieved immense popularity. A large nationwide dealer organization aided immeasurably.

Men of millions who drive the

Hupmobile

GUARANTEED FOR LIFE

Nearly every man whose name is reproduced herewith owns one or more of the four or five fine cars of largest size. None of them, to our knowledge, owns any smaller car save the Hupmobile.

No mere appeal of price—no consideration of a low first cost—could possibly have interested the men whose names appear in this impressive list of Hupmobile owners.

Starting with New York, where men who own Hupmobiles represent wealth aggregating tens of millions of dollars, every large city in the country records its group of leading citizens who have singled out this one popular-priced car for their favor.

It is obvious, is it not, that they have chosen the Hupmobile because it *possesses certain qualities, apart from price,* which renders it attractive and desirable to them?

We have told you, many times, what these qualities are. We have impressed upon you the fact that the Hupmobile is built with such *scrupulosity of method and material* that it concedes nothing, save size, to the costliest cars of seven-passenger capacity.

In this list of names you have indubitable evidence that men of affairs everywhere who own and drive the costliest cars agree with us as to the worth and entire desirability of the Hupmobile.

Can you think of even one other car which appeals at once to the man of moderate means and to the man of unlimited means? In the one case it is smart and efficient enough to travel side by side in perfect equality with its $6,000 running mate. In the other it amply satisfies the buyer who limits himself to one—thoroughly reliable—machine.

F. O. B. Detroit, inc... of electric headlights, electric and oil side ... and batteries; front shock absorbers; fo ... l passenger; 31 x 3½ inch rear tires; hor ...

F. O. B. Detroit, inc ... ols and horn. Special top and windshield, ... generator, etc., extra.

F. O. B. Detroit, inc ... s headlights and generator; oil lamps fo ... hock absorbers; 31 x 3½ inch rear tires, ... dshield, speedometer, etc., extra. Wheel ... ger capacity, four.

F. O. B. Detroit, inc ... tools and horn. Top, windshield, speedom ... k or generator; trunk rack and tire irons e ...

NEW YORK
W. K. VANDERBILT, Jr.
E. H. HARRIMAN, Jr.
LOUIS TIFFANY
DE WITT FLANAGAN
GENERAL JOCYLYN
THOMAS HAVEMEYER
A. VON BRUNIG
C. BARTON WILLINGS
CHARLES TIFFANY
P. O. MILLS
GUY VAUGHAN
TIMOTHY BYRNE, Vice-Pres. N. Y., N. H. & Hartford R. R.
H. B. HOLLINS (2)
NATHAN STRAUSS
WILLIAM GRAY
FRANCES HODGSON BURNETT
ISAAC BACHMAN
THOMAS SLIDELL
LOUIS DE JONGE
HAROLD BROWNING
HENRY SIEGEL
J. C. R. PEABODY
DR. E. H. LYON
C. A. STRALEM
H. C. PHIPPS
W. E. KOTMAN
ARCHIBALD BROWN
HAROLD WESSON
JONATHAN MOORE

BOSTON
J. FROTHINGHAM
ELLIS E. DRESSEL
CONGRESSMAN BUTLER AMES

CHICAGO
H. T. APPLE, Pres. Apple Electric Co.
FRED'K H. BARTLETT, Real Estate
A. H. CRAWFORD, Crawford Transportation Co.
RICHMOND DEAN, Vice-Pres. of the Pullman Co.
EDWARDS-LOOMIS CO.
ROBT. H. INGERSOLL & BRO., Ingersoll Watches
FRED'K McLAUGHLIN, McLaughlin Coffee Import Co.
J. J. MITCHELL, Pres. Ills. Trust & Savings Bank
EDW. S. MOORE, Vice-Pres. Rock Island Railroad
CLIFFORD SKLATEK, Salesman for Locomobile Co. of America
R. W. SEARS, Sears-Roebuck Co.
H. E. THURSTON, Chicago Museum Co.
J. R. TAYLOR, United Cigar Stores
J. S. WOODWORTH, Excelsior Supply Co.
DR. N. ANDERSON
DR. TRUMAN BROPHY, Pres. Illinois Dental Univ.
DR. J. J. CRONIN
DR. W. J. MURFITT
DR. MOE
H. P. NELSON CO., Pianos
W. RAWLEIGH, Mayor of Freeport, Ills.

MEXICO CITY, MEX.
ROBERT DE CASO Y CACHO
LIC. F. DIAZ BARRASO
ANTONIO URQUIZA CONTURIER
JULIO OSIRIO

INDIANAPOLIS
HON. THOS. TAGGART, Ex - Chairman National Democratic Committee, and proprietor of the French Lick Springs Hotel
H. McGOWAN, Pres. Indianapolis Traction & Terminal Co. and Pres. Terre Haute, Indianapolis & Eastern Interurban Railway
L. G. ROTHSCHILD, Surveyor of Customs
W. M. WILKES, Sec. VanCamp Packing Co.
(2) R. W. FURNAS, Pres. R. W. Furnas Ice Cream Co.
J. I. DISETTE, Pres. Realty Investment Co.
A. M. OGLE, Pres. Vandalia Coal Co.

PITTSBURGH
WM. S. STIMMEL
EARL MARVIN
E. H. JENNINGS
J. J. CHILDS
NICH. KOPP
WM. HAMILTON
A. S. COOK
GEO. R. SCOTT
J. R. SPEER
DR. STEPHENS
T. G. ROCENIAK
AL. PACK
S. K. LEECH
W. W. KEEFER
P. S. KIER
J. H. KIRKPATRICK
LOUIS HIRSH
W. R. HADLEY
DR. HEGARTY
J. R. HENDRICKS
C. P. DAVIS
D. CRISSMAN
MRS. BOYLE

DETROIT
NEWTON ANNIS
LAWRENCE BUHL
CHAS. B. BOHN
FRANK A. BRAULT
JOHN E. BAKER
DR. JAMES CLELAND
DR. GEORGE E. CLARK
F. O. CHASE
EDWIN DENBY
R. A. PATRICK
GEORGE A. DRAKE
DON M. DICKENSON, Jr.
H. DuCHARME
JAMES HANNON
H. J. HAYES
D. M. SHAW
H. W. HARDING
JUDGE H. S. HULBERT
GEORGE JOHNSTON
H. M. KEELER
W. A. C. MILLER
GEORGE I. McCLURE
JOHN OWEN
J. WALTER DRAKE
ASHLEY POND, Jr.
W. H. ROBERTS
DR. ROWLAND
W. A. SCRIPPS
DR. H. L. SIMPSON
MARVIN L. STANTON
F. STEVENS
C. L. SMITH
FR. A. P. TERNIS
DR. V. C. VAUGHAN
C. D. WATERMAN
F. A. WESTBROOK
JAMES WARREN
B. H. WEBB

ST. LOUIS
C. VAN DYKE HILL, Sec. West. Adv. Co.
C. M. FOSTER, Mgr. Hyde Park Bwy. Co.
L. DANA, Vice-Pres. Charter Oak Range Co.
G. DUNCAN, Treas. Ludlow-Saylor Wire Co.
LOUIS J. NICOLAUS, Altheimer & Rawlins Bond Co.
H. POTTER, W. R. Compton Bond & Stock Co.
DR. WM. S. DEUTCH
HUDS'N E. BRIDGE, Bridge-Boeck Mfg. Co.
C. N. MOORE, Sec. A. G. Edwards & Sons
F. B. EISEMANN, Treas. Rice-Stix D. G. Co.
A. BRAUN, Jr., Sec. A. Braun Mfg. Co.
E. HAMES, Pres. Peter Hauptman Tob. Co.
F. B. NULSEN, Western Automobile Co.
MRS. T. E. PRICE
DR. JACKSON MILLER
MRS. DR. KITTRIDGE
DR. GEO. KREBS
HARRY POTTER
BART S. ADAMS
OLIVER BLANKE
HENRY NICOLAUS

MINNEAPOLIS
C. A. SMITH, C. A. Smith Timber Co.
P. L. SPOONER, Spooner Investment Co.
GEO. P. THOMPSON, North Star Lbr. Co.
M. J. LAVALLE, Hartig Elec. Co.
W. H. ZINN, John C. Johnson Groc. Co.
E. H. BROWN
C. H. CARPENTER, Carpenter-Deckert Lbr. Co.
DR. GEO. STEVENSON
E. H. McDUFFEE

NEW ORLEANS
J. D. HUNTER
GEO. DUNBAR
H. FITCHENBURG
J. E. PIERCE
W. B. UTLEY
GENE BUSG
D. C. RITCHIE
A. MACKIE GROCERY HOUSE (3)
GEO. E. NORTHDROP
DR. E. L. RICH
F. HOWARD
A. POWELL (2)

CLEVELAND
L. GEDEON, Owner of Hardware Store
S. E. HALE, Pres. & Gen. Mgr. Hale Mfg. Co.
B. L. MARBLE, Pres. The Marble Chair Co.
J. R. NUTT, Sec. & Treas. Citizens Savings & Trust Co.
TOM SWAN, Gen. Mgr. Standard Top & Equipment Co.
J. F. TAYLOR, Pres. Taylor Chair Co.
TELLING BROS., Dealers in Ice Cream
W. G. POLLOCK, Sec. & Treas. Pittsburgh & Lake Angeline Iron Co. and Pres. & Treas. Union Dock Co.
D. E. FULMER, Sec. & Treas. The Landesman-Hirshheimer Co.
CLAUDE FOSTER, Pres. & Gen. Mgr. Gabriel Horn Mfg. Co.
A. H. BABCOCK, Pres. The A. H. Babcock Co. and Pres. Real Estate & General Insurance
R. F. WILLIAMS, President The Williams Bros. Co.

BUFFALO
MANNING, MAXWELL & MOORE
GEORGE S. DONALDSON
WICKWIRE BROS., Wickwire Steel Co.
C. CUTLER, Cutler Desk Co.
W. F. POLSON, Pres. Polson Mfg. Co.
C. B. SEARS, Lawyer
DR. G. HITZEL
DR. BURT C. JOHNSON

VANCOUVER, B. C.
J. J. HANNA
E. PRICE
DR. GOOSETREY
D. W. STINSON
W. L. KEATE
FRED BEECHER
DR. ROBERT McKECHNIE
MR. PORTIER
STANLEY E. MITTON
MRS. NEVILLE
GEO. WALKEM
DR. GLEN CAMPBELL
W. D. MUIR
CHAS. OLIVER
J. T. SUMMERFIELD
CRAWLEY W. RICARDO
DR. ROBERT TELFORD
DR. ROBERT F. GREER

SCRANTON, PA.
C. R. CONNELL, Treas. Lackawanna Mills
JNO. R. ATHERTON, Paymaster Del. & Hudson Co.
C. W. FULKERSON, Piano Dealer
E. R. TROXELL, Physician & Surgeon
J. D. WILLIAMS & BRO. CO., Wholesale & Retail Confectioners

HUPP MOTOR CAR COMPANY   Department P   Detroit, Michigan

Licensed under Selden patent

A listing of some prominent Hupmobile owners.

It Was a RUSHMORE Show!

At the recent Importers' Salon, Hotel Astor, eight foreign and two American makes of cars were exhibited (cyclecars are here omitted).

Five of the foreign makes and one American make were equipped with the

RUSHMORE STARTING AND LIGHTING SYSTEM

The other three foreign makes were not electrically equipped.
Following is the count in detail:

Rushmore-equipped		No Electric Equipment	
DeDion-Bouton	5 cars	Fiat	3 cars
Mercedes	6 cars	Minerva	3 cars
Isotta-Fraschini	6 cars	Peugeot (large)	2 cars
Lancia	8 cars		
Delaunay-Belleville	4 cars	Total no equipment	8 cars
Simplex (American)	6 cars	**Non-Rushmore**	
Total Rushmore equipped	35 cars		
Total Rushmore-equipped foreign	29 cars	S. G. V. (American)	3 cars

Total number of foreign cars of size to employ starters........ 37
Proportion Rushmore to whole foreign exhibit............... 78 per cent
Proportion Rushmore to total foreign cars electrically equipped 100 per cent

An American starting and lighting system was seen among the accessory exhibits, but was not represented on the cars on the floor.

RUSHMORE DYNAMO WORKS Plainfield, N.J.

Trade shows have always been an important part of the automobile business. Above, the Rushmore Dynamo Works notes that a 1914 exhibit was a "Rushmore show."

The Klaxon horn was heavily advertised and was the best-known type of automobile horn. Indeed, "klaxon" became synonymous with automobile horn. Over the years the Klaxon manufacturer was engaged in endless law suits with others who copied the device.

Unless You Buy the *New* Self-Starting HUDSON "33" You Do Not Get the Latest

Three years ago the magneto was sold as extra equipment on most cars.

Today it is regularly furnished with all first class automobiles. It is now considered as essential as the carburetor.

Next year, or as soon thereafter as the change can be made, all automobiles will have self-starters. It will be just as difficult two years hence to sell a second-hand car not equipped with Self-starter and Demountable rims as it now is to dispose of a car not equipped with a good magneto.

What other makers cannot furnish before next year you get now in the *new* HUDSON "33."

Don't overlook this feature in buying a motor car. You may want to sell it in two or three years. The feature that all will want then you can get now if you choose the *new* HUDSON "33."

And Don't Buy a Make-Shift

The *new* HUDSON "33" is a brand-new car—the creation of the foremost engineer in the industry. Howard E. Coffin is its builder. He worked from the ground up. His were all original designs. He was not compelled to utilize old stock. We had nothing that had to be used up.

The bodies were designed for the "33." Every unit is as it was originally planned. Therefore the HUDSON "33" is all new. It is not an old model at a new price—not an old design with a new name.

And best of all, Howard E. Coffin designed it. That in itself establishes its worth. The ablest engineers and the leading specialists in the business gave their aid to him in its building, for they are his assistants.

The automobile world is always on the alert to know what new short-cut to simplicity Howard E. Coffin makes. He is the great constructive builder—the man who, more than any other, has brought about the present high standard of motor cars.

For years he has led. He establishes the trend of engineering practice as certainly as Paris makes the styles and as Edison drives the new mile posts of electrical advancement.

That's the type of car you get in the HUDSON "33" with its almost 1000 fewer parts than are used on the average car — with its dust-proof features, the entirely enclosed motor and its practically noiseless operation—to say nothing of the car's great beauty—the high degree of refinement, soft cushions, easy riding qualities and all the new features not known on any car at its price one year ago. By examining the *new* HUDSON "33" you get an idea of what types of cars will prevail next year and the year after.

The Ideal Is Possible Now

There is no need to wait to buy the ideal car. Under any other name than the HUDSON "33" you cannot get these features earlier than two years.

Many good cars are offered now. Many are the result of the most painstaking, skilled workmanship—but they are not so modern. The usual difficulties experienced in automobiles of three and four years ago have in a measure been corrected by good workmanship — but the cumbersome design still prevails.

In the HUDSON "33" is combined the skill, experience and ingenuity of Howard E. Coffin and his corps of the ablest engineers to be had.

Read Automobile Advertisements
In City Newspapers

The classified advertisements in the Sunday newspapers will give you a true insight into the value at which second-hand cars are held. There are thousands of HUDSONS in use. Yet they are not offered for sale at the low prices at which many other cars are advertised.

The HUDSON "33" is distinctly advanced. It is as modern three years after its delivery to the user as are the then current models of other cars. It has always been thus.

Isn't it worth while to insure yourself against taking a big price sacrifice by buying a HUDSON "33"? Do you think any other automobile is quite so certain to have a market value when you are ready to sell it in order to get the then latest HUDSON?

This Big, Handsome, Noiseless, Self-Starting, Fully Equipped Automobile is Howard E. Coffin's Latest Car—the Simplest and Most Advanced Automobile Built, Regardless of Price

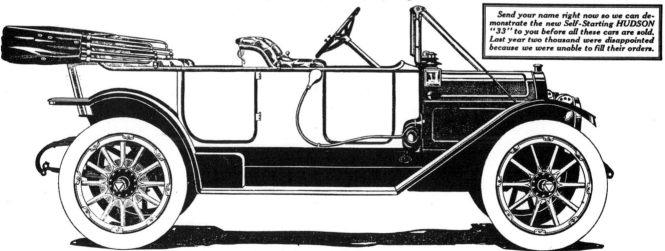

Send your name right now so we can demonstrate the new Self-Starting HUDSON "33" to you before all these cars are sold. Last year two thousand were disappointed because we were unable to fill their orders.

The price for either of four models—Touring, five-passenger—Torpedo, four-passenger—Roadster, two-passenger, or *Mile-a-Minute* Speedster—is $1600. Not a cent more is needed to equip it before it is ready for use, for top, Disco Self-Starter, Demountable rims, BIG tires, ventilated fore-doors, windshield, large gas tank, magneto—dual system—and all things usually listed as extras are included. Write for illustrations showing how the *new* HUDSON "33" is simpler than any other car.

See the Triangle on the Radiator

HUDSON MOTOR CAR COMPANY, 7179 Jefferson Ave., DETROIT

The Hudson line of automobiles was very popular. Howard E. Coffin, whose "opinion" is quoted above, was one of the principals of the company.

HUDSON "33"

**"33"
Pony
Tonneau
$1300**

**"33"
Touring
Car
$1250**

The "33" Torpedo—$1350

Equipment on all models includes 3 oil and 2 gas lamps, horn, tools, pump, quick-detachable rims, gas generator.

Confidence Accounts for the Great Demand for the HUDSON "33"

It is remarkable that the majority of those who have bought the HUDSON "33" knew a great deal about automobile values and yet they placed their orders without investigating the car.

They made their selection just as they would choose a doctor, a lawyer or an architect.

With all their knowledge of automobile values, they were more willing to place their confidence in the skill and experience of the man who designed the car and the company that built it than they were to trust their own judgment.

Surely this is the safest way for an inexperienced buyer to select a car. The details of finish or some attractive yet unessential device may so often influence a buyer as to cause him to overlook the more important features of simplicity, design, materials and other similar qualities.

Even experienced automobilists are influenced by these devices, and that is why the majority of the 687 persons who placed their orders on the first day that the various dealers exhibited their HUDSON demonstrators, have bought more on account of their confidence than because of their own judgment.

It is not remarkable that they have done this. They knew from previous experience the character of cars that Howard E. Coffin has designed. Many of these persons knew, from having driven his earlier cars, the character of workmanship his associates put into his automobiles.

Confidence guides your decision in choosing any article you buy. It should be your principal influence in selecting an automobile. Many qualities of a car are never known until it is put into actual service. Much can be covered by paint. The quality and strength of metals can never be known until the car is actually driven on the road. You must buy an automobile, therefore, just as an inexperienced person chooses a diamond or entrusts his life to a physician or a surgeon whom he knows only by reputation.

Howard E. Coffin is known by the work he has done, to practically every man in the automobile trade. Men in the garages speak his name in connection with some device on an automobile, just as electricians refer to the name of Thomas A. Edison, or as surgeons refer to the Mayo Brothers.

Confidence and not personal knowledge is the safest guide.

Mr. Coffin devised a lubricating system years ago which is today used upon 80 per cent. of the better known American cars. He is recognized as the most advanced automobile engineer in this country. He has been honored by engineering societies and associations in America and abroad. His skill has made for him a fame not enjoyed by any other engineer. The result of his experience and knowledge is shown in the HUDSON "33." It is his greatest car—the one that embodies all that he learned from his previous designs.

The HUDSON "33" is built under Mr. Coffin's direct supervision by the same associates who have been with him ever since the industry began. They have always built good cars. They are doing the same today. They carry out Mr. Coffin's ideas. So in selecting the HUDSON "33" you are selecting not merely the car that you see and drive, but a machine which expresses the training, skill and integrity of an organization that is known wherever automobiles are used.

The demand for these cars is so great that it is doubtful if there will be enough for all who want them, if they delay in ordering.

This year is showing an unexpectedly large demand for automobiles, and the six leading makers will undoubtedly have more orders than they can fill.

This is particularly true of the HUDSON.

Therefore, if you are thinking of buying a car this year, you would better make your investigation now and place your order early, or you will not be sure of getting the car you want, when you will want it.

The Coincidence of the "33"

The remarkable thing about the HUDSON "33" is the way the latest models of the greatest European cars resemble it. Leading engineers of Europe have just exhibited their newest designs at the Paris and London Automobile Shows. Such famous makes as the Renault, Fiat, Mercedes, Isota, Lancia, De Dietrich, Martini and many others, show identically the same ideas that Mr. Coffin, working independently of the European masters, put into the HUDSON "33."

Simplicity the Keynote

Simplicity is evident in every detail.

The number of parts used is 900 less than in the average car.

Oiling places can be reached without inconvenience or soiling the clothing.

Moving parts are all enclosed and dust-proof. This includes the valve mechanism, which is exposed in practically all American cars.

The frame is heavier than is used on any other car of its weight.

The motor and transmission are held together as a unit, giving all the advantages of both the three and four point system of suspension.

Wheels are stronger than are ordinarily used.

Springs are so designed that they are practically unbreakable, yet are easy and flexible

There is greater leg room in the front seat than is provided in most cars.

The steering wheel is extra large, same as on the biggest, costliest, cars.

Don't these facts make you want to see the HUDSON "33"?

Think what it means to obtain for $1,250 the masterpiece of such an engineer as Howard E. Coffin.

Think what it means to obtain a car at that price that embodies the ideas that the leading European engineers this year are putting on their cars, any one of which sells for from three to five times the price of the HUDSON "33."

Then think what is indicated by the 687 orders taken the first day.

Doesn't that look as though it would be hard to get prompt delivery of a HUDSON "33" in the spring?

Therefore, reserve your HUDSON now.

Mohair top, Prest-o-Lite tank instead of gas generator and dual system ignition, with famous Bosch high tension magneto, $150 extra for either model.

Write for complete detailed descriptions and address of your nearest dealer.

See the Triangle on the Radiator

HUDSON MOTOR CAR COMPANY

6010 Jefferson Avenue, Detroit

The Hudson 33, shown above in a 1911 ad, was one of the earlier Hudson models.

$930,000 Per Week
Paid for HUDSON Cars

$235,600 Paid
by Users in One Day

On September 15 — the day before this is written — dealers sold to users 152 HUDSON Six-40's. That is, yesterday buyers of new cars paid out $235,600 for HUDSONS.

The average has long been $930,000 per week — because that is the limit of output. We are building and selling 100 per day. That is five times as many — five times, mark you — as we sold at this season last year. And we had no war then. Our average sales have more than trebled since August 1st.

Means That Hudsons
Rule This Field

In July — when we brought out this new model — we trebled our output to cope with demand. Thirty days later — despite our best efforts — we were 4,000 cars oversold.

We shipped by express nearly 1,000 cars to minimize delays. That is unprecedented. But thousands of men waited weeks for this car when other cars were plentiful. No other could satisfy men who once saw this new-model HUDSON Six-40.

Five - Fold Increase
An Amazing Thing

Consider that the HUDSON has long been a leading car. Every model for years has been designed by Howard E. Coffin. He has brought out in these cars all his new advances. And the demand for his models — long before this Six-40 — gave HUDSONS the lead. The first HUDSON Six, inside of one year, made us the largest builders of six-cylinder cars in the world.

Think what a car this must be — this new HUDSON Six-40 — to multiply this popularity by five in one year. And to do it at a time like this. Think how far it must outrank all the cars that compete with it. Think what a tremendous appeal it must make to car buyers.

Think how it attracts — how it must excel — when in times like these they pay $930,000 per week for it. And they would have paid more had we had the cars to deliver — as shown by yesterday's sales of 152 cars.

The HUDSON Six-40 is today the largest-selling car in the world with a price above $1,200.

See the Car That Did It
Howard E. Coffin's Best

Go now and see this model — the car whose record is unmatched in the annals of this line. You will see a quality car sold at a price which is winning men by the thousands from lower-grade cars.

You will see a class car — in many respects the finest car of the day — sold at one-third what class cars used to cost.

You will see how clever designing and costly materials have saved about 1,000 pounds in weight. And in this light car — the lightest seven-seat car — you will see one of the sturdiest cars ever built. You will see a new-type motor which has cut down operative cost about 30 per cent.

You will see new beauties, new ideas in equipment, new comforts, new conveniences. You will see scores of attractions you have never seen before.

They are all in this masterpiece of Howard E. Coffin, who has long been the leading American designer. This is his finished ideal of a car, and many count him final authority.

Mr. Coffin has worked for four years on this model, with 47 other HUDSON engineers. Part by part, they have refined to the limit every detail of the car.

This is the acceptable proven type. This lightness, beauty, economy and price are new-day standards which men are demanding. And this quality — Howard E. Coffin's level best — is the least men will take when they know.

Now is the Time

Now is the time to pick out your new car. Next year's models are out now. You see what the field has to offer. And the best touring months are before you — the Indian Summer days. Get your new car and enjoy them.

If you buy a class car, this new HUDSON Six-40 is the car you'll want. The exclusive features which have won so much favor are bound to appeal to you. Your dealer will see that you get your car promptly if we have to ship by express.

Five New-Style Bodies:

7-Passenger Phaeton, $1,550
3-Passenger Roadster, $1,550
3-Passenger Cabriolet, $1,750
4-Passenger Coupe, $2,150
Luxurious Limousine, $2,550

All f. o. b. Detroit

Canadian Price: Phaeton or Roadster, $2,100, f. o. b. Detroit, Duty Paid.

Six-40
HUDSON
$1,550

This ad notes that over 100 Hudsons were built and sold each day.

HUDSON Touring Car

$1150

"Look for the Triangle on the Radiator" This price includes three oil lamps, two gas lamps, generator, horn, tire repair outfit, tools and jack.

Material—Design—Overhead Charges
Manufacturing Cost and Profit—Agents' Commission

When you buy any motor car, you pay in some proportion for these six factors. Now then, let us see how much of each you get for your money in the Hudson Touring Car at $1150.

What You Get In Material

There are 123 fine steel forgings in the Hudson. No car selling for less than $1,500 has as many. The Crank Shaft is a one-piece, heat-treated drop forging, tested to a tensile strength of 100,000 lbs. The Crank Case and Transmission Case are of the finest aluminum, unlike the cheap cast iron used in many low-priced cars. The Driving Gears of the rear axle are of the finest nickel steel. A special grade of gray iron is furnished in the pistons and piston rings, insuring unusual wear. The Running Boards, Steps and front Foot Boards are of beautifully polished aluminum. They will never wear out or need attention. Our paint and finish specifications are particularly rigid. And so on throughout the entire car—the utmost care is exercised in the selection of materials.

Fine material involves the best of judgment in buying. Mr. H. E. Coffin, our Vice-President and head of our Engineering Department, personally oversees the specifications for every ounce of Hudson material. Mr. Coffin has designed three of America's foremost cars. His yearly trips abroad keep him in touch with the best of European methods and ideas. His reputation as a motor car engineer is International, and any expert will tell you that his O. K. on material is sufficient proof of its quality, and proof of its particular adaptability to the purpose.

So much for Hudson material.

What You Get In Design

It should cost no more to build a good looking automobile than another kind. It is simply a question of engineering and designing ability. The Hudson Touring Car at $1150 is not only the best looking in its class, but we believe one of the most beautiful automobiles built, regardless of cost.

Note the straight line body—the sweep of the fenders—the big, clean cut hood—the wide side door—the tilt of the steering post—the unusual length of foot room in the front seat. These points are hard to match even in much higher priced cars.

Sit at the wheel of any car you know. Then do the

same in the Hudson. You will appreciate the Hudson comfort. The main features of high-class design in the Hudson are the powerful, 4-cylinder, long stroke Renault type motor (Renault motors are the pride of Europe)—a selective sliding gear transmission, instead of a common, cheap, planetary type—a semi-floating rear axle like the best European cars—big, expensive, three-quarter elliptic rear springs—and a length of over 9 feet between front and rear axle. The two later features make the Hudson as easy riding as the highest priced car.

Hudson Manufacturing Cost

"That Hudson car is the simplest, most clean cut of any on exhibition." That remark was heard innumerable times at all the big, recent automobile shows. The very simplicity of the Hudson means low manufacturing cost. In the Hudson, you find no superfluous rods, bolts or wires. Nowhere are two or more parts used where one will do. You do not have to be a manufacturer to know that the absence of complications and the use of few parts saves time and labor and cost.

Simplicity is the very key-note of good engineering practice. No car is so simple mechanically as the Hudson. That's why Hudson manufacturing cost is low in proportion to the quality. And there are no freakish ideas in the Hudson either. You cannot afford them. Neither can we. **Hudson features and Hudson refinement are new in a car at the Hudson price,** but they are not new or sensational in the sense of never having been used before. They have been tried, tested and proven out on the highest priced cars, both in America and in Europe.

Hudson Overhead Charges

Overhead charges include all salaries, and expense incurred in marketing a product. Every officer of the Hudson Company is a stockholder. They are all active in the business. They must get their profits in dividends, not in salaries. Every officer has been in the manufacturing end of the automobile business since automobiles were first built in this country. They have built good cars and know by actual experience how to keep Hudson overhead expense at a minimum. You can find out who they are and what they have done from the Hudson Catalog.

In the Hudson price, there is included no item charged up to distribution—for the getting of agents. We did not have to spend money to get them. The

agents of the country knew us and the best among them came to Detroit to get the agency for Hudson cars. The distributing end of our business will cost us neither worry nor money, because we will continue to give so much for the money that the Hudson agency in any city will always be eagerly sought.

A Word About Profit

We do not claim that we are the largest automobile manufacturers. We never expect to be. But we do claim to be among the largest producers of high class cars. Because we insist upon a quality car, we must be content with a moderate profit. *An examination of the car itself will verify this statement.* The men who own the Hudson Company have faith in the future. Hudson cars are being built to justify your confidence. Every Hudson sold to date has sold others. Owners have found unusual value *in* the car.

In the Hudson the value is all there before your eyes in good, sound, automobile design, material and finish. You do not have to go into the books of the Company to find your "value received."

Neither do you have to accept the reputation of the men in the Hudson Company as part of your value received. But because of their reputation and their ability, you can rely on their continuing to give you in the Hudson cars, the most possible for the money.

Agents' Commission

We say nothing about the sixth item, Agents' Commission, as practically all makes of cars are sold on the same commission basis. But we do wish to say, however, that every Hudson dealer invites you to make the most careful examination of Hudson cars. The dealers know from their own broad experience that in the Hudson you get more for your money than in any other car. Remember the six factors which enter into the selling price when you are examining the Hudson. You will see for yourself that you are asked to pay for the right proportion of each of them.

You owe it to yourself to examine the Hudson —as soon as you can conveniently do so. In the meantime, the Hudson catalog will give you further evidence in support of our claims. We invite you to send for it to-day, the coupon being for your convenience.

Hudson Motor Car Company, Detroit, Michigan
Licensed Under Selden Patent

Hudson advertised widely. The above ad appeared in Success Magazine.

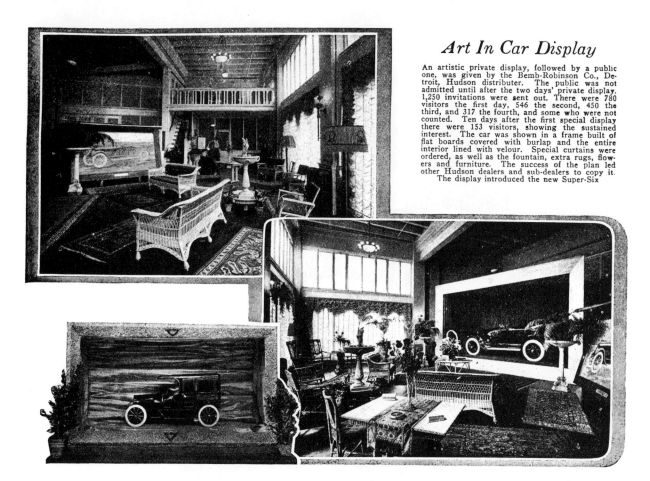

The elaborate display of a Hudson dealer in Detroit.

This ad by the Coey Motor Company asked, "Why not market your own car under your own name?" In 1916 dozens of new automobile companies were being formed each month.

The eighteenth annual announcement of the

1893 HAYNES 1912
Automobile

Haynes 40 Touring Car, Model 21, 5-passenger, $2100, fully equipped.

Haynes 40 Close-Couple, Model 21, 4-passenger, $2100, fully equipped.

Haynes 40 Limousine, Model 21, electric and oil lighted, $2750, fully equipped.

Haynes 40 Colonial Coupe, Model 21, electric and oil lighted, $2450, fully equipped.

Haynes 50-60 Touring Car, Model Y, 7-passenger, $3000, fully equipped.

Haynes 50-60 Fore-door Limousine, Model Y, electric and oil lighted, $3800, fully equipped.

All models are so designed as to accommodate dynamo electric lighting equipment, which we will install for purchasers at nominal cost.

THE 1912 Haynes car, product of America's oldest and most experienced automobile manufacturers, is bigger in every way, more powerful and more pleasing in its lines than any of its splendid predecessors. The time-tested, sweet-running Haynes motor has been built with greater stroke and bore, giving more power, greater flexibility and decreased vibration. The wheel base has been lengthened. The brakes are larger, providing 1 square inch braking surface to every 13 lbs. of car. And with these improvements there are many refinements in style, such as the rich black body and running gear, with black enamel and nickel trimmings throughout.

The 1912 Haynes is now ready for delivery. You can see the new models at our branches and agencies, or we shall be glad to send you a catalogue and name of nearest dealer.

SPECIFICATIONS HAYNES MODEL 21

Motor. 4 1-2 inch bore, 5 1-2 inch stroke, T-head Haynes type cylinders cast in pairs, offset 1-2 in. Flexible four-point suspension.
Wheel Base. 120 inches.
Ignition. Eisman dual magneto, with dry cells for starting.
Carburetor. Stromberg 1 3-8 in., Model B.
Lubrication. Splash and force feed, oil reservoir in lower half of crank case and filled through bleeder pipe in center of crank-case.
Steering Column. Worm-and-gear type, Timken roller bearings on shaft, corrugated hard black rubber rim, aluminum spider, 18-in. wheel.
Clutch. Haynes contracting steel band

on bronze drum. Supported by crank shaft. Easily adjusted and lubricated.
Transmission. Selective type, three speeds forward, one reverse. Timken roller bearings.
Rear Axle. Timken full floating type, pressed steel housing supporting full weight of car. Shaft, nickel steel.
Front Axle. Single piece I-beam 2-inch, drop forged. Spring seat forged integral. Spindles 5-16 inch diameter. Timken roller bearings.
Wheels. Artillery type wood, twelve spokes front and rear. Boss spokes alternating in rear wheels.
Tires. 36 x 4 inch, front and rear. Demountable rims.

Springs. Front, semi-elliptic: 40 inches long, 2 inches wide, 7 leaves: rear, 41 1-2 inches long, 2 inches wide, 6 leaves. Fitted with grease cup, both front and rear.
Brakes. Internal and external on rear wheels. Drum 14 x 2 1-2 face.
Colors. Body black, 18 coats of paint all hand rubbed. Wheels black same as body. All metal equipment, gun metal, black enamel and nickel.
Equipment. Eisman dual magneto, Stromberg Model B Carburetor, silk mohair top, wind shield, Prest-O-Lite tank, five lamps, Warner 60-mile dial Speedometer, extra Dorian Remountable Rim, Tanner automatic gasoline gauge.

HAYNES AUTOMOBILE COMPANY

NEW YORK—1715 Broadway   **Dept. K, KOKOMO, IND.**   **CHICAGO—1702 Michigan Avenue**

Haynes Model "21" Limousine

Haynes Model "21" Colonial Coupe

Haynes Model "Y" 7-Passenger Touring

Haynes Model "Y" Limousine

Advertisements for Haynes, Glide and Havers cars.

BENZ DISPUTES DAIMLER'S GLORY

Celebration in His Honor Evokes Pointed Protest—Historical Dates That Have Been Called Into Question.

March 4th last was celebrated by the German town of Untertuerkheim as the twenty-lfth anniversary of the appearance of the gasolene automobile. The Daimler works closed for the day and festivities of a more or less joyous nature marked the occasion, which, however, served to bring public protest from the Benz company, which maintains that Untertuerkheim was not the proper place for such a celebration, and that the twenty-fifth anniversary in question occurred in 1910, almost two years before.

According to the Daimler side of the controversy which has arisen over the historical date, it was on March 4, 1887, that Gottlieb Daimler for the first time traveled over the streets of Esslingen and Cannstatt with his "benzin motor carriage," although two years before he had succeeded in propelling a tricycle by means of gasolene; but the tricycle, not being a fourwheeler, it does not, according to the German viewpoint, rank as a true forerunner of the present automobile.

The Benz protest flouts all of the Daimler claims. The Benz people state that it is a matter of record that the first automobile left the Benz factory in Mannheim in December, 1885, which original car at present reposes in the historical museum at Munich, Germany, flanked by copies of two patents issued on its construction in January, 1886, and April, 1887. The second patent covers a selective, two-speed transmission. The Benz interests also point out that at the great industrial exhibition held in Munich in 1888, a Benz automobile was displayed, thereby taking rank as the first one to be publicly exhibited.

For the Man Who Smokes Cigars.

The idea of discouraging the production of sparks on a motor car does not sound exactly orthodox, but it is just what the Nospark Co., of Oshkosh, Wis., has gone into business to do. The purpose of its device, however, is to subdue the unruly cigar spark, which is a source of no little discomfort and annoyance in the rush of air caused by the rapid motion of a car. The "Nospark" is a small aluminum screen cap that fits over the active end of a cigar and prevents the ashes and sparks from being whisked away by the wind. Ventilating holes provide for plenty of air on all sides.

To Teach Motor Engineering in Pittsburgh.

The importance of automobile engineering has made itself felt in Pittsburgh, Pa., and as soon as Machinery Hall at the Carnegie Technical Schools is completed, a course in this work will be underatken. The new course will be under the dean of the School of Applied Design.

DETROIT GIVES BIRTH TO "DODO"

It Is of French Extraction but American Adapters Radically Alter Its Make-up— Lightweight at Low Price.

While there has been no little adverse comment abroad regarding the "invasion" by American small cars of foreign markets, it is so seldom that a foreign small car "invades" in return, that when such a thing happens it is almost in the nature of an event. But if the putting forth of the little car shown in the accompanying illus-

THE DODO, SHOWING TANDEM SEATS

trations is considered in the light of a diminutive "invasion," then it must be granted that the attack is an extremely mild one, for the Autoparts Manufacturing Co., of Detroit, which is responsible far the car, has so altered the design of the French "Bedelia," that served as a foundation, as to leave little of the original except the tan-

FRONT VIEW, SHOWING DRIVE

dem seating arrangement and a general reminiscent appearance. The car has been christened "Dodo." So far only the one photographed has been constructed, but preparations are being made to manufacture Dodos in quantities.

The most important change in the design consists in concentrating the entire driving plant, including the driving wheels and intermediate mechanism, at the front, thus making the machine a front-drive car and eliminating the somewhat crude system, originally used abroad, of rear drive through belts which were slipped and allowed to run loose in lieu of a clutch. The air-cooled motor is rated at 10-12 horsepower and has two vertical cylinders; its position at the extreme front end facilitates air cooling, the opening in the front of the hood admitting an ample supply of air for the purpose. As the rear wheels are relieved of driving duty, they run on an axle that is a simple straight steel tube. There is no frame, as the term usually is understood in motor car design; the body itself is so constructed as to make a separate frame unnecessary. In fact, the concentration of the power and transmission mechanism at the forward end makes the body and rear wheels a sort of trailer, which has nothing to do but carry the passengers and be pulled along by the front wheels. As in the original Bedelia, the passengers sit tandem, this arrangement facilitating light construction. The regular tread will be 56 inches and the wheelbase 100 inches. It is proposed to build a narrow-tread model for European trade, with a distance of 50 inches between the wheels. The wheels are 28 inches in diameter. Tires are 3-inch.

In addition to the touring body shown in the illustrations, the Dodo will be built with parcels delivery body, and, possibly, with a diminutive coupe body, if it is found that the wind resistance is not too great.

Rare Cause of Compression Loss.

Loss of power, occasioned by loss of compresion has been charged to a variety of causes, probably the most prolific being the gumming or sticking of the piston rings. Another cause of loss of compression which is rare, though it may not be as rare as generally is supposed, recently was discovered by an harassed owner and his experience may serve others to advantage. "The piston rings in my engine," he says, "are supposed to be prevented from turning by small pins screwed into the pistons and projecting into slots in the rings. The holes in the piston castings are drilled through the whole thickness of the piston wall and one of these pins under the top ring had come adrift and disappeared so that the gases from the cylinder head passed right through the hole into the crankcase. Examination of the remaining rings revealed that a pin had disappeared from each but the rings had turned so that the holes were covered." "It is possible," he adds, in discussing a crankcase explosion that all but wrecked his engine, "that the cause of the accident may have been somewhat similar."

How General Electric Carries Patents.

Although since its organization the General Electric Co. has expended more than $20,000,000 in the purchase of patents and in defending them, its balance sheet shows that since the close of the 1906-7 year the patents have been carried at a nominal value of $1, which in these days when patents and goodwill usually are carried at enormous sums, is such a radical state of affairs as to call for general remark. Since extinguishing its patent account five years ago, however, the General Electric Co. has charged $4,039,600 to earnings to represent the cost of acquiring new patents and patent litigation.

50 H. P.—7 Passenger, Torpedo Touring Car, $2,700—Full Equipment

Distinctive Features of the "High-Quality-Sane-Price" Car

The entire personality of this car cannot be here described; the rest of the story is told in a handsome catalog, which will be sent upon request.

The features of construction of the models given below are merely a few of the Inter-State's most striking components.

The "high-quality-sane-price car" briefly describes the Inter-State. We claim, as do operators of these cars, that in the Inter-State the greatest automobile value in America is given. The Inter-State, with its medium price, possesses the characteristics and refinements of cars costing twice as much.

MORE Power, More Years of Service, Additional Refinements—*at the price that should be paid.*

Seven 40 H. P. Models

A Few of Many Superior Points of Construction

Bore of Motor 4½ in. Stroke 5 in.

(1) This ½ in. greater stroke gives more horse power for lighter weight motor. (2) Motor of longer life. (3) Greater economy of gasoline—20 miles to the gallon under favorable road conditions. (4) Fine radiating surface. (5) Smoother running, less noise. (6) Reduced speed of action means reduced wear on bearings, valves, valve-stems, cams and crank shaft. (7) Longer stroke results in reduced temperature at exhaust valves. Thus, valve-grinding is rare. (8) Increased compression and resultant economy of operation. (9) Better mixing and vaporizing of charge gives greater flexibility; motor can be throttled down to lower speed and a steadier, more quiet and smooth pull on hills.

Integral Clutch and Gearset Runs in Oil (found only in a few of the highest-priced cars). Greater rigidity and absence of friction—no loss of power, as clutch and gearset are of integral or unit design.

Power Transmission by Enclosed Propeller Shaft. Eliminates distance rods and torsion bars; no destructive sand or dust can work into crevices.

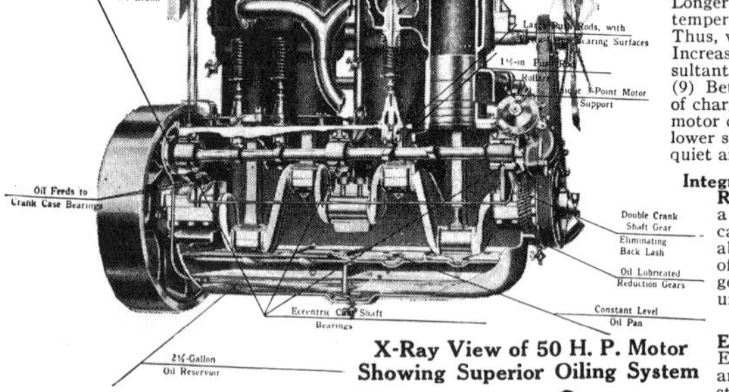

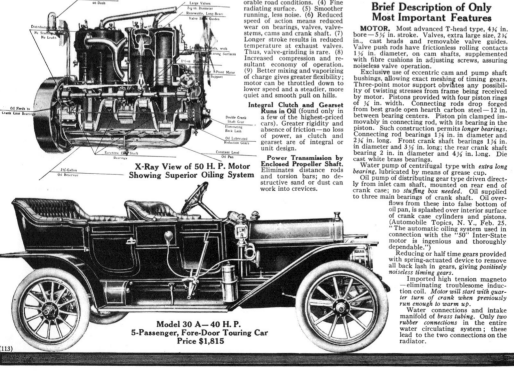

X-Ray View of 50 H. P. Motor Showing Superior Oiling System

118-in. Wheel Base. 2 to 8 in. longer than in cars anywhere near price of Inter-State.

Wonderfully Easy-Riding Springs. Front Springs semi-elliptic, 42 in. long; Rear Springs ¾ elliptic and 45 in. long.

Proper Distribution of Weight. 10,000 to 15,000 miles of service to original tires are result of car's lightness and even distribution of weight.

50 H. P. Model

Brief Description of Only Most Important Features

MOTOR. Most advanced T-head type, 4¾ in. bore—5½ in. stroke. Valves, extra large size, 2¼ in., cast heads and removable valve guides. Valve push rods have frictionless rolling contacts 1½ in. diameter, on cam shafts, supplemented with fibre cushions in adjusting screws, assuring noiseless valve operation.

Exclusive use of eccentric cam and pump shaft bushings, allowing exact meshing of timing gears. Three-point motor support obviates any possibility of twisting stresses from frame being received by motor. Pistons provided with four piston rings of ¼ in. width. Connecting rods drop forged from best grade open hearth carbon steel—12 in. between bearing centers. Piston pin clamped immovably in connecting rod, with its bearing in the piston. Such construction permits *longer bearings.* Connecting rod bearings 1⅞ in. in diameter and 2¾ in. long. Front crank shaft bearings 1⅞ in. in diameter and 3½ in. long; the rear crank shaft bearing 2 in. in diameter and 4½ in. long. Die cast white brass bearings.

Water pump of centrifugal type with *extra long bearing,* lubricated by means of grease cup.

Oil pump of distributing gear type driven directly from inlet cam shaft, mounted on rear end of crank case; no *stuffing box needed.* Oil supplied to three main bearings of crank shaft. Oil overflows from these into false bottom of oil pan, is splashed over interior surface of crank case cylinders and pistons. (Automobile Topics, N. Y., Feb. 25. "The automatic oiling system used in connection with the "50" Inter-State motor is ingenious and thoroughly dependable.")

Reducing or half time gears provided with spring-actuated device to remove all back lash in gears, giving *positively noiseless timing gears.*

Imported high tension magneto—eliminating troublesome induction coil. *Motor will start with quarter turn of crank when previously run enough to warm up.*

Water connections and intake manifold of *brass tubing.* Only *two rubber connections* in the entire water circulating system; these lead to the two connections on the radiator.

Fly wheel 16 in. diameter—larger than is used for motors this size—*gives superb auxiliary cooling system.*

Enclosure of wiring in fibre tubes, supported by cast brass brackets of handsome design.

Ten-inch diameter multiple disc clutch, running in oil bath; bronze discs, supplied with cork inserts; friction surface, cork against steel, used by highest-priced cars manufactured.

Gearset and clutch, unit construction, two compartments, separated by oil-tight retaining wall, allowing use of different and suitable oils for gearset and clutch. Transmission of selective sliding type; gears of *exceptional strength* and *heavy pitch;* clashing gears of chrome-vanadium steel, *scientifically hardened* to minimize wear. Three speeds forward, one reverse. All gears run on highest grade imported annular ball bearings.

Gear ratios, approximately 3½ to 1 on high; 5¾ to 1 intermediate; 9½ to 1 on low speed; 13½ to 1 on reverse, giving most practical and satisfactory speed regulations under all conditions.

Rear axle, full floating with differential gears of chrome-vanadium and high carbon steel, so supported in housing as to permit their removal intact. Generously proportioned nickel steel axle shaft. Driving shaft, nickel steel, enclosed in torsion tube. The enclosed shaft eliminates torsion bars and distance rods—positively *insures correct alignment of propeller pinion shafts* at all times. *Every possible adjustment and positive locks* on axle to insure permanency. Front and rear wheels mounted on annular ball bearings, so assembled and provided with bushings that should *bearing ever become defective, weight of car will be carried on bushings until new bearings can be fitted.*

Brakes—*far in advance of general practice.* Both service and emergency brakes internal expanding, *dirt and waterproof type. Noiseless in operation. Either brake sufficient to lock wheels.*

Steering gear *quickly* and *easily adjusted* and designed *with* maximum degree of safety for every possible road condition; provided with large ball thrust bearings to compensate for end thrust.

Vanadium steel springs, front 40 in. long, 2¼ in. wide; rear 48 in. long, 2¼ in. wide.

Pressed steel frame channel section, heat treated after forming, provided with four cross-members *insuring perfect alignment and yet flexible to conform to every condition* of road service.

Wheel base, 124 in. Tread, 56 in.

Complete Equipment

Silk mohair top, wind-shield, speedometer, clock, black enameled Solar gas headlights of large size. Combination oil and electric side lamps and tail lamp, storage batteries for lighting. Robe and foot rail, tire irons; large, well-filled tool box, extra demountable rim, Prest-O-Lite tank and horn.

Tear off Coupon as a reminder to send for beautiful free Catalog.

INTER-STATE AUTOMOBILE CO.
MUNCIE, IND.

Branches	**Canadian Branch**
153 Massachusetts Ave., Boston	Hamilton Mach. Co.
310 S. 18th St., Omaha	Hamilton, Ont.

COUPON

S.E.P. 56

INTER-STATE AUTOMOBILE CO.
Muncie, Indiana

Send me new catalog of your eight (1911) "40" and "50" models.

Name ________________

Address ________________

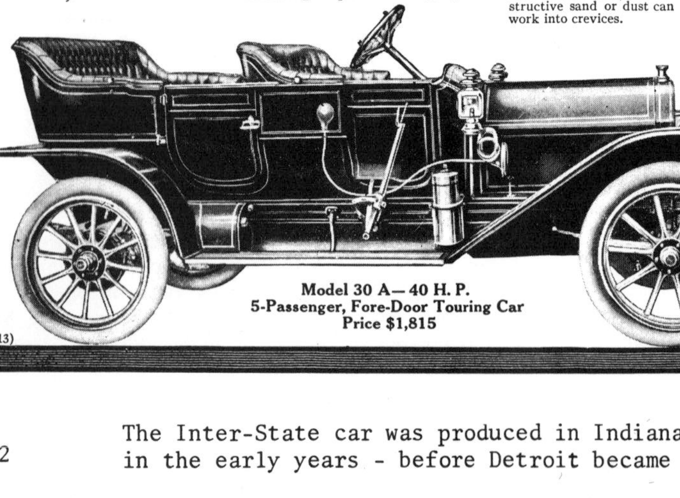

Model 30 A—40 H. P.
5-Passenger, Fore-Door Touring Car
Price $1,815

(113)

The Inter-State car was produced in Indiana. Many manufacturers located in Indiana in the early years - before Detroit became dominant in the field.

The Jordan Sport Marine appealed to the adventurous.

SEE THIS CAR and if possible, persuade a good motor car mechanic to go with you. Its stream-line beauty and roomy luxury captivate, but we want you to go over the chassis with a man who KNOWS machinery.

MODEL C, "The Car of No Regrets." Everything you want in an automobile at a price that makes the motor world wonder

$1075 WITH **EQUIPMENT** Famous Ward Leonard Starting and Lighting System, $90 net additional. Prices F. O. B. Detroit

HAS CANTILEVER "COMFORT" SPRINGS
30-35 HORSE-POWER. :: :: :: TOURING CAR AND ROADSTER

DEALERS! Wire now for territory on this new model The KING'S 1914 success is about to be repeated manifold

KING MOTOR CAR COMPANY, DETROIT, MICH.
New York Agency and Showroom, Broadway at 52nd Street
New York Service Department, 244-252 West 54th Street

The King was billed as "The Car of no Regrets."

Cantilever "Comfort" Springs Eliminate
Jolts and Hold the Car to the Road

$1075
Famous Ward Leonard
Starter and Lighter
$90 net additional
Prices F. O. B. Detroit

30-35
Horsepower

*Touring Car
and Roadster*

KING

ANNOUNCEMENT OF MODEL C

THE CAR OF NO REGRETS

Pure European stream line body.
Flush "U" doors. No moldings.
Concealed hinges and latch
handles.
Full floating rear axle.
Combination head lamps.
Instrument board.
Special crown fenders.
Gasoline tank in cowl.
Hyatt roller bearings.
Honeycomb radiator.
113" wheel base.
Center control.

**New price, new body,
new chassis refinements, but
retaining all the sturdiness, reliability,
and special mechanical features that made
the 1914 model a success the world over.**

The KING chassis has always been built to give many years of faithful,
economical service. Now it comes with a body of a type pronounced
by the majority of engineers to be the *ultimate* motor car design.
In Model C you will be buying for a decade.

All stock of the KING MOTOR CAR COMPANY is owned by the active
executives of the Company. These stockholders prefer solid, successful growth
rather than large, immediate profits. To this end they insure careful, high grade
manufacturing by including every employee in an annual distribution of profits.
The KING was first to do this. With this painstaking and responsible manufacture, go materials of such high quality that only by cash buying and modest
profits can such a price as $1075 be made possible.

Dealers Should Not Delay

in arranging for territory yet unallotted. The KING'S 1914 success is
about to be repeated manifold. A handsome, dependable, economical car
of popular name and price, produced by a financially solid factory, and
generously advertised, is a combination that will mean big 1915 profits.

King Motor Car Company

1300-1324 Jefferson Avenue, Detroit, Michigan
New York Agency and Showroom, Broadway at 52nd St.
New York Service Department, 244-252 West 54th St.

Multiple disc cork insert clutch.
True ventilating, rain-vision
wind-shield.
Extra deep tilted cushions.
Silk mohair one-man top.
Option on two gearings.
Flush-top upholstery.
Gemmer steering gear.
Stromberg carburetor.
3¹⁵⁄₁₆" x 5" motor.
Extra heavy frame.
18" steering wheel.
Full equipment.

CANTILEVER SPRINGS

KING 1894

KING MOTOR CARS
are operating efficiently and economically in England, Germany, Australia, India,
Switzerland, Guatemala, Philippine Islands, New Zealand, Chile, South Africa,
Uruguay, Java, Martinique, Colombia, Sweden, Brazil, Ceylon and Denmark

The above King ad sought dealers to handle the King line. A large dealer system
was the keystone to success.

KING
EIGHT
ANNOUNCEMENT—1918

The same reliable chassis, with minor improvements—The
same four body models, still further refined—That is the
simple manufacturing program of the King for the
new year

King war-ambulances and armored cars now in military service; successful performance all over America and in fifty-
six foreign countries; the fact that there are more King
Eights in operation than any other Eight save one;
remarkable economy in up-keep: These are facts
which should weigh heavily in the King's favor
when the selection of a car is under consideration.

Touring Car Foursome
Sedan Roadster

**KING MOTOR
CAR COMPANY**

DETROIT

THE CAR OF NO REGRETS

King also made "war-ambulances and armored cars" the above copy notes.

The New "Six-48" Keeton Seven Passenger Touring Car

KEETON
THE TWO CARS THAT WILL INCREASE YOUR SALES
CAR-NATION

The volume of your sales depends largely upon the attraction value of the cars you handle. Some cars feature power, some economy, some quietness, others speed, appearance, price, etc., but in no other car will you find these qualities blended in such harmonious proportions as in the new "Six-48" Keeton.

A limited number of these "distinctive" cars will be produced for the coming season and dealers will find it greatly to their advantage to get in touch with us at once.

KEETON SPECIFICATIONS

Motor—Six cylinder, 4 in. bore, 5 in. stroke, cast en bloc, "L" head.
Ignition—Eisemann Dual High Tension Magneto, Automatic Spark Advance.
Electric Starting-Lighting — "Jesco" Starting and Lighting System, single unit type.
Cooling—Centrifugal Pump and powerful fly-wheel insure ample cooling.
Front Axle—Elliott type, ball thrust bearing in yoke head.
Rear Axle—Full floating type, gear ratio 3¾ to 1. Imported annular bearings.
Brakes—Brakes cam actuated internal expanding, large diameter.
Control—Left side drive, right hand control.
Steering—Worm and full Gear Type with thrust bearings, 18 in. or 20 in. walnut wheel.

Clutch—Cone shaped steel disks running in oil and housed in fly wheel.
Transmission—Selective type, 4 speeds forward and reverse, direct on third, imported annular bearings.
Wheels—Five interchangeable wire wheels, 34 in. in diameter, 4½ in. tires.
Speedometer—Warner Autometer with clock combination.
Horn—Large Klaxon.
Air Pump—Mechanically operated, two-cylinder compressor.
Wheel Base—136 inches.

PRICES—F. O. B. DETROIT
2 Passenger Roadster, completely equipped $3250
7 Passenger Touring Car, completely equipped 3250
A full line of open and closed bodies.

$495 CAR-NATION $495
"The Car for the American Public"

More Than a Cyclecar

The Car-Nation has all the features hitherto only found on large expensive cars, yet it is light, snappy, economical (25-30 miles to the gallon) and the price is within the reach of the great majority of buyers.

The Car-Nation is made of standard parts, every one of which has been time tried and proven by use in bigger cars costing $1000 and over. Just think of what this means in **every day service** to an owner.

Read the specifications and go over them part by part with any car you can think of. The 4 cylinder block motor with 3 speed forward and reverse, selective type transmission and multiple disk clutch as a unit power plant—wire wheels. Left hand drive, center control—V-shaped radiator with a sloping hood and cowl—in fact every part is a "feature" in many larger cars.

Two Passenger "Car-Nation" Plowing Mud

CAR-NATION SPECIFICATIONS

Unit Power Plant—Motor—4 cyl. en bloc, 3⅜ x 3¾, "L" head—large valves and bearings. Very quiet and powerful.
Ignition—Magneto—Fixed Spark.
Lubrication—Constant Level Splash—Plunger Pump.
Carburetor—Approved Type—very economical.
Cooling—Thermo-Syphon. V-shaped radiator, adjustable belt-driven fan.
Clutch—Multiple steel disk type running in oil.
Transmission—Selective type 3 speeds forward and reverse—One lever control.

Drive—Bevel gear through concentric Torque tube with one universal joint.
Rear Axle—Semi-Floating Type, Hyatt Roller Bearings.
Brakes—Emergency, Internal Exp. on 10 in. drum on rear wheels. Service, external contracting on transmission shaft.
Wheels—Detachable wire—30 x 3 in. clincher rims and smooth tread tires.
Control—L. H. drive, center control.
Wheel Base—104 inches.
Tread—48 inches.

Standard Equipment—Horn—Head Lamps and Tail Lamp, with set of tools.

PRICES
Model A—2 passenger Roadster...... $495.00
Model B—2 passenger Tandem Type.. 510.00
Model C—4 passenger Touring Car.... 520.00
Extra Equipment: Top $25—Windshield $10.00
DEALERS—We are now producing these cars and the territory is going fast. You can make a very advantageous connection by closing your territory for this line.

Write or wire now.

Manufactured by Keeton Motor Co., Detroit, U. S. A. See Our Exhibits at New York and Chicago Shows

1913 Keeton and Car-Nation advertisement. "Plowing mud" was an all-too-familiar experience in motoring at that time.

Car-Nation

The Car for the Nation

$495 ROADSTER

"More than a Cyclecar"

$520 TOURING CAR
as Catalogued

The Low Priced Car that in Design, Construction and Detail Ranks With Big Expensive Motor Cars

The Car-Nation is a car that any one would be proud to drive. It embodies all the "up to the minute" ideas in both European and American practice, while the price brings it within the reach of the great majority of buyers.

The light weight—great economy in operation—25-30 miles to the gallon of gasoline —ease of handling—low initial and upkeep cost—long life of the tires—speed and hill climbing qualities, make the Car-Nation unsurpassed for general utility.

There is nothing freakish about the whole car — every part is standard — four cylinder block motor—multiple disc clutch—3 speeds forward and reverse—selective type transmission—floating rear axle—wire wheels—left side drive—center control—in fact everything about the whole car has been approved as the best practice.

Dealers throughout the whole country can make a very advantageous agency connection by writing or wiring now.

$3250 FULLY EQUIPPED

The 7 passenger "Six-48" Keeton Touring Car

The New "Six-48" Keeton

The Keeton has that distinctive French type of construction that has always made the strongest appeal to people of culture and refinement, both in Europe and America, as the criterion among motor cars.

The mechanical excellence of the Keeton and the completeness of the equipment insure the maximum endurance and comfort in use.

Write for "THE TRIPLE TEST" booklet.

MANUFACTURED BY

THE AMERICAN VOITURETTE COMPANY
DETROIT, U. S. A.

The Car-Nation was a typical cyclecar - half motorcycle and half automobile. Cyclecars were lightweight and often utilized motorcycle parts such as tires. Their chief selling point was the low price - just $495 in the above instance.

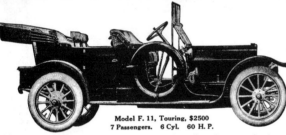

Above and left: The KisselKar was "Every Inch a Car." Kissel was one of the most heavily advertised makes.

Below: The plant of the Knox Automobile Company was offered for sale in 1914.

$2100
F. O. B. Cleveland

The Light Weight of the "H. A. L. Twelve"

The shipping weight of the "H.A.L. Twelve" is 3555 pounds.

The scientific design has sacrificed nothing in the way of strength to permit this weight

All attempts in several long and terrific tests to find a weak spot in its construction have been without result.

That, you will agree, is an unusually light weight for a car of its strength, power, luxurious roominess (115 inch wheelbase) and elegance of equipment.

That weight, 3555 pounds, is from 200 to 1000 pounds less than the weight of virtually all other cars of similar capacity and a power approximating the power of the "H.A.L. Twelve."

That light weight, with the tremendous strength, power and flexibility of the motor, gives the "H.A.L. Twelve" its wonderful pick-up, its buoyancy and thrilling sense of life.

Light Weight and Sturdiness are Vital Factors Today.

With the increased cost of tires and many other upkeep expenses rapidly and continually soaring,

The car of light weight with great power will naturally dominate.

The prospect's first question of the dealer will be "How much does the car weigh?"

Then he will ask "How does the weight correspond with the power of the motor?"

The dealer without a car light in weight and with the strength and power properly proportioned, works under a handicap.

That is one reason why the "H.A.L. Twelve" will be the big seller.

That is why the "H.A.L. Twelve" will readily appeal to all classes of buyers.

Back of the "H.A.L. Twelve" are men of wide manufacturing experience and sound financial standing. Back of the "H.A.L. Twelve" are the reputation, the prestige and the achievements of Harry A. Lozier.

The H. A. Lozier Company
Cleveland, Ohio

Distributors for Greater New York
Hollander-Randall Co., 1744 Broadway

The Lozier was one of the most desired sporting-type cars. The above copy notes that the H.A.L. Twelve has wonderful pick-up, bouyancy and a "thrilling sense of life."

Marmon 34 ad from the Saturday Evening Post.

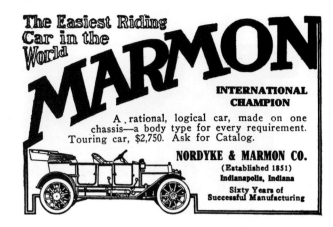

Marmon, Mercer and McIntyre ads. The Mercer Race-about is one of the most sought-after vintage cars by collectors today. The $400 high-wheel McIntyre at the right looks more like a horse-drawn buggy than a car (circa 1909).

A Combination of Construction Features Unequalled at Double the Price

With the Monroe Car you get a 4-cylinder motor, valve-in-head type, small, powerful, highly refined,—equally efficient and smooth-running at 3 miles an hour and at 60.

You get a pressure oiling system which adjusts the lubrication of the cylinders to the amount of power being generated, preventing over and under lubrication.

The Monroe

An M & S differential securing equal traction, except when turning and preventing skidding, spinning and sticking.

Cross compound cantilever springs and deep frame construction, giving exceptionally easy riding qualities.

The Brush patented chassis structure—in which the frame is conformed to the shape of the body in a way to secure extra rigidity and stability and at the same time permitting lighter frame and body construction.

The Monroe Car is an extremely light weight car for the power it generates and its carrying capacity. Every high grade standard unit necessary for efficiency has been installed in the Monroe.

Where else can you get such a combination of up-to-date features and good construction for $985?

THE MONROE MOTOR COMPANY
PONTIAC   MICHIGAN

The Monroe, 1917.

Moon closed cars are out-fitted with as many of the conveniences of a gentle-man's club and a lady's boudoir as it is possible to include in their compara-tively limited space.

Ladies and gentlemen will appreciate the careful planning and clever work-manship which has fur-nished Moon closed cars with so many dainty and handy comforts — which are highly valued by all those who understand the niceties of life

Elegance Within Reason

Moon manufacture builds elegant, luxurious and comfortable motor cars at prices which are within the bounds of reason.

The interior decoration of the Moon Sedan and the Coupe is unquestion-ably correct. Their design is delight-fully new—the big, wide doors and all cabinet-work as carefully finished as a fine, old, grandfather's clock.

Moon closed cars have the warmth and snug comfort of a cheery living room—just as if it were set on wheels

and driven along by the famous Red Seal Moon Continental Motor—that famous, flexible power-plant, always dependable for the spurt, pick-up, or long, steady pull.

And the big Moon windows drop at a moment's notice to bring you the sunshine and fresh air of beau-tiful weather.

The Touring Car rounds out a trio of Moon Models—notable for their elegance—and obtainable at reason-able price.

Built by MOON MOTOR CAR COMPANY, *St. Louis, U. S. A.*

This advertisement emphasizes the luxury features of the Moon car.

The Mitchell Line

Model			Price
Model R—Roadster, 3 passengers	.	.	$1,200
Model R—4 passengers	.	.	1,250
Model T—5 passengers	.	.	1,500
Model S—7 passengers, 6-cylinder	.	.	2,250

The First Three Thousand Mitchells

sold this spring have given such splendid reports of themselves that our early prophecies of a "Mitchell Year" are already *more than half verified.*

Again we have proved that it is possible to build a high-class car at a reasonable cost and to keep on improving it *without increasing the cost to you.*

We have watched these cars with hawk-like vigilance through the eyes of our "Trouble men" scattered throughout the country, and we have yet to hear of a solitary Mitchell going wrong *without the aid of fool-driving* or *unavoidable accidents.*

The Mitchell Car didn't achieve greatness in a night, a month or a year. It has advanced steadily and surely over *a period of years,* and this experience has taught us how to build the kind of an automobile that the American public wants. *Ask the American Public!*

We believe—and we have the facts to warrant the belief—that we have the best car for general all around purposes and maintained-service that this country affords. And there are *twenty thousand owners* who will gladly confirm our opinion if you will take the trouble to ask them.

One established feature which has had much to do with our success is the Mitchell-Make-Good-Policy which guarantees a new part for every part that proves defective, and this policy has been— and will be—adhered to *without evasion, argument* or *technical question.* This is vastly superior to the ordinary, every-day guarantee.

Reserve your Mitchell now and bind the bargain with your agent for immediate delivery. We won't have a car left by July 1 if the present demand continues, and we know at this writing that we won't be able to make within thirty per cent of the cars our agents have asked for by peremptory telegram.

"A Word to The Wise is Sufficient."

Mitchell-Lewis Motor Co.

Racine, Wis. U.S.A.

COMPARE Motorette material, part for part, with that used in similar places on the best known automobiles.

MOTORETTE

As well built as a $6,000 automobile

Frame: Same material as used in the Packard, Cadillac, and Chalmers-Detroit.

Springs: Made by the same people as are those of the Pierce-Arrow, Packard and Simplex.

Bearings: Made by William Cramp & Sons, Philadelphia, the same as used on the Pierce-Arrow, Packard and Locomobile.

Cylinder Castings: Same grade of material as used in the Lozier.

Gears: Same material as used in Cadillac.

Crank Shaft: Same as Chalmers-Detroit, Cadillac and Matheson.

These parts are assembled in our plant under the most rigid inspection.

Each Motorette is thoroughly tested before shipping and is in running order ready for the road.

Guaranteed for one year—Price $385

Send for a catalogue. It gives information and specifications in detail. Look up your local Motorette dealer. Ask us his name, if you don't know it.

The C. W. Kelsey Mfg. Co.

190 Morgan Street, Hartford, Conn., U. S. A.

Dealers—Get into the branch of the Automobile business where there is no competition. Sell the Motorette. Send for information today.

Mitchell, Kelsey Motorette and Moline-Knight ads.

MAXWELL TESTING
LEAVES NO ROOM FOR DOUBT

EVERY Maxwell Car that leaves our factories is a tried and known unit. We definitely determine, as far as is physically possible, just what every Maxwell Car will do in the hands of its owner. Each Car must pass the dynamometer test, an unfailing guarantee of efficiency (see illustration at top).

Every part of the engine and then the assembled engine, the chassis, the wheels, the transmission, the starter, the steering gear, the brakes and finally the finished Maxwell Car—all of these are examined and tested many times and in many different ways.

So that when you buy a Maxwell you know what to expect of it. It has passed our tests which are more severe than any tests you will ever put it to. You have complete confidence in it because it has already fulfilled our exacting requirements.

We cannot afford to take chances. We do not assume anything. We find out and *know*.

This manufacturing policy, faithfully pursued, has earned for the Maxwell an invaluable reputation for dependability, for exceeding serviceability.

Moreover, this manufacturing policy is an important contributing cause to the actual fact that the Maxwell is *"The World's Greatest Motor Car Value."*

MAXWELL ENCLOSED CARS: Sedan, $985; Town Car, $915; Cabriolet, $865.
All models completely equipped, including electric starter and lights.
IN CANADA: Touring Car, $850; Roadster, $830, f. o. b. Windsor, Ontario.

Touring Car

$595
F.O.B
DETROIT
•

Roadster

$580
F.O.B
DETROIT
•

Maxwell Motor Company, Inc. Detroit, Mich.

Maxwell publicized the testing of its cars. The Maxwells were best sellers.
In the early 1920's Maxwell was combined into the Chrysler Corporation.

Before you make your Selection Consider the Marion Record

LOOK at this partial list of Marion victories. There is Boyce in his famous Marion that thundered through the mud and driving rain from Charleston to Indianapolis without a hitch—363 miles—in 26 hours. There is Monson, in the car that took second place in the Elgin National Road Races, and also the Marion that flew in just three seconds behind the 90 H. P. Simplex—at Brighton Beach—taking second place. Here are the Milo and Algonquin Hill Climb trophies captured by the

And so we could go on—listing victory after victory.

The strength and durability of the Marion is the result of the work of a thousand picked men. We have no one special feature that we harp on. The **MARION** is above that. Every detail—every part—is a feature—every part is the best that can be gotten. For instance, our 40 H. P. car is equipped with the Continental Motor, because we know from exhaustive investigation that it is the most reliable and most efficient motor made. Every test has proven this to be a fact. And so it is with the entire car. Part for part, the car represents the best that the industry is producing.

When you purchase the Marion the chassis you get is identical with the chassis that performed such wonderful work in the big motoring events of the world—that won so many victories. The Marion factory has never turned out a special racing car. The cars that do the racing are identical with the cars you buy from the Marion dealer in your town.

The Marion car is handsome to look upon. Take the "45"—at $1,700.00—shown below. It is the masterpiece of our thousand picked men. It is a good, large, roomy car—one that is built for comfort as well as to stand the strain of the most severe usage. Every line, every curve, shows its distinctiveness.

Make it a point to see the Marion car. Our nearest dealer will be glad to take you for a ride and answer specifically any questions or doubts you might have in mind. Get in touch with him, or write us for the Marion book on the "Thousand Man Car."

The Marion Sales Co.
Indianapolis, Ind.

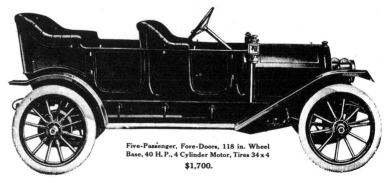

Five-Passenger, Fore-Doors, 118 in. Wheel Base, 40 H. P., 4 Cylinder Motor, Tires 34 x 4
$1,700.

Road racing and endurance contests were just as much a part of automotive salesmanship in 1911 when the above Marion copy was written as they are today.

This illustration indicates the location of the oiling points of a motor car (the number and location of these points vary in different types of cars). Unless properly lubricated with suitable oil and grease, an automobile will give trouble and soon wear out.

The Importance of Lubrication

PROPER lubrication is of vital importance to the successful operation of a motor car. Manufacturers and dealers realize this. A large number of those owning or operating automobiles do not, and as a result, over 65 per cent of automobile troubles are due to insufficient lubrication or to the use of unsuitable lubricants.

Every automobile owner or driver should bear in mind that each separate mechanism of the car requires its own type of lubricant. Further, that the use of cheap or unsuitable lubricants will, sooner or later, land the car in the repair shop.

Automobile lubrication has been studied exhaustively by the experts of this Company. As the result of these studies and the experience gained during years of extensive manufacturing of oils for every use, the Standard Oil Company has put on the market the most efficient automobile lubricants yet produced. These are sold under the name

Polarine Oil (frost and carbon proof) furnishes perfect lubrication for all types of gasoline engines and for all wearing parts. It is delivered in sealed cans—gallon and five-gallon sizes—or in barrels and half-barrels.

Polarine Transmission Lubricants are prepared in three consistencies. "A," for Summer and Winter use on transmissions where conditions permit a *semi-fluid* oil. "B," for Summer and Winter use, on transmissions and differentials where a *semi-solid* lubricant is required. "BB," especially recommended for *Summer use* on transmissions and differentials. The cans are of convenient size.

The **Polarine** Brand covers Oil, Transmission Lubricants and Greases. These **Polarine** Lubricants have been produced by our experts after thousands of laboratory and practical tests. We believe that they are the best automobile lubricants on the market.

Polarine Oil is an oil rich in lubricating quality. Feeds perfectly at any temperature down to zero. Gives freedom from destructive carbon deposits. Lengthens the life of cylinders, piston rings and bearings.

Polarine Transmission Lubricants and **Polarine** Greases have been specially manufactured for the parts of the car requiring lubricants of a heavy consistency. These products are unequalled for

the lubrication of the special parts for which they are recommended.

Use **Polarine** Lubricants this season. They will add to the pleasure of motoring. They will enable you to save repair bills, increase your speed, climb hills easier and do away with the many petty mishaps due to the use of unsuitable lubricants.

All dealers sell **Polarine** Lubricants or can get them for you.

Our Booklet, **Polarine Pointers** contains facts about the care of motor cars, including hints on lubrication and the causes of engine troubles.

If you own a motor car or motor boat send for this booklet. Write our nearest agency.

Polarine Cup Grease is a solid lubricant for use in cups and where a heavier grade than "BB" is desired. **Polarine Fibre Grease** is a solid lubricant of high melting point, particularly adapted for use on universal joints. Delivered in round cans.

More information in our booklet. Send for it.

Standard Oil Company

(Incorporated)

A few of the many early Standard Oil Company products for the motorist.

MARION·HANDLEY

Six-40

$1350

120 Inch Wheel-
base
4 Inch Tires

7 pass. Touring or 4
pass. Roadster
f. o. b. Jackson

Six-60

$1650

125 Inch Wheel-
base
4 ½ Inch Tires

7 pass. Touring or 4
pass. Roadster
f. o. b. Jackson

AWAY from the rank and file and emphatically in the class of cars of dominant
character and personality stands the **MARION-HANDLEY**.

Clean, sweeping lines — perfect balance — restful riding comfort — - luxurious
appointments — characterize and individualize

"The Six Pre-Eminent."

Send for Catalog or see your nearest dealer.

New York Motor Sales Corporation

33 Burdett Building, Troy, N. Y.

A. J. KAMPF, Albany, N. Y.   **H. A. SNOW, Binghamton, N. Y.**

CHARLES RANDOLPH, Rome, N. Y.   **C. E. DOOLITTLE, Ticonderoga, N. Y.**

STALEY FORMSBEE CO., Johnstown, N. Y.

PERRY MOTOR SALES CO., Syracuse, N. Y.

Built and Warranted by   The Mutual Motors Co., Jackson, Mich.

The Marion-Handley as advertised in Motordom, a publication sent to New York
state motorists.

90

Matheson, Lexington, Moline and Michigan ads. The Michigan Buggy Company, manufacturer of the Mighty Michigan Forty, originally made horse-drawn vehicles.

METZ "22"
NON-STOP RUN

✦

BOSTON
TO
MINNEAPOLIS

METZ "22"
NON-STOP RUN

BOSTON - MINNEAPOLIS

I said, before I started, that I could drive a Metz "22" 1,600 miles, from Boston to Minneapolis, in 4 days—or 96 hours.

This meant, of course, that it would have to be a non-stop run.

Some of my friends thought I was cutting the schedule pretty short, and among the business enemies of the car there were those who smiled contemptuously.

I will admit that sitting in your office mapping out a schedule for a long cross-country run, and driving a car up to that schedule, are two different things.

Driving to schedule always reminds me of the Irishman who was walking to Boontown and, upon inquiring at a farmhouse, was told that it was about ten miles further on.

After walking an hour or so, and not seeing

any evidence of church spires in the distance, he stopped at another farmhouse and asked, "How far is Boontown?"

"About ten miles," he was told.

So he journeyed on and after another hour or so met a farm rig coming from the direction in which he was going. "How far is Boontown?" he asked.

The driver pulled up, and after careful calculation replied, "Well, I should say it's nigh onto ten mile."

"Ten miles?" repeated Pat, cheerfully. "Good! I'm holding me own, anyhow."

And just so, at times, in driving a car, it seems difficult to keep the schedule from getting ahead of you. If you can keep even with it you are usually doing pretty well.

However, I had laid out what I considered a reasonable driving schedule for a non-stop run, and, having absolute confidence in the car, was

An adventure story, 1913 style. "Metz '22' Non-Stop Run Boston to Minneapolis" was originally issued as a booklet by the Metz Company. As it gives some interesting sidelights on cross-country travel a half century ago we reprint it on this and the next few pages.

not at all doubtful of my ability to keep up with it.

The "night before the Fourth" held no attractions for me, this year, as I had in mind more important business than celebrating. I put in my usual amount of sleep, and "took it easy" on the Fourth. But in the evening I gave my faithful "22" a final try-out, and shortly before midnight tossed aboard my luggage and supplies, adjusted the search-lights, and was soon eating up space between Waltham and the City Hall of Boston, where I received a letter of greeting from his Honor Mayor Fitzgerald to his Honor Mayor Nye of Minneapolis.

The Official Start

Many friends were at the Boston City Hall to see me safely off—if there had been fifty thousand of them, I couldn't have been any more embarrassed; and at the last stroke of twelve, ushering in the morning of July 5, 1913, the Mayor's message was thrust into my hand, and we were off.

Mr. M. C. Barrett, of Springfield, Mass., was my companion in the car, it having been ar-

ranged that he should accompany me as far as Albany.

The streets were still alive with those who had been celebrating Independence Day, and cautious driving was necessary for the first few miles. But we soon reached the open country where the cool night air and the scent of the new-mown hay in the fields proved delightfully refreshing. To one who has never experienced the pleasures of a night ride under such conditions, especially after a hot day, I can only say —don't miss an opportunity to enjoy it.

Across the Connecticut

As we pulled into the square at Worcester, 44 miles from the start, I noted the time and found we were a little behind schedule. We reached Springfield, 98 miles from the start, just at dawn, where several of Barrett's friends were on hand to see us pass through. The police officers did not object to our maintaining a brisk pace at this early hour, when most of the city was still in peaceful slumberland, and in a twinkle we were across the long bridge over the Connecticut River, and on the open highway to Westfield.

Oh, the joy of this new morning before Old Sol came peeping over the hills of the Berkshires! The car seemed all animation as it

dashed up the grades and down on the smooth roadway, ever winding, twisting, and entwining itself in its playful course with the river, forest, and mountain.

Lee, Lenox, and Pittsfield, with their hosts of summer resorters, were already in the near distance when the first rays of sunlight began casting long shadows ahead. The rhythmic hum of the motor must have been soothing to the ears of my companion, Barrett, for long before reaching Albany he had fallen asleep, and so sound were his slumbers that when he awoke, on my stopping the car to pay toll at the bridge crossing the Hudson into Albany, he asked in bewilderment, "Where are we?" I replied: "You're a good guide to keep me from losing the road."

Faster than Railroad Time

Nearly 200 miles had now been covered, and for most people the day had only just begun. It lacked ten minutes of eight, and a mental calculation disclosed the fact that I had beaten the train (the Chicago Special) leaving Boston at 11.15 P.M., and pulling out of Albany at 7.20, by fifteen minutes.

To many it may seem strange that in these days of modern railroading a first-class through train on an up-to-date railroad should be slower by fifteen minutes than a car costing less than five hundred dollars traveling over the highway between Boston and Albany. Nevertheless, safely and sanely done, without once opening the motor's throttle to its fullest extent.

Truly, the automobile is coming into its own when independent, economical, and comfortable travel is thus placed within reach of almost every one.

Through the Mohawk Valley

My brother Edwin was waiting for me at the toll gate in Albany. He had a pail of water ready in case any was needed, but it was found that only a pint was required to fill the radiator; so hardly a minute elapsed before we were again under way. Edwin had been over the road between Albany and Syracuse several times, so was familiar with every mile of the route, and the only piece of bad going we encountered was between Fonda and Palatine Bridge. New York State is certainly to be congratulated on its progress in good roads.

Edwin wanted to take the steering wheel to relieve me of the monotony of driving, but to me there is no monotony in directing such a car as my "22," full of life and ginger. So I thanked

him and said I preferred to stick to the wheel. Under his guidance I followed the road in the famous Mohawk Valley, passing through Schenectady, Amsterdam, Little Falls, and Herkimer to Utica, where we stopped for gasoline.

More than 30 Miles per Gallon of Gasoline with Two Passengers

It required 9¾ gallons to refill the tank; and as I had started with a full supply, the consumption was 9¾ gallons for 295 miles, or at the rate of 30¼ miles per gallon—the cost for gasoline being $1.95, while the fare on the train for two is $12.80.

We arrived in Syracuse at 1.50, ten minutes ahead of schedule.

But one cannot stay forever on duty, no matter how fascinating the work. Muscles and nerves need relaxation. So I reluctantly turned over the guidance of the car to Jack Connelly, who was waiting for us at the terminal square in Syracuse. Right here I am reminded that human ingenuity has outdone nature itself; for while I needed rest to recoup, the car was as fresh and as eager to continue as at the start.

Speed Traps

Connelly came armed with information from the Syracuse Automobile Club that speed traps were being operated in some of the towns west; and the Club requested that in case fines were imposed the victim take a receipt and pass the same to the Secretary of the Club, who would see that the amount was diverted into its proper channels for the good roads' fund of the State.

This, by the way, is a wise act on the part of the New York State lawmakers, for there is some satisfaction in knowing that a fine, often unjustly imposed, is to be used for such a good cause. I think, too, that under this regulation there is apt to be much less aggressive activity on the part of the local constable than where the booty becomes partly his own.

However, there was no hold-up for us as we proceeded, and none was called for, as we were not out to see how many miles per hour we could drive, but to demonstrate the reliability of the car on a long, steady, continuous drive.

Through Auburn, Geneva, Canandaigua, Le Roy, and Batavia we sped without particular incident, except to note a very poor stretch of

road through the town of Waterloo and another at Batavia, with several detours on account of road-making.

This brought us into Buffalo a little later than we expected, but we reached the city limits before dark, and drove the last 15 miles over a fine brick highway to the heart of the city.

Engine Was Kept Turning

Here we rested a few minutes, but our motor was not allowed to stop. We closed the throttle, so the motor would turn over slowly, and informed those around us who were curious to know, that we had left Boston that same

"We found we had struck into a picnic party at a resort on Lake Erie." See page 16.

morning, had covered up till then nearly 500 miles, and intended to get somewhere into Pennsylvania before midnight.

I had previously been over this road to Erie, and felt sure of not losing the way. Several detours were necessary, however, on account of road improvements after leaving Buffalo, and I soon felt like a stranger in a strange land, for the road was no longer familiar.

From the location of the north star I knew we were going in the right general direction, but about 10.30 P.M. we became utterly confused. The sky had clouded over, so that the stars were no longer visible, and we were obliged to head for a cluster of lights in the distance to get our bearings.

Arrived at this point, we found we had struck into a picnic party at a resort on Lake Erie. It was composed mostly of young ladies in a holiday mood, and they were inclined to jolly us when we made inquiry as to where we were, and as to how we might find the road to Erie.

Thought We Were Fooling

A great shout of incredulity and merriment went up when we informed them that we had

come that day all the way from Boston, and were trying to get into Pennsylvania before midnight. We were obliged to treat the crowd to sodas before they consented to give us the information we wanted, and at that it was rather indefinite.

We managed, however, to find our way to Silver Creek, and on to Ripley before midnight. We were then close to the State line, and I imagine had crossed into Pennsylvania before Father Time had counted off a full toll of twenty-four hours.

A sound mind, even with a constant supply of invigorating fresh air, cannot forever ward off sleep, and I found myself dozing now and then, and the road finally became simply a factor in a confused dream. Connelly is a skilful driver, and carefully avoided the rough spots and "thank-you-ma'ams," so that I realized only the sense of floating along as if coasting in the air.

A Narrow Escape

Suddenly we stopped. A quick left turn of the road had been overlooked, and we managed to stop just before bumping into a barbed wire fence. Connelly blamed the sharp turn in the road, but I have misgivings that he, too, was slightly under the influence of drowsiness, for when I suggested taking the wheel he was perfectly willing to give it up. His head nodded forward, and he was soon lost to the world.

I tried to keep awake by rubbing my eyes, but found that sleep is a powerful fighter, and

several times I dozed with the car bowling along at a twenty-five mile clip, and each time awoke with a start. Intuition seemed to keep me on the road, for I am certain that I covered, all told, a good ten miles while practically unconscious.

Toward the west the sky was taking on a ruddy glow, and we surmised that it was the reflection of the electric lights of Erie. Such was the case, and in another five miles we reached the outskirts of the city and made our way to a garage for gasoline.

It was by no means an easy job for two drowsy fellows, as we were, to inject quick action into the sleepy garage attendant, but we finally got him to fill the tank while we swallowed the last few morsels of the lunch we had brought with us.

"What You Want to Know, For?"

Have you ever tried to get exact information from a person half asleep? I have. We tried to pump this garage attendant about the best roads to Cleveland, but the "mess of gibberish" which this chap handed us was past understanding. So we were obliged to strike out for ourselves, and fortunately did not have much trouble in finding the road.

We soon began to encounter stretches of muddy roads, showing that rain had preceded us. The mud became worse as we went on, and the going was very treacherous through

Conneaut, Ashtabula, and Geneva; but by daylight there was some improvement. In going through Mentor I tried to point out to

Connelly the old homestead of President Garfield, but the place had changed so since my last visit that I could not make it out.

Again miles of brick pavement led the way into the great city of Cleveland. It was early Sunday morning, and the streets were pretty well deserted as we pulled up in front of Hotel Hollenden at ten minutes past eight—over 700 miles from the start in 32 hours total elapsed time.

End of First Lap

We had been having some trouble with our search-light, so had the gas tank replaced at Cleveland. This consumed some time, and it was past 9 o'clock when Lawrence Cathcart, with his guide, took the car in hand for the next lap, nearly 400 miles, to Chicago.

After a refreshing breakfast at the Hollenden, Connelly and I departed for the railroad station, he going back to Syracuse, while I headed for Chicago, to meet Cathcart and again take the car for the last lap to La Crosse and Minneapolis. I slept all the way to Chicago, and for some time after my arrival there at the hotel; but early the next morning I went over to

Michigan Boulevard to be on hand when Cathcart came in. He arrived about 7 o'clock.

"How far did you say it was from Cleveland to Chicago?" he burst out, pulling up the car.

"About 360 miles," I answered.

"Well, you just add another hundred onto that," he assured me, "and you'll be somewhere near right."

As a matter of fact, he had covered many miles extra because his guide had taken him from the regular course we had mapped out. After the 22 hours of steady driving over the none too good roads of Ohio, Indiana, and Illinois, Cathcart arrived in Chicago a pretty tired boy. The guide, however, although tired, was enthusiastic and said to me: "I did not believe we could get here inside of a day. It was a great ride."

Beginning of the Third Lap

It was not difficult to find the road as far as Madison, Wisconsin. The route took us through Elgin, McQueens, Belvidere, Rockford, Beloit, Janesville, Evansville, Oregon, and Madison, Sauk City and Baraboo, and nightfall brought us to Reedsburg, where we landed after traveling

over some very sandy stretches, and a detour which finally took us through some back yards in the village to again reach the main road, which had been fenced off for repairs.

We had grown very tired of ham sandwiches

and hard-boiled eggs, which had been our steady menu aboard the car, so we sought out a restaurant and had a genuine "feed," such as two hearty New Englanders are able to make away with. Johnny McGann was with me now. He drove the stretch from Chicago to La Crosse.

I like to ride with McGann, for I always know in advance just how he is going to take a rut or a bump or any unusual road obstruction. He negotiates these exactly as I would, and it is a pleasure to ride with any one who drives the same as yourself. The person who is not familiar with cars possibly may not fully appreciate my meaning, but it is a fact that automobile driving becomes an art, and a false move on the part of the driver is as discordant to the nerves of a passenger who knows as a false note is to the ears of a trained musician.

Trouble Brewing

Darkness had grown to inky blackness by the time we left Reedsburg, on our way to La Crosse. We lost time in reaching Wonewoc, being obliged to inquire frequently at a lonely farmhouse. Elroy, some 15 miles further,

we made after a round-about chase in which we could have saved at least half the distance if we had known the road. And at Kendalls I stopped in front of a hotel, only to find that every one had retired. We were badly in need of information regarding road directions, and I shouted, and hammered, and rang the dinner bell, but no one responded, although all the doors were left open.

I came to the conclusion that travelers were supposed to help themselves, as they do in some places down in Florida. If you want a room, the rule in such case seems to be to grab a candle and take the first bed not occupied; in case all are occupied, select one with a single sleeper, take off your boots and turn in under the quilts with him. Such a procedure sounds strange, but it is true, nevertheless.

Guessing at the Road

However, I was not looking for a night's lodging, but for information. Failing to get an answer, we were obliged to resort to our route book, so continued along as best we could—little suspecting that we were going farther and farther out of our way every minute.

After a time we were brought to a stop at the end of a road, and I took out my flash-light to hunt for a sign-post. Turning to the right, I encountered a tremendous grade and a very rough road.

"That certainly cannot be the way," I remarked to McGann; "it looks better to take the road to the left." We did this, and proceeded only a short distance when suddenly the motor stopped. McGann locked the brakes, and announced quietly, "Out of gas!"

I realized the same thing at the same instant, for I would bank on my motor running indefinitely if given sufficient gasoline and oil.

A nice predicament!

No one realizes the consternation caused by running out of gasoline in an absolutely strange place, with impenetrable darkness all around you. Here we were, in the wilds of Wisconsin, miles from nowhere, and out of gasoline!

One Ray of Hope

But wait! Not quite out. The outlet to the gasoline pipe in my tank is one-half inch above the bottom of the tank. By careful driving

on the sloping side of the road there would be a slight inclination of the tank, and the remaining gasoline would flow to the lower end. So, having decided that we were on the wrong road,

we turned around and, by keeping well on the right-hand slope, managed to return about three miles to the last farmhouse we had passed.

We turned our search-light full onto the front of the house, and I made bold with my electric flash lamp in hand to arouse the inmates.

A child's voice was heard, and I knew the household must be awake; but what did they think of this outfit, with a powerful search-light turned full on the house and a none too gentle-looking stranger approaching at midnight? I felt as though I ought to shout "Don't shoot; I'm not a robber." But I knew McGann would never forget that, so I quietly walked up to the door and called "Hello!"

We Had Missed the Main Road by About Seven Miles

For response came a woman's voice, asking what I wanted, and when I explained that it was gasoline, she replied that they hadn't any. Further inquiry brought out the fact that we were about 7 miles from the main road, the Ridgeroad, as they call it, and that several

miles farther along on this Ridgeroad lived a farmer by the name of Reicheim who had a machine that he used for sawing wood—and perhaps he might have some gasoline.

After thanking the lady very kindly, and apologizing for the midnight invasion, we started our motor with the meager supply of gasoline still left and made 6 miles of the journey back toward the Ridgeroad before our dear old "22" made its last gasp and refused to budge another foot without replenishment of the life-giving fluid that makes the wheels go 'round.

Gasoline or Bust!

It was past midnight. I looked up into the sky, thinking I might locate East, West, North, or South from the position of the stars, but only occasionally did one or two peep through the parting clouds. So with my little flash-light I set out to find Farmer Reicheim, who sawed wood with a machine. I gained the main road, and turned in the direction we would have taken if we had kept to our true course.

The reader may think it strange that we should not have provided ourselves with an ample supply of gasoline while it was procurable by daylight, and I will admit we were a little careless in not watching the supply; but as we had previously traveled over 400 miles on a tankful, and as we were expecting to cover only 300 miles or so on this lap of the journey to La Crosse, we gave no thought to the matter. After filling at Chicago, bad roads, heavy sand, and losing our way used up our supply faster than we realized, and so we found ourselves stranded.

McGann was to keep watch by the car while I went on the hike for gasoline. The first house I came to was deserted. Nothing about the barn looked like a machine that used gasoline, so I continued for about a mile to the next house, where they said the man a few rods farther along the road could probably tell me where I could get what I was looking for.

"A few rods up the road!"

I walked and walked, until I began to think I must be going in the wrong direction. Finally I discerned the outlines of a house and, upon awaking the inmates, was told that they didn't

know of anybody that had a machine, didn't know Reicheim, and only ventured to suggest that their neighbor across the road, and a little to the westward, might be able to give me some information.

"How far is it, and which way do you call westward?" I inquired.

"Well," they said, "which way did you come from?"

"I'm hanged if I know whether you would call it up or down the road," I replied. "All I know is, I've got a car stalled about four miles from here, and I want some gasoline to make it go."

"Sorry we can't help you," they replied, "but if you will turn west and walk a few rods, you will come to a house where they may be able to tell you where you can get some."

Unable to get any definite information from these people, I again looked at the sky with further hopes of learning the points of the compass. Westward, indeed! They might as well have told me to go heavenward.

Not to bore the reader with the details of that hour of struggle, I finally reached "the house to the westward" as the first rays of

dawn were forcing back the dark robes of night. My first rap on the door brought no response. I repeated, several times, and then came a woman's voice: "Who's there?"

Can any one tell me why it is that in every case where I roused households that night it was the woman who answered first? Are the men more timid, or are they less anxious to help one in distress? Whatever the reason may be, God bless the women for their willingness to respond.

Mr. Reicheim Was Not a Bit Interested

At last I had located Mr. Reicheim, for in answer to my question I found that it was indeed his house. As soon as he came to the door I started my hard luck story, but it did not seem to impress him very much.

"I will pay you any price you ask," I explained earnestly, "but I must have gasoline."

"Well, I haven't got any, now," he drawled. "I put the last two gallons I had in the engine about a month ago."

"But you say you have not used the engine since then," I persisted, "so the gasoline must still be there."

"Oh, yes, it must still be there, all right," he admitted, "but I don't believe I could get it out."

I saw by his manner that he wanted to go back to bed, but I was determined to get that

gasoline, if there was a quart of it about the place.

"Now look here," I argued, "my car is about four miles back on the road. I must have gasoline to get to La Crosse before 8 o'clock this very morning. I have been tramping this neighborhood since midnight looking for YOU, and now I must have that two gallons of gasoline. Tell me where it is, and I will get it myself, and pay you your own price for it."

He mumbled something to his wife about being forced to get up at that hour of the morning, and as I saw him prepare to go out to the barn with me I nearly collapsed with joy. You may well believe that that midnight tramp had pretty nigh exhausted me, and I had now located probably the only two gallons of gasoline within a radius of 10 miles of where we were stalled.

We had some trouble in getting the gasoline out of his engine. There was nothing for it but to disconnect the pipes and work several valves; but the precious fluid soon came trickling down into a milk pail which we had pressed into service, and as that pail filled my spirits rose accordingly. For I had secured enough "life" to carry us on to La Crosse.

At my long absence McGann became alarmed. He thought I might be lost from him, as well as lost in the Wisconsin woods, and he tried to signal me by throwing the search-light in fantastic sweeps across the sky. Then he tried calling, and finally lay down in the car for a

sound sleep—which was just as good for me, and better for him. He awoke as I came marching up triumphantly with my milk pail filled with "gas."

It did not take long to set the stuff to work. We poured it into the tank, cranked up the engine, and were again on our way at a little after 4 o'clock, with La Crosse about 50 miles distant.

Some stretches of the road now became abominable. Heavy rains had preceded us, and numerous washouts, deep-cut ruts and gullies were encountered. But at St. Joseph we secured more gasoline, and the roads improved very much into La Crosse, where I was fortunate in picking up Archie Oldberg, who knew every foot of the remaining distance, 175 miles, to Minneapolis.

No Important Adjustments Were Required

We deemed it wise to again look over the car in order to assure ourselves that nothing had worked loose after the hard punishment it had received during the night's run; but a couple of nuts holding down the seat were the only adjustments to be made.

A good breakfast at the Stoddard did much toward alleviating the hardships of the past, and we were soon on our way and across the Mississippi, on the last leg of the journey to the twin cities.

It was a sweltering day, as we could see by the withered look of the inhabitants of the small towns through which we passed, but the swift pace of our "22" whipped action into the air for us, and we did not feel the effects of the heat until afternoon, when sandy roads were encountered, slowing down our progress somewhat.

At last, away in the distance, Oldberg pointed out the dome of the Minnesota State House, at St. Paul, and it is needless to say that a thrill of delight ran through me; for although hours had been lost, on account of inexperience with the roads, nevertheless I was still within the time schedule which I had made before setting out on the trip.

We now recrossed the Mississippi into St. Paul and passed through this city and out into the short stretch of country which separates it from its twin sister, Minneapolis, our objective point, where we arrived at the Hotel Radisson at 5.33 P.M. on July 8th.

I had said that I could cover the distance in 96 hours, and I had actually performed the feat in 89 hours and 33 minutes, thus beating my schedule by 6 hours and 27 minutes.

It is a record that reflects much credit upon the METZ "22," and the trip itself is one that will always be remembered as one of the pleasantest experiences of my life.

Four Sizes of Announcement Used by Detroit Dealers

The Bemb-Robinson Co. (upper right) used a small sign inside the window with "1915" in a Hudson triangle on the window—The Regal dealer (upper left) made a bare announcement—The Oldsmobile (lower left) went more into detail—The Oakland (lower right) made a big display and covered the entire window, pending the arrival of its new models

Above: Window displays for the new 1915 cars.

Right: A precaution against theft.

Below: Red Head spark plugs were one brand of many on the market.

National

SIX— $2375

Simplicity, Convenience and Ease

Have **you** ridden in, or driven this new National Six? Until you have you simply can't realize that our claims for its ease of riding, graceful operation, and comfort and convenience are not over estimated. If we told you all that owners say about this beautiful car we fear you would think we were exaggerating.

Note the picture in the lower circle. You see the center control, left side drive, convenient and well arranged dash equipment, access to both front doors, and smart sloping lines to cowl and hood.

When we say, "You don't have to raise the hood," we mean that with a National car you get mechanical confidence; we mean, that our fourteen years' manufacturing success warrant your putting faith in our engineering achieve-ments. We put the right material in the correct place; we give you performance instead of mere specifications; we give you results and freedom from having to go over the car with a "fine tooth comb" to make sure there are no mechanical mistakes in it. We say that with a National you get 100% pleasure and service, because of the fact that your car is reliable and does not cause you worry about its operating mechanism.

The driver of a National does not have to worry about what is taking place beneath the hood or under the seat. His attention is required no farther than what you can see in the picture in the circle above; the wheel, levers and instrument board. The rest of the car operates with the driver's unconsciousness, because the National company built and guarantees it.

Five models of famous National 40 cars, $2750 to $3400

Write Us for Illustrated catalog

National Motor Vehicle Co., Indianapolis, Indiana

The 1914 National.

Third Series of Twelves
A *NEW* MODEL

National built motors have always been abreast, and generally ahead of the industry. When four cylinders were the proper thing, National built the world's Champion Fours. When sixes came into vogue, it was National that built the first American Sixes, and National Sixes of today are the highest development of that type. National was a pioneer in the latest type motor—the Twelve Cylinder.

National Twelve Cylinder cars are today in operation in every state in the Union and in eleven Foreign countries. Owners everywhere testify to the success of the Twelve.

The same corps of engineers who have produced previous successes, have within the last year, concentrated on improvements for this third National Twelve.

NEW FEATURES

Removable cylinder heads to facilitate cleaning and inspecting.

Increased size of cylinder with corresponding increase in power.

Balanced crankshaft—another power increasing improvement.

Heated intake manifold to handle effectively the low grade fuel.

Larger main bearings reduce the vibration in a practically vibrationless motor.

Valves on outside of V continued together with new design valve lifters make National Twelves most accessible of all V motors.

Independent electrical units—

Delco for Ignition and separate, independent Starting and Lighting units.';

To Dealers: **Some excellent territories still available. Others now subject to revision.**

Silent Power
Silence of Skill *vs.* Noise of Crude Power

THIS new National Twelve cylinder motor is the last word of all multi-cylinder efforts to achieve perfection. Its undemonstrative power entirely abolishes engine distraction and annoyances. It is infinitely more refined and dignified; infinitely more serviceable.

From low to high speed—at every stage between—there is the same *high pressure* of power, even, supple and subject to your perfect control.

You are not reminded of the mighty and faithfully working motor under the National's hood, because no mechanical effort is observable.

Quality Without Extravagance

EVERY time National sets a new style in body creations, there are always added new accommodations, for National body designs are essentially practical. They are not conceived alone for the sake of striking appearance, but for the *sake of the passengers' welfare*.

The inspiration behind the National gives you outdoors the same status your drawing room gives indoors.

Six or Twelve Cylinder "Highway" Models

THE marvelous success of the National Twelve is the greatest boon for the Six. Paradoxical? Isn't it logical the engineers who master multi-cylinder problems by perfecting a Twelve are best qualified to build the most efficient Six? National, too, had the advantage over all others by building America's first Sixes. Let a demonstration convince you National's Six is a superior Six in *every* respect.

Furnished in Touring Car, Roadster, Phaeton, Coupé and Touring Sedan in both Six and Twelve Cylinder Models.

National presents the advantages of its 12-cylinder car.

WAR!

As desperate a war as ever waged in the industrial history of America is now on—has been growing more intense for months. It is just as foolish as it is fierce. Its cost is shamefully fabulous. Its cause is fallacy. Its effect is destruction.

Mighty industrial giants, armed with enormous advertising appropriations, are fighting one another while the public looks on and realizes the foolishness and the waste of the needless battle of the—

SIX vs. FOUR

Here Is Common Sense

Why do you care about the mechanical insides of your car? Not because you want a cylinder or more, a gear, an axle or a transmission in themselves. These things are worthless to you except as they combine to make a whole automobile.

Think how ridiculous it is that large manufacturing concerns, some building six-cylinder cars, others making four-cylinder cars, should lose sight of their purpose in life (to give you good WHOLE cars) and go headlong and frantically into a rough and tumble fight over those two extra cylinders.

Their very actions betray them. They weaken their own arguments by staking everything on the presence or absence of those two extra harmless cylinders.

The Truth Is—

the ultimate test of a car's quality is its performance; its operation as a complete car. The number of cylinders is not of most importance. A single mechanical feature is good only when all the other parts help to make it good. There must be harmony of parts. A good Six is a good car and a good Four is a good car. That's all there is to it.

In fact, the best car is the one that gives you such maximum service and pleasure that you forget it has such things as cylinders under the hood or machinery beneath the seat. We say you can buy a National, "without raising the hood," because we put the correct mechanical part in the proper place; because of our long, successful experience; because we build whole cars guaranteed to perform satisfactorily.

National 40 proved superior in tests, including In-Motor 4⅞x6; electric starter and lights; a most luxurious and dependable car.

National Six is beautiful, graceful in design, the ternational 500-mile race. Five models, $2,750 to $3,400. most comfortable car you ever rode in—roomy, convenient, noiseless. Motor 3¾x5½; 132-inch wheelbase, electric starter and lights; left side drive, center control; complete in every detail, full equipment, **$2,375.**

National Motor Vehicle Company

Indianapolis, Indiana

The old question of six cylinders vs. four cropped up continuously in advertisements circa 1915. This National ad is an example.

"BOWER SAVES POWER"

In the Lightest Pleasure Vehicles
"Bower Saves Power"
In the Heaviest Commercial Cars

BOWER ROLLER BEARING COMPANY
Detroit, Michigan

The Bower Roller Bearing Company - an important supplier to the industry.

Remember Man's Name and Make It An Asset

Calling Prospect By Name Makes Him Like You and Your Methods, Says Reilly—Helps in Selling.

By Ray W. Sherman

"Wait a minute, I've got to see this man."

Henry Bennett, who commenced handling the Redman car a couple of months before, left Reilly sitting at a desk on the salesroom floor and moved toward the man who had just come in the door.

"How'dy do, Bennett?" greeted the visitor.

"Fine! How are you?"

"How's business?"

From that the conversation went to numerous things, but mostly to the car the newcomer was thinking of buying. When he left he was in much the state of mind he was in when he entered—and he probably would be so for days to come, for he was the type of man who has to worry so much over all the cars built before he can buy a 1906 runabout for $80. Tommy Trumbull would call him a fussbudget.

Reilly's Neighbor.

"Who's that?" asked Reilly after the man had gone and Bennett had returned to where Reilly sat.

"Don't you know him? That's Harold P. Heffernan, the contractor He lives out in your end of the town. You ought to know your neighbors better than that."

"I've got something else to do besides running around calling on all my neighbors."

"Oh, very well," drawled Bennett, with assumed sarcasm; "that may be so, but we've heard different. We know you."

"Maybe," smiled Reilly.

"But you ought to know Heffernan."

"I do know him, but ever so slightly," replied Reilly. "I haven't seen him in a long time. I thought I knew him when he came in, but I couldn't place him. No one ever could forget that face if he saw it a couple of times—big, ruddy boy that he is."

"I guess he leads a pretty strenuous outdoor life," was Bennett's comment.

"How long have you had him in tow?"

"Not long. Why?"

"Why don't you call him by name when he comes in? Don't you ever do that?"

"Why didn't I? I don't know. I don't know whether I do so or not. What difference does it make, anyway?"

"Quite a lot, Henry, quite a lot."

"Whaddyuh mean? Quite a lot?"

"IT MAKES YOU MORE SOLID WITH THE MAN—IT HELPS YOU GET ALONG WITH HIM—IT HELPS SELL HIM A CAR"

"You ought to do that always—if you can," said Reilly. "It's good business. It helps out."

"Helps out? How?"

"Oh, you know"—Reilly made funny little gestures with his index fingers extended—"it makes you more solid with the man. It helps you get along with him. It helps in selling him a car."

"It does?"

Likes Idea of Being Known.

"Didn't you ever go into a cigar store, or a haberdashery, or a barber shop, of a hotel, or a restaurant, or anywhere else? And don't you remember that in some of these places you were called by name every time you went in? Didn't the proprietor or some clerk greet you and call you Mr. Bennett—or Bennett, if he knew you well enough—and didn't you rather like the idea of feeling that you were known?"

"Ye-s-s," slowly and thoughtfully admitted Bennett. "I do remember such things now that you speak of them."

"And you liked it, didn't you?"

"I must admit that I did. I must also admit that unless I'm mistaken I take pleasure in giving my trade to those places. I like them."

"Now answer your own question!" asserted Reilly. "Why did you do it? Why did you like it?"

Why Did He like It?

"Hum-m-m," mused Bennet. "Darned if I know—but I liked it just the same, didn't I?" And he looked up at Reilly and laughed good-naturedly.

"You certainly did." Reilly laughed in return. "And," he added, "it works the same way with almost anyone. Try it. See if it doesn't."

"But what's the why of it?"

"The why of it doesn't matter; and I don't know that I know what it is anyway. It just works, that's all. Not everyone can do it; I'm a little weak on it myself, but heaven knows I've tried hard and am still trying. I never used to be able to remember a name while I was being introduced to a man, and it has been an awful drill for me to get so I can remember a name at all. I know it is a big help and that not being able to do it is a weakness and I do the best I can. I do believe, however, that I am getting better slowly.

"But a man who deals with the public should be able to remember names. And if he can remember them—as I think you can—a man should make use of them. When a man walks in, say 'Good afternoon, Mr. Heffernan.' It is many times more effective than a plain 'Good afternoon.' It sets you several steps forward with him. He is more favorably inclined toward you."

"Remember Man's Name and Make It An Asset" was one of an extensive series of dealer aids published regularly in the trade publication, Motor World.

"Just why, I don't know. It flatters him somewhat to think that he is so well known that people call him by name when he walks into a public place. You know how that little thrill of self-congratulation goes through you when you walk into a restaurant after the theater and the head waiter says, 'Good evening, Mr. Bennett.' It's the same thing. Being called by one's name in public places is pleasing to a man."

"I'm sure of it. I can recall lots of instances now."

"If there are two business places side by side and both are equally good and have the same line of stuff, but if in one the customer will be pleasantly greeted and, above other things, called by his name when he goes in, I'll guarantee the customer will drop into this place more frequently than he does into the other. This being called by name sort of makes the binding tie stronger.

"It gives the customer the impression that he stands a little better with this store than some other customers, that he is personally acquainted there, and that he will be well taken care of. The other store might be just as ready to take care of him and do anything for him that the first store would, but the mental impression that the customer gets often means a lot more than the service he actually receives. If he thinks he likes

a place, that settles it, no matter what his reasons are.

"When you dig up a prospect one of the first things you should do is get his name indelibly inscribed on your memory. Get it there so it won't come off. Then, having got it, make it an asset. What good does it do to remember the prospect's name if you aren't going to use it? It may be handy to be able to go to the right prospect card after he goes without having had to ask his name, but that is an infinitesimal part of its value.

"It is acquiring greater efficiency without the expenditure of any extra effort if you use the name to greet the man when he comes in. It helps in a varying degree—and if you're anxious to sell a car every little helps a lot. If you have a big name acquaintance with a large circle of people it will help you amazingly in building up your business."

"I am good at remembering names and faces," said Bennett.

"Young Tommy Trumbull is a regular wizard at it," continued Reilly. "He just naturally remembers names. If he hears a man's name once he never forgets it and can always hook the right name up with the right man. I naturally can't remember names and faces——"

"Why don't you try some of these object memorizing stunts?"

"A-g-g-h-h!" grunted Reilly. "I've tried 'em. They won't work. At least I never could make them work."

"I've heard they were very good," asserted Bennett. "I never tried the schemes because I never had occasion to, but I've heard they were a great help."

"Yes, they're fine!" exclaimed Reilly, disgustedly. "I've tried 'em and I know. Do you know Underhill, who lives four miles out on the Midtown road? Runs a big lumber and grist mill at the foot of the hill?"

"Yes, I know him. Why?" Bennett sensed something and laughed.

"Well, I tried this object memory stuff on him," stated Reilly. "The first time I met him I said 'Underhill, Underhill, Underhill; let's see, how can I remember that?' Then I figured it out like this: He runs a mill, the mill is at the foot of a hill. I had it! Simple as day—Mill—under the hill—Underhill. Easiest thing you know."

"Yes."

"Well, the next time I saw him coming I got to arranging my objects. I could get the hill and the mill under it and that made me think of a piece called Jerry the Miller that I used to speak when I was a kid in school. So I figured—Mill—hill—miller—Jerry the Miller—name can't be Jerry—it certainly isn't Miller—Ah! Got it! Jeremiah! Mr. Jeremiah. Good afternoon, Mr. Jeremiah.

"Bah! It won't work!" exclaimed Reilly. "You've just got to remember, that's all."

National Adds Six-Passenger Body

Novel Extra Seats — Front Divided—Plenty of Room.

By way of increasing the scope of its line, the National Motor Vehicle Co., Indianapolis, Ind., has brought out a new model that is new only insofar as the body is concerned—that is to say, it is

a new body on the same six-cylinder chassis which mounts the four- and five-passenger bodies.

The latest body is practically identical, so far as its lines are concerned, with the other bodies, though it is somewhat longer in order to permit the extra passenger accommodation, and a little larger in nearly all its dimensions.

A neatly worked out feature is the arrangement of the two extra seats, which, when not in use, fold forward into the backs of the front seats, the recess then being covered with curtains which are buttoned down. The most striking feature of the body, however, is the separation of the front seats, which are divided by an aisle which permits passengers to change about from front to rear or vice versa without leaving the car; the aisle is large enough to permit easy passage, but there is still ample room for the occupants of the front seats, which are left wide and roomy.

In the mechanical details of the chassis, wheelbase, tires and so on, the car is identical with the other Nationals.

BACK OF FRONT SEAT SHOWING FOLDING AUXILIARY SEATS

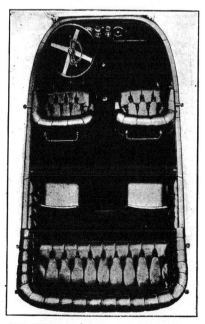

TOP VIEW OF NEW NATIONAL BODY SHOWING DIVIDED SEATS

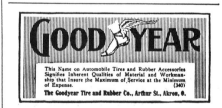

Advertisements in Motor World, 1912.

Motorist's Column

Automobile Bureau

By R. B. JOHNSTON

Readers desiring information about motor cars, trucks and delivery wagons, accessories, routes or State laws, can obtain it by writing to the Automobile Bureau, Leslie's Weekly, 225 Fifth Avenue, New York City. We answer inquiries free of charge.

AGITATIONS against the promiscuous use of the muffler cut-out have been recently started in various parts of the country and all motorists should aid in suppressing this nuisance. The racket of the free exhaust has been responsible for many accidents, as horses have been frightened by the noise when some heedless motor-car driver has suddenly opened his muffler cut-out and raced his engine.

There is seldom any excuse for this too-prevalent practice, which ought to be indulged in only when a car is in a garage or a repair shop. When it is necessary to adjust a carbureter or when the ignition system needs attention, the work can perhaps be done quicker if the cut-out is used. In such cases whoever is making the adjustments will probably save time, as he can tell easier when his task has been finished to his satisfaction.

The fact that many manufacturers do not fit their cars with muffler cut-outs is proof enough that there is no real necessity for their use. Designers of cars, both here and abroad, have been trying for years to eliminate all noise and produce cars that would run as silently as possible. They have done their work well, but heedless drivers in these days often give the impression that they wish their cars to make as much noise as all cars did before gasoline machines had reached their present state.

It is the practice of some drivers, especially those who use their cars in city streets where there are many pedestrians, to use their muffler cut-outs as warning signals. There are some advantages of this plan, but it is still none the less a dangerous one, owing to the almost ever-present likelihood of frightening horses. Horns or some of the numerous mechanical signals are better for this purpose and should be used instead of the muffler cut-out.

The widespread and growing objection to this practically uncalled-for nuisance makes it seem likely that State Legislatures and boards of aldermen will pass laws to stop it, unless the motorists render such action unnecessary by voluntarily putting an end to it. A number of cities now have ordinances against smoking exhausts, which surely do not annoy so many people as the noise from muffler cut-outs. Especially at night, the use of the cut-out is a needless annoyance to a great many men, women and children, and shows a lack of regard for others that no considerate driver should be willing to have charged against motorists as a class.

Motorists who drive their own cars should be very careful to keep oil and grease away from their tires. Men who keep their cars in their own garages or stables ought to be especially careful about allowing oil or grease to get on their tires, as grease softens rubber so that it wears out very rapidly. It is a good plan to wash the tires off every day or so, as the tires will not only look better for the attention, but the danger of oil or grease damaging the casings will thus be practically eliminated.

It will not be necessary for the individual motor-car owner to purchase polished brass or copper pans to keep under a car in a private garage, as cheaper and just as efficient ones of tin or galvanized iron can be bought for much less money. The highly polished floor pans seen under cars in salesrooms are very ornamental, but such elaborate ones are not needed in garages. These pans not only catch any oil or grease that may drip from a car and thus make it an easy matter to keep the rubber-destroying fluid from damaging tire casings, but they also serve the almost equally valuable purpose of keeping the floors cleaner than they would be without the pans.

Among other things connected with driving which is apt to be neglected is reversing or driving a car backward,

says a writer in the *Automobile*. Usually a car is never reversed for more than a few yards at a time and the maneuvering involved requires no great skill. Steering a car when running backward is diametrically opposite to that when running forward. A turn of the wheel to the left steers the car in the opposite direction, to the right, and vice versa. The usual mistake made in reversing is in turning the steering wheel too far and describing zigzags in the road as a result. The autoist should remember that the reverse gear of a sliding change gear should never be engaged until the car has been brought to a full stop.

When tops are kept raised for any length of time, a good deal of dust will accumulate on the upper part, and it is a good plan to sweep this off every week or so. If the dust is allowed to remain on the top it is very likely to discolor it, especially if the dust is of a different hue than the top material. Even though the top and its layer of dust may escape wetting, the car owner ought to have the top swept clean with a broom after every trip over dusty roads, as a motor car with a dusty top presents an odd appearance when its coach work has been washed and the metal work polished. When dust has been gathering for a week or more, a shower will almost surely result in a stained top.

A good many motorists who use metal-studded non-skid tires will fit these tires to both of the rear wheels of their cars. A famous French tire manufacturer declares this is not the proper way to get the most benefit from non-skid tires. His advice to motorists who use non-skid tires is to fit one of the front and one of the rear wheels with the metal-studded casings. The non-skid casings ought not to be both on one side of the car, but should be fitted to opposite sides. If the right rear wheel is fitted with one of the non-skid tires, the other one should be fitted to the left front wheel.

Oil is bad not only for tire casings, but for inner tubes as well. For this reason extra tubes should always be carried in oilcloth bags or cardboard boxes, and never, under any circumstances, shoved into a tool box, where they may come in contact with oily or greasy tools or oil cans. A little care devoted to the proper disposal of spare tubes will repay an automobilist in the greater service he will get from them.

Unless an automobile owner knows a great deal about machinery, it will be best to get and follow the advice of the car manufacturer regarding lubricating oils and greases. The manufacturers make careful and long-continued tests before they adopt any particular make or grade of oil or grease, and as they wish to have their cars give the best possible service to owners, their advice on this subject can be followed without question.

Joe Tracy, the famous racing driver who retired from competitive driving and is now a consulting automobile engineer, declares that many automobile users are too economical with lubricating oil. He says many a good car has worn out before its time because the driver did not pay the proper amount of attention to keeping its moving parts lubricated. His friends often make joking remarks concerning the amount of oil he uses on his own personal car, but Tracy's usual reply is, "It's much cheaper to buy oil than machinery—and, besides, I don't have to lay my car up every so often while new parts are fitted to it."

R. McM.: I know of no automobile manufacturer in search of "patents for gasoline engines." Any maker would consider a suggested improvement on his engine.

On this page: (left) "Motorist's Column," a regular feature of Leslie's Weekly. Upper right: An interesting windowshade-like device for dimming headlights. Lower right: An automobile starting device for cold weather.

The Owen Magnetic was the "Car of a Thousand Speeds."

The OWEN

The fine motor-cars of America and Europe are indeed well built, and substantial, and elegant; but a ride of any length in such cars without a sense of fatigue or strain is very uncommon.

There is clearly a place for a car devoted to comfort, and this place is filled by the Owen.

The Owen is built according to the same general factory practice—the same materials, the same kind and amount of workmanship, but not the same weight.

Instead of 5000 pounds the Owen weighs but 3400; therefore it can have those smooth, easy, springs which convert an unpleasant jolt into an agreeable and gentle undulation. Instead of the small wheels, which feel every depression of any size, the Owen has 42-inch wheels; and passes over as if the road were entirely level. The long-stroke motor (6 inches) moves slowly and smoothly, reducing the vibration to the minimum, and making the rider absolutely unconscious of the engine. The double drop frame (possible only in a car with high wheels) lowers the center of gravity and gives the car a firmness and closeness to earth that adds immensely to comfort and the sense of security.

Driving is made easy by placing the driver on the left-hand side, where he can see better; and the single lever at his right gives him absolute and easy control of the car.

The Owen is the most economical of the cars that may properly be ranked in the highest class. This is due to the high wheels, which are very easy on tires; to the long-stroke motor, which works slowly and uses almost every particle of gas; and to the comparatively light weight of the car.

The Owen, built on certain new ideas, is neither a new car nor an old one. It is the result of years of thought and experience. Only one hundred cars were built last year; but these cars have been carefully watched, any faults which appeared have been eliminated; and, based on this actual experience in the hands of owners, the Owen has been further developed in the directions so much needed in the motor world.

Price $3200. Send for catalogue.

R M Owen & Company Lansing Michigan
General Sales Agents for
Reo Motor Car Company

UNITED STATES NOW USING MORE THAN 1,000,000 CARS

Number More than Doubled in Two Years—Empire State Still in Lead with 132,000—New York Official Gathers Data.

Since 1911 the number of automobiles in the United States has advanced from 522,939 to 1,127,940, an increase of 605,001, or 115 per cent., according to a compilation recently completed by Secretary of State Mitchell May of New York. Careful estimates in States where registration is by counties or municipalities places the number of cars in the hands of dealers at approximately 50,000, which leaves about 1,097,940 automobiles in daily use. This includes both pleasure and commercial vehicles.

New York State still leads, with 132,579, and of this number the metropolitan territory, which includes Greater New York and adjacent sections, has 60,000. The registrations in New York State by horsepower were: Less than 25, 49,473; 25 to 35, 42,211; 35 to 50, 18,770; 50 and over, 1,360; this does not include the half-rate registrations after August 1.

Illinois has the honor of second place in the list with 95,582 cars, and Ohio ranks third with a total of 86,153; Nevada is last with 1,141. The comparisons of the registrations by States in 1912 and 1913 follows:

State.	1913.	1911.
Alabama	5,314	....
Arizona	3,132	....
Arkansas	5,100	1,500
California	....	14,566
Colorado	13,297	....
Connecticut	20,136	13,500
Delaware	2,145	1,228
District of Columbia	11,614	2,230
Florida	3,720	1,333
Georgia	12,919	5,700
Idaho	2,426	....
Illinois	95,592	42,000
Indiana	61,177	12,000
Iowa	77,269	29,323
Kansas	12,937	....
Kentucky	7,551	2,680
Louisiana	8,139	....
Maine	11,112	2,678
Maryland	12,567	7,097
Massachusetts	57,197	36,975
Michigan	41,394	27,664
Minnesota	45,054	19,000
Mississippi	2,217	....
Missouri	39,541	18,225
Montana	6,102	....
Nebraska	34,943	7,766
Nevada	1,141	....
New Hampshire	7,254	4,489
New Jersey	50,491	48,266
New Mexico	1,972	....
New York	132,579	81,655
North Carolina	7,710	1,452
North Dakota	12,504	7,185
Ohio	86,153	45,150
Oregon	14,114	6,156
Pennsylvania	79,846	43,074
Rhode Island	10,000	5,866
South Dakota	14,700	3,250
Tennessee	8,900	1,000
Texas	28,000	....
Utah	3,400	442
Vermont	5,913	3,298
Virginia	9,023	3,909
Washington	21,000	8,000
West Virginia	5,007	2,041
Wisconsin	34,647	7,241
Wyoming	1,585	....
Totals	1,127,940	522,939

Left: More about the Owen. Right: 1913 U.S. automobile registrations.

NORTHWAY'S MOTOR CAR
STANDARD OF THE WORLD

The Wise Ones Choose The Crescent (Motor Co.'s) Royal Ohio Models

The Crescent joins together Northway's manufacturing skill with Paxson's selling organization. Time's noblest offspring is the latest. This is Northway's latest.

After years of experience, exhaustive tests and expensive experiments, the greatest of all designers and inventors,

OHIO ON THE MAP

Mr. R. E. Northway, the founder of the Northway Motor Co. and original designer of that now famous motor, which is acknowledged by the best engineers and experts to be the greatest motor in the world, now brings out his latest and greatest of all motors, to be used exclusively by the Crescent Motor Co. of Cincinnati, O.

Northway's Latest and Greatest Crowning Glory

ROYAL MODEL, $1,985
MOTOR—Six-cylinder, 4 x 6.
AXLE—Full floating on annular bearings.
TRANSMISSION—Four speeds ahead and one reverse.
CLUTCH—Multiple disc.
CONTROL—Center and left hand drive.
SPEEDOMETER—Warner, flush.
TIRES—35 x 4½ and 36 x 4.
WHEEL BASE—132 inches.
ELECTRIC STARTER, LIGHTS and HORN.
RIMS—Demountable.

OHIO MODEL, $1,275
MOTOR—Four-cylinder, 4¼ x 4¾.
AXLE—Floating on roller bearings.
TRANSMISSION—Three speeds ahead and reverse.
CLUTCH—Multiple disc.
CONTROL—Center.
SPEEDOMETER—Stewart.
TIRES—34 x 4.
WHEEL BASE—116 inches.
ELECTRIC STARTER, LIGHTS and HORN.
RIMS—Demountable.

We are now ready to contract with good, reliable, live wide-awake dealers and distributors on this greatest of all lines.

Address All Sales Correspondence to

THE CRESCENT MOTOR COMPANY
W. T. HUNTER, Pres., Cincinnati, Ohio

C. D. PAXSON, Gen. Sales Mgr.,
1900 Euclid Ave., Cleveland, O.

BELLAMORE & TOOMEY CO.,
10 Bridge St., New York City.

The Royal and Ohio models of the Crescent Motor Company utilized "the greatest motor in the world."

OhiO 40-A—Five-Passenger Touring Car
$2150, Fully Equipped

Output Limited Without High Price

THE output of OhiO cars is limited as to numbers, but not as to quality—for every OhiO is a thoroughly tested high-grade car at a moderate price.

To insure accuracy, interchangeability and low cost with limited production, the OhiO factory is equipped with high-priced machinery, jigs and tools, and manned by high-grade, experienced men; and our *limited production permits a series of tests such as we couldn't give if we were turning out thousands of cars a year.*

Before it leaves the factory every OhiO car must successfully withstand the strain of at least 200 miles of road-testing over rough, rocky roads, up-hill, down-hill and straightaway—first the engine and chassis, and then the car completely equipped, even to the wind-shield and speedometer. No OhiO car is shipped until we *know* it is ready to run and to keep on running.

If you believe that integrity in little details is essential to good construction, you should investigate the OhiO. Write today for Catalog 37, giving complete specifications, and telling how every little detail measures up to a high standard.

OhiO 40-L—Torpedo
$2450, Fully Equipped

OhiO 40-K—Roadster
$2150, Fully Equipped

OhiO 40-B—Close-Coupled
$2150, Fully Equipped

The OhiO Motor Car Company
Licensed under Selden Patent
Elmwood Station, Cincinnati, Ohio

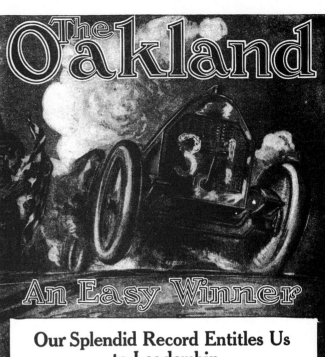

The Oakland
An Easy Winner

Our Splendid Record Entitles Us to Leadership

OAKLAND Cars have won 25 hill climbs, road and track events, in competition with the cream of American Motor Cars. The big majority of these were hill climbing contests, and its continuous victories are the talk of the racing world—just as its wonderful touring qualities have made it first in the minds of well informed motorists.

Can you think of a stronger test than hill climbing? Motor, clutch and transmission must show a continuous 100% of efficiency—if victory is to be won. Hill climbing is the supreme test—and 25 continuous victories prove an absolute superiority of construction—honestly and fairly won.

Contest after contest was added to our string of victories—not easy ones but the hardest kind of road and hill climbing events—anywhere—everywhere.

No one else has dared to claim this leadership, because no one else can show such records as those won by the Oakland at Los Angeles, Algonquin Hill (Chicago), Baltimore, Washington, Cincinnati, Cleveland, Dead Horse Hill (Worcester, Mass.), Seattle, Giant's Despair, at Wilkes-Barre, and many others.

What does all this mean to you? It means honesty of manufacture, excellence of material, the finest of workmanship, closest attention to detail and, above all and foremost, it means that the fundamental principles of design are correct—and stand so proven before the world to-day.

Accessibility and simplicity are the two most pronounced qualities of the Oakland chassis. Motor, clutch, transmission, magneto and pump are all easily at your hand. Your eye takes in the whole chassis at a glance. Its simplicity means a saving of time and money to you.

These cars are priced far below other machines that have less power, are more complex, less get-at-able—and therefore, less modern.

30-H. P. Runabout
$1000

40-H.P. Touring Car
$1600

For 1911 we are marketing a 30 and a 40 horsepower chassis with seven body mountings. The 30 horsepower will be made in a five-passenger Touring Car, detachable fore-doors, at $1200 (detachable tonneau if preferred); a Toy Tonneau, four passenger body, at $1150, and a two-passenger Runabout, the fastest car of its kind to be found anywhere, at $1000. The 40-horsepower chassis will be furnished with a five-passenger, fore-door body, at $1600; a speedy Roadster with fore-doors at $1550, and Model K, five-passenger touring car, $1500.

Compare the car, compare the record, compare the price. We invite your closest inspection and most careful thought—on this most important subject—to you—and to us. If you will do this, we *know* what the result will be.

Be sure to mail this coupon to the factory.

**Oakland Motor Car Co.
Pontiac, Michigan**

Please send me copies of "Little Stories of Big Victories;" "The man who has driven one;" "The 1911 Catalogue."

Name _____
Street _____
City _____

Oakland Motor Car Co.
Pontiac, Michigan

OhiO and Oakland cars, 1910 and 1911 respectively.

Oakland
Sensible Six

Get the *real* thrill of the open road in an *Oakland Sensible Six*. The valve-in-head motor develops full 41 h. p. at 2500 r.p.m.—one h. p. to every 53 pounds of car weight.

And every mile is an easy mile. The big, over-size tires, 32 x 4, the long, semi-elliptic springs, 51" in rear, 112" wheelbase, all make the *Sensible Six* one of the most comfortable and easy riding cars of its size ever built.

It has the power, comfort, good looks, reliability you want in an automobile—yet it is sensibly priced—$875, and built to operate at moderate cost.

*Oakland Eight—$1585—*is a big luxurious 73 h. p., 7-passenger touring car for those who demand the utmost in power, speed and luxury.

OAKLAND MOTOR COMPANY, Pontiac, Mich.

"Sturdy as the Oak"

The Oakland Sensible Six.   Oakland was a division of General Motors.

Oakland, National, Motokart and Overland ads. The Motokart was designed for delivering parcels and small packages.

Overland Closed Cars

FOR the winter? A closed car —by all means.
For the summer? An open car—most assuredly.

The Overland Light Six Sedan and Coupé are *both*—closed *and* open cars.

And they are smart appearing cars either closed or open—in no sense makeshifts, either way.

The side windows—all of them— and the uprights that support them—fold away entirely out of sight when you want an open car.

The Overland achieved immense popularity. This two-page ad originally appeared in color in the Saturday Evening Post.

Overland

Light Six
Touring Sedan
(Springfield Type)

$1585

Touring Coupé $1385

f. o. b. Toledo
Subject to change without notice

The Full Round of Seasons in Luxurious Comfort

The sides of the car above the body are entirely open from end to end whenever that is your humor.

And it's so little trouble that you'll shut the car up tight for even a light shower and have it all open again in a jiffy as soon as it's over.

Then there's the solid comfort all winter long of a perfectly enclosed car with all the protection of a limousine and the richness of closed car upholstery and interior finish.

Mounted on the economical Overland Light Six chassis. These are ideal every-purpose cars.

The motor—a six cylinder power plant of the most modern type—is remarkable for its velvet-soft smoothness—a marked characteristic especially pleasing in closed cars.

You'll be delighted with the performance of the Overland Light Six Touring Sedan and Coupé.

And you'll be delighted with their luxuriousness.

The unusually comfortable seats of the Sedan are upholstered in a soft, rich, gray, fine striped cloth. Sides and ceiling are lined to match and a thick gray carpet covers the floor.

At the rear window, there is a rich gray silk roll-up curtain. A dome light in the ceiling softly but amply lights the interior at night whenever desired.

Enjoy the full round of the seasons in luxurious comfort.

See the Willys-Overland dealer about one of these cars today.

Willys-Overland Inc., Toledo, Ohio
Willys-Knight and Overland Motor Cars

Five Times Last Year's Call for Overlands

The demand for Overland automobiles is five times last year's record. Yet the Overland last year was one of the big-selling cars. It is a wonderful thing when an output jumps so quickly to 140 cars daily. When a car does that, against today's competition, you ought to know that car.

Our Amazing Sales

The four Overland factories, employing 4,000 men, turn out an Overland every four minutes. Yet during February—ending just before this was written—our orders received for immediate delivery amounted to twice our production. And February is a midwinter month.

Now a fifth Overland factory is being equipped. We are preparing to work nights and days. The Overland dealers—in 800 cities —are going to be kept supplied.

The demand for Overlands is twenty times as large as two years ago. It is five times as large as last year. It is larger now, and is growing faster, than for any other car on the market.

And all this demand is solely due to the records the cars have made. Each car has sold others, and the others sold others. For, until two months ago, there was no Overland advertising.

The car which is winning these legions of buyers—which has so outrivaled a hundred competitors—is bound to win you when you know it.

The Main Reasons

The Overland was designed by a mechanical genius, after most other cars had been fully developed. He was able to compare the work of a hundred designers by actual results in use. Thus for every part he chose the best device that the best engineers had worked out.

Then he created a wonderful engine—powerful, simple and all-enduring. Next he reduced the number of parts as the best way to minimize trouble. A single part which he invented did away with 47.

Then he simplified the operation. Three of the Overland models operate by pedal control. Push a pedal forward to go ahead, and backward to reverse. Push another pedal forward to get on high speed. The hands have nothing to do but steer.

As a result, a child can master the car in ten minutes. A novice can run it the first time he takes the wheel.

And the Overland is almost trouble-proof. Give it oil and water and it will always keep going. We have run one of these cars 7,000 miles, night and day, without stopping the engine. Many an owner has run from 7,000 to 10,000 miles without even cleaning a spark plug. The car has been run as far as 28 miles on one gallon of gasoline.

That is why Overland owners sell these cars to others. They are as faithful as horses, as economical as horses, as easy as a horse to drive and to care for.

Our Costly Machinery

About $3,000,000 has been invested in plants and machinery to produce the Overland car. The parts are made by automatic machines, so that error or variation is out of the question. Accuracy is secured—just as in watch making —to the ten-thousandth part of an inch.

The various parts of the car, in the process of making, pass more than 10,000 inspections.

Then every chassis, before the body is added, is given a thorough test on hard roads. As a result, every Overland car goes out in perfect condition.

The Cutting of Cost

In the past year alone we have cut our costs 20 per cent. We have done this through multiplied output, labor-saving machinery, and through making the parts which other makers buy.

This year we are selling a 25-horsepower Overland, with a 102-inch wheel base, for $1,000. No other car of equal power and size is sold at near this price.

We sell a 40-horsepower Overland, with a 112-inch wheel base, for $1,250. For $1,500 we are selling a car with all the power and speed— all the style and appearance—that any man can want. All prices include five lamps and magneto.

No other maker can afford to give what the Overland gives for the money. We use four separate cylinders, employ a five-bearing crank shaft—use for every part the very best that men know. But our modern machinery and enormous production give us a vast advantage.

Ask for the Facts

We have two books which every man should read if he wants to keep up with motor car progress. They are fascinating books and they tell a wonderful story. Cut out this coupon as a reminder to ask us to send them free.

Overland Model 38—Price $1,000. 25 h. p.—102-inch wheel base. With single rumble seat, $1,050—double rumble seat, $1,075—complete Toy Tonneau, $1,100

The Overland

Two of the many Overland Models

All prices include Magneto and full lamp equipment

A 40 h. p. Overland with 112-inch wheel base. Price with single rumble seat, $1,250—double rumble seat, $1,275—with 5-passenger Touring or Close-Coupled body, $1,400
(47)

The ads on this and the facing page attest to the popularity of the Overland.

1000 Car Loads

Overland cars

For One Dealer

WE have one dealer who takes 1000 carloads of Overlands every twelve months.

That's 5000 cars.

This dealer wired us a few months ago and wanted 7000 cars. But we could not supply them.

Other dealers take 2500, 2000 and 1500 Overlands apiece.

Even the 1500-car dealer takes more cars than the largest single factory in Germany turns out.

There are over 200 American automobile manufacturers, who do not make in a year as many cars as our one single 5000-car Overland dealer takes in the same period.

If you think this over for a moment these figures will mean something to you.

It certainly is reasonable to assume that we must be giving more car for less money than any other manufacturer in the business.

If we were not, we could hardly be doing the largest business.

That's sound logic.

If you will just take the time to make a few specification comparisons you will find the cost of the Overland is 30% less than that of any other similar car made.

Our catalogues will be sent on request. Please address Dept. 50

The Willys-Overland Company, Toledo, Ohio

Manufacturers of the famous Overland Delivery Wagons, Garford and Willys-Utility Trucks. Full information on request.

$950				$1075
Completely Equipped f.o.b. Toledo	Electric head, side tail and dash lights Storage battery 35 horsepower motor	33 x 4 Q. D. tires 114-inch wheelbase Mohair top, curtains and boot	Stewart speedometer Clear-vision windshield Electric horn	*With electric starter and generator f. o. b. Toledo*

Overland

The First Step In The Purchase Of An Automobile

A CAR may look beautiful and apparently act splendidly as you see it hum around the corner, but what do you know about its regular day in and day out performance? What do you know of its reliability—of its general behavior? And what does it cost to keep in operation? When you buy an automobile, these conditions have a direct effect on your pocket book — one way or the other. Don't fall into the costly habit of taking things for granted. This hinders your better judgment. Get the *facts* and then you can determine the value of any car.

And you don't have to be a technical expert to select the best machine. You don't have to know all the ins and outs of a motor. Nor do you have to be able to write a treatise on the transmission. When a careful business man buys a typewriter, he does not pretend to intimately know the mechanism, but he *does* know that the machine he buys is standard and that it has a concern behind it who is responsible.

The selection of the best car for your money is merely a case of simple analysis and common sense comparison. Take several of the leading popular priced cars — separate the facts from the fiction — compare one with the other and the car that shows the best balance is the machine you can invest in with a feeling of security. Remember that the facts represent the real value—the fiction the false. When you purchase your car use your mind as well as your eye. Combine your reason with your sense of sight. This seldom fails to get you the most for your money.

The Overland is the most highly standardized car on the market. For instance, compare the Overland priced at $1250 with any of the popular priced cars selling around $1500 to $1700. Take each list of specifications—compare item for item and see how you can make twelve hundred and fifty dollars go as far as seventeen hundred. Then compare this car with all other makes selling at about the same price and see the added Overland value. Then keep the fact in mind that more than 25,000 Americans own Overlands. On top of this remember that The Willys-

Overland Company makes all of their parts in their own plants. The motor, body, steering gear—in fact the entire chassis right down to the tiniest screw is made by Overland machinery.

The Overland plants are the greatest of their kind in the world. They employ over 4000 men. The factories cover 30 acres. This great institution, with its scientifically managed army of skilled men is today turning out the best car for the price that can be made.

Make the simple comparisons we point out above and be governed accordingly. Take no risks. Automobiles cannot be bought every day. When you buy, *buy right.* The more you leave the matter to guess work, the weaker your investment will be. Get the Overland facts and you'll get the value you are entitled to.

Look up the Overland dealer in your town or drop us a line today for an Overland book. It shows the full line of cars—Roadsters, Torpedo Bodies, Small or Large Touring Cars with Fore-Doors and Open Fronts. Priced from $775 to $1675. Let us send you the facts about these cars.

The Willys-Overland Co., 136 Central Avenue, Toledo, Ohio

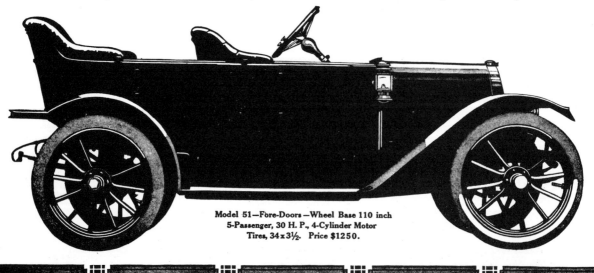

Model 51—Fore-Doors—Wheel Base 110 inch
5-Passenger, 30 H. P., 4-Cylinder Motor
Tires, 34 x 3½. Price $1250.

The above text emphasizes the reliability of the Overland and its manufacturer.

A Touring Tip

For fourteen years Firestone users have been spreading the good news. Year by year the army of Firestone Regulars has increased. It is whole-hearted appreciation of extra merit that is responsible for the growth of Firestone—the largest exclusive tire and rim makers in America.

The economy of the most miles per dollar—freedom from tire mishap—increased riding comfort and car-protection afforded by the extra life in Firestone Rubber—these are the facts you learn by experience.

You learn, too, that you can absolutely depend on Non-Skids for an amazing amount of extra service. It is not luck or chance—these factors are practically eliminated by the process of making. It is Firestone principles that earn success.

Firestone Red Inner Tubes, of pure, Up-River Fine Para Rubber, have proved their excelling power of heat-resistance, strength and "come-back" quality. This is "the tube above comparison," for reducing tire trouble and insuring most miles per dollar.

Firestone Quick-Detachable, Demountable Rims have been adopted by the big majority of car-makers. They alone meet all requirements for simple, dependable operation and sure tire protection.

All Types—All Sizes—Always on Hand

Firestone
Tires—Tubes—Rims—Accessories

The Firestone Tire and Rubber Co., Akron, Ohio—All Large Cities
"America's Largest Exclusive Tire and Rim Makers"

Firestone pneumatic tires are guaranteed when filled with air at the recommended pressure and attached to rims bearing either one or both of these inspection stamps. When filled with any substitute for air or attached to any other rims than those specified, our guarantee is withdrawn.

Firestone Tires were made of "Up-River Fine Para Rubber."

Making the Salesman Fit the Prospect

Low-Voiced, Quiet Man for Women - Suburban Man for Suburban Trade.

Physician's Equipment

FIG. 1—COVER DESIGN OF CIRCULAR FOR PROSPECTS WHO ARE PHYSICIANS

That the successful selling of electrics requires a live selling organization, a hustling sales manager and a meritorious product with proper representation, is evident from a day's study of the methods employed at the factory branch of the Anderson Electric Car Co., Chicago retailers of the Detroit electric. A Motor World representative had been seated next to Sales Manager George R. Veeder but two minutes, when he ordered "Get after Mr. Wilson quickly, or some one else will clinch the sale. Smith will take care of Mr. Jones for you, but don't delay in getting to Mr. Wilson's office at once and tell him I sent you." The salesman left.

"Selling electrics," said the sales manager, "is an all year round job. We have no seasons in our business. Our force is always busy, winter and summer, spring and fall. Our eight salesmen must keep busy to handle our 5,000 prospects, for that is the number always on record in our files. When we lose a deal it is because the salesman has failed

to follow the deal closely enough, and our competitor has been on the job. I will say a large percentage of prospect losses can be attributed to this cause alone." With this finished, the sales managed proceeded to outline the entire selling system.

The eight salesmen at this branch are busy and on the job all the time. Each salesman reports at 8:30 in the morning and proceeds to lay out his work for the day. He makes a list of his prospects he is to call on that day, and this list is turned over to Mr. Veeder, is checked up the following morning, and a written report made on each prospect. By this method the house keeps in close touch with every live deal the salesman has on record. By 9 o'clock the salesman has made his appointments for the day and goes out on the firing line.

Salesmen Kept on Outside.

"No salesman remains around the sales office unless by appointment, because," says Mr. Veeder, "if a man must visit we want him to visit with his customers or prospective customers."

Each salesman has a day assigned him on the sales floor, during which time he is responsible for taking care of every-one coming in relative to the selling end of the business. On this day he is entitled to whatever sales come in to the house and to all the prospects of this day.

These eight salesmen are individually adapted to the handling of certain classes of trade. Two of these men are particularly suited to the handling of ladies and have characteristic ways which appeal to the feminine sex. They are low voiced and quiet in their manners. An-

other salesman successfully handles the Jewish trade, and has a large acquaintance in this field, in both a business and social way. A fourth man can and does handle all the high class trade in Evanston and the North Shore. He resides in Evanston, has been selling Detroit electrics for years and has a large following and devotes his entire time to the North Shore aristocratic sections.

The other four men are decidedly fitted for handling all classes and types of customers. A spirit of co-operation exists in this selling force, and in many instances, when one man is unable to land a hard customer, another salesman volunteers to help clinch the deal.

Salesmen Make Regular Visits.

The most difficult problem, according to Mr. Veeder, is not in getting prospects, but in keeping the men in touch with these prospects. The Detroit electric branch has a system in force regarding the working of prospects, whereby the salesman has to make a personal call on a prospect every 30 days, otherwise he loses his identity with this prospect, and it may be claimed by, or given to, another salesman. This method has a tendency to keep the salesman working at all times on live stuff, does not tie up a lot of prospects in one salesman's name, and injure the business by this reason. Every prospect reported on is dated ahead by the sales manager's department, and through this system these prospects are brought to the attention of the sales manager daily, and the salesman is notified to see them.

This house has a prospect file containing 5,000 names, all of which at some time have shown an interest in the purchase of an electric. These prospects are systematically circularized from two to four times every 30 days, with either a form letter, a booklet, or some attractive piece of literature gotten out by the factory in Detroit. These prospects are classified, and literature of a definite nature is sent them. The illustration herewith (Fig. 1) shows the type of liter-

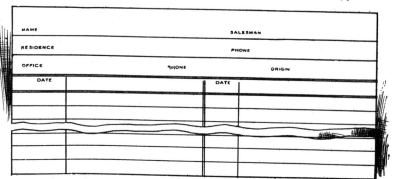

NAME		SALESMAN	
RESIDENCE		PHONE	
OFFICE	PHONE	ORIGIN	
DATE		DATE	

FIG. 2—CARD FOR RECORDING PROGRESS OF WORK ON PROSPECT

ature sent to physicians, whose needs are studied in writing the booklets.

At this time the branch is sending a series of five pamphlets (Fig. 3) to prospects, these pamphlets representing talks on "Summering in Chicago." These pamphlets are written in the first person and tell about the pleasures of electric car driving about Chicago during the summer and why it is not necessary to leave for the country when one has an electric.

Circulars Sent Out Systematically.

Besides the circularizing of 5,000 prospects each week, every salesman and the sales manager keeps a classified list of physicians, lawyers, bankers, publishers, etc., who are owners of Detroit electrics. When a salesman has a prospect who is a banker he does not fail to show his list of banker-owners to the prospect, and this is said to influence the buyer.

The salesman, after obtaining a prospect, must fill out a blank which is carboned twice. This blank (Fig. 2) gives all the information about the prospect. One blank is kept by the salesman, one by the sales manager and a third is placed in a vault for safekeeping.

There are three things a salesman must know before any definite selling is begun. The first is the size of the family, so that he may know the type or model of car to show, the second, where the prospect lives, so as to get a line on what list of customers live in his neighborhood and use this as a selling point, and the third, is there a trade involved. If it is a trade deal the customer is asked to bring his car to the shop, so that the appraiser may set an estimate on its value, and this in connection with the market value for that particular vehicle determines the price at which it is to be taken in trade.

Prospects Who Already Are Owners.

Another question which comes up in connection with trades is "has the prospect a gasolene or an electric car?" If he has a gasolene car he must be handled as a convert, while the former electric owner is not hard to carry over. If a man and his wife come into the deal, the woman must be sold first and then the man. The woman is not considered when price is stated, but the man is handled as a financial proposition.

The salesman makes it a point to visit the buyer of one of his cars periodically. From 5 to 10 owners a week are visited and in this way the owner is always advised about his car. When a new one is to be bought the Anderson company is immediately brought to mind because

the salesman makes periodical visits to the house.

Each salesman is required to stop at

FIG. 3—CIRCULARS THAT HAVE BEEN HELPFUL IN THE SUMMER CAMPAIGN BY POINTING OUT PLEASURES OF SUMMERING IN CHICAGO WITH AN ELECTRIC

public electric garages whenever he is in the neighborhood. In this way many

prospects are picked up. Mr. Veeder stated that he could call on any first-class electric garage and be able to secure from 5 to 10 good live prospects. The sales manager has daily talks with each man about his prospects. He asks if Smith, or Jones, is showing much enthusiasm, etc. Mr. Veeder has found that a little personal talk helps matters considerably. There are no definite rules about keeping in touch with the office when out, but every salesman does so because it is for his own and the company's good.

Qualities That Make the Salesman.

"I have found," says Mr. Veeder, "that the two great qualities necessary for the making of the successful salesman are determination and application. A man with these and the required amount of ability for presenting a proposition in a businesslike and logical manner to the electric car purchaser cannot help but make a big success in Chcago to-day."

Simple Night Window Display.

A certain Eastern dealer who does not believe in covering his show window glass with lettering has hit upon a novel method of getting window display at night for the name of his company.

Far enough back of the window to prevent interference with such displays as he may have in it he has had hung white linen shades which run on guy ropes at the side so that they will remain still. At night these are pulled down and a row of overhead lights illuminates them and shows up the name of the company, which is painted in black on the white shade. It is visible for a greater distance than was possible with a sign painted on the window itself. During the daytime the shades are rolled.

Pennsylvania Bans Roadside Signs.

Pennsylvania, in common with several other states, long has had a law which prohibits the placing of advertising on state property along the highways, but up to the present time the measure has never been actively enforced. Now, however, State Highway Commissioner Bigelow has sent out notices to all supervisors and township commissioners instructing them to enforce the provisions of the act. This act was approved March 10, 1903, by Governor Pennypacker. It provides a penalty of not more than $20 nor less than $5 for placing upon property belonging to the State of Pennsylvania, or to any county, township or borough therein, any written, painted, printed advertisement or other notice, sign or poster.

Motor World

Vol. XXXVIII   New York, U. S. A., Thursday, January 15, 1914   No. 4

FORD TO BUILD THAT LONG LOOKED FOR ELECTRIC CAR

Plans Well Laid for Popular-Priced Vehicle Selling for About $600— Will Employ Special 100-Mile Edison Battery.

Notwithstanding reports to that effect, the Ford Motor Co., of Detroit, does not purpose producing electric vehicles. However, while many men, some of them manufacturers of electric vehicles, have discussed the desirability of an electric car at a popular price, Henry Ford, as an individual, has been actively preparing to produce one. He himself confirmed the report late last week. It had been current for several days, always associated with the Ford Motor Co., but inquiry at that fountainhead brought the technically correct reply, "Absolutely no truth in report that Ford Motor Co. will build electrics," and thus partially disarmed suspicions.

Meanwhile Henry Ford personally was in consultation with none other than Thomas A. Edison, at the latters' laboratory in East Orange, N. J., and when the fact became known he admitted his intention to enter the electric vehicle field with a popular priced car—one selling for about $600. At the same time, he made known that Edison, for a year or more, has been developing a battery especially for the purposes of the Ford electric and has succeeded so well that a 400-pound battery, capable of operating 100 miles without recharging, is assured. It will permit the construction of a car weighing approximately 1,100 pounds.

The car will be built in either Detroit or Dearborn, Mich., but it is not expected that anything beyond the work of perfecting it will be done for a year at least. When it is ready for the market it will be produced by a company other than the Ford Motor Co., which, however, will be dominated by Henry Ford

and managed by his 21-year-old son, Edsall.

Meanwhile, as has been known for more than a year, Ford is developing a one-man gasolene plow, with which he will next startle the universe, in all human probability.

Yuster Forms Axle Company in Ohio.

M. L. Yuster, former general manager of the Hess Spring & Axle Co., and several other men of equal prominence in the automobile industry, have organized the Yuster Axle Co., in Cleveland, O., for the manufacture of axles for both cars and trucks. They already have acquired the former Royal Tourist car plant in Cleveland, which is uncommonly well adapted for their purposes, and the necessary equipment having been installed operations have commenced.

W. R. Hopkins, of the Cleveland Short Line Railway Co. and the Cleveland Underground Rapid Transit Co., is president of the Yuster company; E. H. Parkhurst, former vice-president of the Peerless Motor Car Co., is vice-president; E. W. Farr, treasurer of the Perfection Spring Co., second vice-president; Ben F. Hopkins, of the Belt & Terminal Railway Co., treasurer, and M. L. Yuster, secretary and manager. E. E. Muller, is assistant general manager and purchasing director, while R. E. Fries, formerly with the Weston-Mott and Lozier Motor Car companies, will have charge of the engineering department.

Grand Rapids Man Buys Disco Assets.

At the receiver's sale of the Disco Co., in Detroit, yesterday, the property was bid in by C. H. Bender, of Grand Rapids, Mich., His offer of $17,200 probably will be confirmed by the referee on Saturday, when it is Bender's immediate intention to organize a new company and continue the manufacture of Disco starters. It will be backed by a group of Grand Rapids business men. The assets acquired were inventoried at $100,133.57 and were appraised at $75,140.82.

MICHIGAN BUGGY'S SIXTEEN MOST OBLIGING DEALERS

One of Them Signed Undated Notes for $1,000,000—Receiver Bares More Figures Showing Extent of Rottenness.

Nearly everyone connected with the industry has at least a fairly good idea of the remarkable high financing which kept the Michigan Buggy Co., of Kalamazoo, afloat until the crash came on August 6th last; but it was not until this week when the receiver, the Detroit Trust Co., through its vice-president, Joseph Bower, issued a report to the creditors that the many ramifications were fully disclosed.

While it was already known that undated dealers' accommodation notes to a large amount had been made use of, Bower's investigation uncovered the fact that, apart from those which had been negotiated, the Michigan company had attempted to fortify its future with almost literally a bale of such paper. He found signed but undated notes of the sort bearing the names of sixteen Michigan Buggy dealers and distributers, to the amount of more than $2,462,000, of which Dewey & Co., who handled the Michigan car in the little town of Plano, Ill., furnished more than $1,000,000 worth.

It was believed that there were many other notes of this nature but they could not be found. None of them had been entered on the books, but nothing serves better to show how the Michigan officials proposed to keep their rotten ship afloat. When the company failed, its liabilities were placed at approximately $3,000,000, to say nothing of the $1,600,-000 debts accumulated by Victor L. Palmer, its secretary-treasurer, who later was personally forced into bankruptcy. As originally reported, the company's assets were $2,780,000, which the

News items from the January 15, 1914 issue of Motor World... Henry Ford and Thomas Edison confer about electric cars...the bankruptcy and unorthodox accounting procedures of the Michigan Buggy Company...

first appraisal scaled down to the sum of $1,260,000.

According to the receiver's report, while the Michigan Buggy Co.'s statement of January 31, 1913, which is used for the purpose of comparison, charged off five per cent, of what is termed balance of accounts receivable, the investigation indicates that it is more likely that from 60 to 70 per cent. of the entire debt balance should be charged off, in view of statements made by creditors concerning their indebtedness.

The January 31st statement shows that items carried as merchandise sales were also included in the inventory, but this is difficult to prove owing to the fact that many of the inventory books giving physical details have disappeared. It has been found that included in the assets were such items as interest charges, advertising expenditures, office expenses, etc., to the amount of $144,000, the notorious "velvet" payroll, carried in the name of J. Roach & Co., appearing in the general accounts receivable though charged to advertising.

As one of the many other instances in which the books were juggled, it is pointed out that February sales were carried as accounts receivable for January, to the extent of $521,900.

While the books showed a profit for the year, amounting to $287,000 in round figures, the inflations of inventory and other errors are such that instead of a profit there was a net loss of $74,000. The inventory inflations amount to $510,-200, while accounts payable, omitted from the January 31st statement, amount to $417,600, making it necessary to deduct from the assets reported by the Buggy company the sum of $1,529,000, which deduction will be still further increased, says the receiver's report, when the correct depreciation on accounts receivable and other inflations is reached.

The full report of the Detroit Trust Co.'s audit covers 258 pages and, needless to say, it does not accompany the report submitted to the creditors this week. It is, however, available at the offices of the Trust company in Detroit and Kalamazoo. The report to the creditors is accompanied by a check for the first six per cent. dividend to all creditors whose claims have been approved.

The receiver does not expect to realize more than the guaranteed bid of $225,000 from the auction sale of the personal property of the bankrupt company. A bid of $40,000 has been received for the real estate, which the receiver has reported to the court, but without recommendation.

SPARK PLUG ASSOCIATION TO BE FORMED IN CHICAGO

Tentative Arrangements Made at New York Show to be Followed by Definite Action in the West —Name Already Chosen.

Preliminary steps already have been taken, as was told in Motor World last week, and the final organization and election of officers of the association of Canfield spark plug patent licensees will take place at the Chicago automobile show; the meeting for this purpose will be held January 29, at 2 o'clock in the afternoon in the Auditorium Annex.

The licensees already have decided that their body will be called the Association of Spark Plug Manufacturers and Attorney William A. Redding, who is counsel for A. R. Mosler, the owner of the Canfield patent, is drafting bylaws which will be acted upon at the Chicago meeting. The objects of the association, which are to permit an interchange of ideas, to bring about greater harmony in the spark plug trade, to correct existing abuses and to standardize manufacture and make possible a better and cheaper plug, will also be put into concrete form at that time.

The matter thus far is in the hands of the committee, which was named at the Mosler luncheon in New York during the show; its members are: D. B. Mills, Rajah Auto Supply Co.; Albert Champion, Champion Ignition Co.; R. A. Strohnnehan, Champion Spark Plug Co.; David Smith, Standard Co., and Otto Heins, Bosch Magneto Co.

Following its appointment, the committee made preliminary arrangements and reported its progress to the licensees last week Friday. The project is receiving enthusiastic support from the spark plug men.

Westinghouse Seeks a Kissel Plant.

Negotiations are under way whereby the Westinghouse Lamp Co., of New York, probably will become possessed of the factory recently established in Milwaukee by the Kissel Motor Car Co. and which is admirably suited to the manufacture of globes for motor car and other lamps which the Westinghouse company has in view.

While admitting that the negotiations are pending, President Kissel states that their consummation depends entirely on other deals which are in contemplation and which, if terminated, will result in further extension of the Kissel business.

It is probable that the Westinghouse transaction will come to a head about the end of the present week.

The Kissel company, of course, still maintains its original plant in Hartford, Wis., and it is stated that if it relinquishes its Milwaukee factory to the Westinghouse agents it will build a still larger structure in that city.

Rolls-Royce Earns Handsome Profits.

During its fiscal year which ended October 31st, according to its report just made public, Rolls-Royce, Ltd., which is probably the most notable of the high grade manufacturers in Great Britain, earned a net profit of $456,845, as compared with $355,310 during the corresponding twelve months of the previous year. The directors recommended the payment of a dividend at the rate of 30 per cent. per annum on its capital stock of $1,000,000. The Rolls-Royce reserve fund now stands at $680,630. Among other things, the annual report brings out that the item of good-will, carried at $200,000, is to be eliminated.

Pope Receiver Reports Cash Increase.

According to the report of Colonel George Pope, receiver for the Pope Mfg. Co., in Connecticut, the balance on hand on December 31st was $106,091.67, as against $85,404.32 November 29th last. During December, receipts from sales of the Hartford factory products amounted to $35,889.62. Other receipts bring the total income for the month to $55,987.38. The expenditure during the corresponding period amounted to $35,-300.03, the largest item being $19,337.72 for factory payroll.

Oathout Becomes Silver's Partner.

Charles W. Oathout, at one time the Jackson agent in New York, has acquired an interest in the rights of the C. T. Silver Motor Co., the Overland agent, which recently took over the Peerless agency also and with it the palatial Peerless branch on upper Broadway. Oathout has been elected treasurer of the Silver company and will also serve as sales manager, which indicates that he will play an active part in the business.

American Starters for Renault Cars.

Although the Renault factory in France is not yet supplying electric starters as stock equipment, the Renault Selling Branch in New York has found the demand too formidable to resist. Accordingly, it has placed an order for Ward-Leonard electric equipment for all cars brought into this country.

Indispensable to motorists on the road.

As necessary a part of the equipment as an extra tire or tire pump.

In constant use throughout the day while touring.

Known everywhere by auto owners.

Covers 250,000 miles of tourable roads with detailed route directions.

Out two months earlier than last year—to catch the early spring tourists.

INCREASE YOUR ACCESSORY SALES
WITH A SUPPLY OF

1914 Automobile Blue Books

The Standard Road Guide of America. Purchased each year by over 90 per cent. of the touring motorists. Helps to increase your accessory sales. Each sale of a Blue Book means sales of equipment for the tours to follow.

New Edition Thoroughly Revised
First Shipment to Dealers April 25th

To insure having your supply on sale as soon as your competitors, write the nearest office today for sales proposition. Liberal dealer discounts. Effective co-operation.

THE AUTOMOBILE BLUE BOOK PUBLISHING CO.
912 S. Michigan Ave., Chicago   2164 Broadway, New York

The Automobile Blue Book was published annually.

Broadway Makes Noise About Its 1915 Cars

When the New Cars Come the People Know It.

No Sign Too Small When Season Is Opening

WHEN the 1915 cars began to arrive in New York City the salesrooms along Broadway took on renewed life with a jump. Big signs flared forth and the dealers could not make too much noise about the arrival of their demonstrators.

The Buick branch covered its front with big canvas signs. No cars were on hand but the signs said the cars were coming.

C. T. Silver put up two Willys-Knight signs that could be seen for blocks; the higher one is visible from Times Square. It says little—but enough. It tells the whole story well.

The Cutting-Larson Co. was free with paint and canvas when the new Oldsmobile struck town and proceeded to grab publicity while the time was ripe. The marked-up card shown below the Olds store front is an enlargement of the card shown on the windows. It looked like a rush job and was strong because of it.

How did you announce your new cars? Send us a picture! Write us a letter! If you have a good idea, pass it along!

The introduction of 1915 cars in New York City.

The PASSING of the HORSE

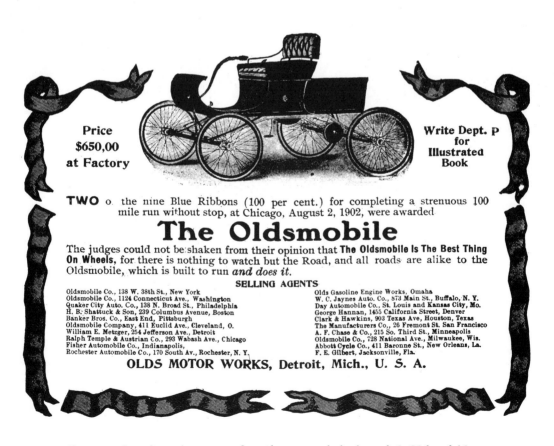
Very early advertisements for the curved-dash model Oldsmobile.

Announcing the New Seven-Passenger OLDSMOBILE

$1367

f.o.b. Lansing

THIS light weight, eight-cylinder car combines power, acceleration, speed, economy, comfort, beauty, and luxury in a measure hitherto undreamed of in a light car. The eight-cylinder motor, developing 58-horse power at 2,600 r. p. m., with the light weight of the car—3,000 pounds—presents a proportion of power to total car weight of approximately one horse power to every 51 pounds—an unusually favorable ratio.

This relation of weight to power, together with the high frequency of the power impulses—one to every five inches of car travel—is the reason for the wonderful hill climbing ability of the car—for its dependability on all sorts of roads—and for control so responsive that gear changing is seldom necessary.

Careful refinement of mechanism insures almost absolute quiet, while the counterbalanced crankshaft, light weight, balanced, connecting rods, and aluminum alloy pistons reduce internal resistance, bearing pressures and vibration to a minimum.

The comfort of the car is beyond description. Long, flat, flexible springs and perfect balance of chassis insure easy riding under any kind of going. The seats, upholstered with fine, long grain French leather, stuffed with pliant springs encased in linen sacks, increase comfort to the point of luxury.

Economy results from light weight and motor efficiency—economy both of fuel and tires. The new Oldsmobile is now on display by Distributors throughout the United States. Illustrated catalog on request.

Details of the Car

Wheel Base—120 inches.

Weight—3,000 pounds.

Motor—Eight-cylinder, V-type, high speed motor, with counterweighted crankshaft, developing 58-horse power at 2,600 r. p. m.

Cooling—By centrifugal pump.

Radiator—Honeycomb, with solid German silver jacket.

Lubrication—Force feed.

Electric System—Delco—In three units, starter, generator, and distributer, each unit independent.

Spark Control—Automatic, with hand lever for extreme ranges.

Carburetor—Automatic compensating type.

Gasoline System—Vacuum feed, with gas tank in rear.

Transmission—Unit with motor.

Gear Ratio—4 11-12 to 1.

Clutch—Cone type, leather faced.

Drive—Hotchkiss type.

Frame—Cold pressed steel, deep channel.

Front Axle—I-beam, with Timken tapered roller bearings.

Rear Axle—Full floating, spiral bevel type. Timken bearings.

Brakes—Foot, external contracting, emergency, internal expanding.

Wheels—Selected hickory, natural wood finish.

Springs—Front, semi-elliptic; rear, three-quarter elliptic, long and flat.

Steering—Left hand, semi-irreversible, worm and half-nut type.

Fenders—Crowned type.

Doors—Twenty-three inches wide.

Upholstery—Finest French leather, stuffed with springs encased in linen sacks.

Dash—Circassian walnut, with silver finished instruments.

Finish—Paint and varnish, applied by hand.

Equipment—In addition to regular items, includes double bulb headlights, dash light, tonneau light, double tire carrier, and side curtains, opening with doors.

OLDS MOTOR WORKS, LANSING, MICH.

ESTABLISHED 1880   INCORPORATED 1899

Many of the geniuses of the automobile industry are the product of the House of Oldsmobile—a school where men are trained to be thorough and accurate

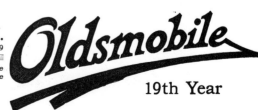

19th Year

1917 Oldsmobile ad. At this time Olds was a division of General Motors.

1914 Oldsmobile Six
4 or 5-Passenger Phaeton
Boston Boulevard
Detroit

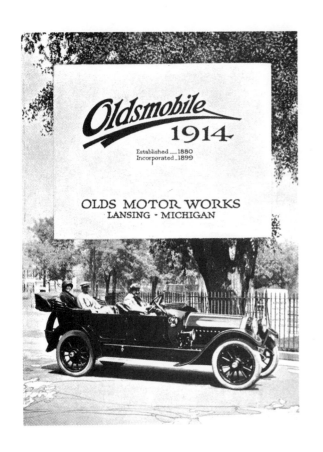

OLDSMOBILE was conceived in Lansing, Mich., a thriving, prosperous city renowned for its industrial progress and widely known as the capital of the State. Grand River, wending its way through the city, about divides it in half. On the bank of this river, overspread by ancient willows, is a two-story affair of brick—the townspeople will tell you that this modest little old building, the birthplace of Oldsmobile, was a typical manufacturing plant in the Lansing of thirty-three years ago. From this you can easily gather that Olds Motor Works was founded in 1880. The working force then consisted of six men, and they worked in a building not larger than one corner of the body shop of the present factory.

It was in 1887 that the first Oldsmobile was given to the world—though the world, as ever, was skeptical and disposed to look a "gift horse in the mouth." It was a tricycle on wooden wheels, and weighed 1300 pounds. This, so far as is known, was the first American vehicle driven by a gasoline motor.

After experimenting for the next two years, the second Oldsmobile made a more formidable and confident appearance upon the road.

In 1892—twenty-two years ago—the first Oldsmobile was sent abroad. A London patent medicine firm

On this and the following nine pages are excerpts from the 1914 Oldsmobile catalogue.

Demonstrating—1901

First Oldsmobile—1894

1902-3

1903-4

First Six Cylinder Oldsmobile—1908

130

bought the car. It was shipped to Bombay and never heard of again—although the factory has never really construed this as a misfortune. The third Oldsmobile model, with a cumulation of experience and improvements, was introduced in 1894.

By this time it was more than a matter of conjecture that Oldsmobile should take its place among other industries of the world.

Making of past records, memories and tribulations a closed book, it was now determined to begin anew the task of creating, perfecting, and marketing an Oldsmobile which would weigh less than 600 pounds and sell for less than $700. This was done, and in such a manner that an epoch in the industry was established which marks the greatest achievement in the history of automobiles.

In 1902, about 2500 Oldsmobiles were sold. In 1903 the production was increased to 3000. By 1905 there was a still greater demand, and the quota that year was 6500 cars.

Beginning with 1905, great strides were made in matters of refinement; and from that time to the present, comfort and beauty have been as much a part of the car as efficiency and power.

At Madison Square Garden, New York, we pioneered the first four-cylinder medium-priced car—this was in 1906. We were at that time experimenting with a six-cylinder model, which was finished in the late fall of 1907 and placed successfully on the market in 1908. In 1909

we built and sold more successful six-cylinder cars than any other manufacturer in America or Europe. By 1910 Oldsmobile was a recognized leader among high-priced four- and six-cylinder cars. This leadership we have retained up to the present.

In 1913 we met the growing tendency of the times and produced a high-grade car at the actual selling price of a cheaper make, and by means of simplified manufacturing methods brought forth a car competing in every way with the highest priced—at a figure which made the devotee of the low-priced car thoughtfully consider the advisability of adding just a little more to his original purchase price to secure a high-grade automobile of more than ordinary reputation and merit.

Oldsmobile is a name recognized as one of the oldest in the annals of the motor car industry. Though age alone does not indicate any material facts regarding the construction of an automobile, it does signify one feature of importance, and that is: On its merit alone has Oldsmobile retained through all these years a high place in the esteem and respect of the motor purchasing public, who have substantially indicated their approval, despite their so-called fickleness, which has caused the passing of many new comers in the field.

During the past decade motor and body design has changed, but to an institution backed by years of experience these changes have never been radical, but have been

The Factory

Grounds 56 Acres
Total Floor Space, 426,177 sq. ft.

Final Inspection

Final Test

Looking Down Division Street

Loading Platform

1914 Oldsmobile Six
7-Passenger Touring
in Detroit

Under the Washington Elm,
Concord

1914 Oldsmobile
7-Passenger Touring Car

instituted as improvements when the merit of the change has been proven. Standards are the natural outgrowth of developments, and developments of permanent worth have been born of experience which all leads back to the value of the name Oldsmobile.

While standards are the outgrowth of development, there is one standard which has made Oldsmobile development possible, and that is the desire and the ability to build each year a car just a little better than anything else on wheels—not only from an engineering standard but from an artistic viewpoint as well. Each new model is a creation as far advanced in ideas of line and beauty as the present state of the art and our conception of beauty will permit.

Skilled workmanship and good materials are the foundation for the long life of an Oldsmobile. You cannot wear one out. We receive letters from all parts of the United States from owners who are driving their original purchases—made six, eight, ten and fifteen years ago—and in many instances the repair bills have been less than the price of the license tag. Isn't there something in a name when the name has records like this?

Oldsmobile was a pioneer in the six-cylinder field, and has proven the conviction of its engineers that the six is the logical type of motor car to fulfill every purpose of an automobile — to give comfort, ease of operation, smooth starting and acceleration; tire economy, power and a satisfaction not to be found in any other type of motor.

Just a Few Quality Features of the 1914 Oldsmobile

QUALITY costs money, but it creates satisfaction. The features contained in an article of quality serve a definite purpose in a manner which defies imitation.

RIMS—For instance, there are many makes of rims—we use Baker rims because they are the lightest rims on the market and embody practically all the advantages of other makes in addition to their own. A fact worth remembering in this connection is that the reduction of 100 pounds weight on the wheels is equivalent to 300 pounds on the chassis. This means a longer life for the car and increased mileage for the tires.

CURTAINS—Jiffy curtains can be put up in a few seconds without any necessity for the motorist to get out of the car in rain and mud. They give the maximum of light, and are stored in a convenient pocket in the peak of top in such a manner that the celluloid is in no danger of being broken or cracked.

BOWS—The bows on the Oldsmobile top are of solid construction, made extra strong so as to do away with the necessity of reinforcement.

JACK—We furnish a geared jack capable of raising 3000 pounds more than will ever be called for in raising the wheel of an Oldsmobile.

LOCKS—Our body designer, with the assistance of the lockmakers, designed for the 1914

In the woods at Belle Isle

Minneapolis Branch

Los Angeles Branch

Detroit Branch

San Francisco Branch

Specifications Oldsmobile Model 54

Wheel Base, 4—5 passengers	132 inches
Wheel Base, 7 passengers	139 inches
Wheel Base, Limousine	132 inches
Carrying Capacity (passengers)	4—5—7
Horse Power	50
Number of Cylinders	6
Bore	4¼ inches
Stroke	5¼ inches
How Cast	In pairs
How Cooled	Water Cooled
Engine Mounted	Main Frame
Engine Suspended	Three Point
Type of Radiator	Honey Comb
Carburetor	Float Feed Type—Special design
Magneto (name)	Delco
Storage Batteries (name and cap.)	Delco—6 Volt
Spark Coil (name)	Delco
Lubrication	Splash
Clutch, Style	Cone
Style of Drive	Shaft
Style Change Speed Mechanism	Selective
How Operated	Hand
Type Front Axle	I Beam
Type Rear Axle	Floating
Brakes, Operated	Foot and Hand
Size Front Tires	36 x 5 inches, Fisk or Goodyear
Size Rear Tires	36 x 5 inches, Fisk or Goodyear
Name and Type of Rim	Demountable (Baker)
Front Wheel Bearings	Timken Roller
Rear Wheel Bearings	Ball—Imported and Domestic Special Oldsmobile Design
Steering Wheel, Diam. and Position	19-inch, Right
Brake and Change Gear Lever Location	Right Hand
Spark Control	Automatic Delco
Springs, Front	Semi-Elliptic
Springs, Rear	¾ Elliptic Underslung
Road Clearance	11 inches
Frame	Press Steel Channel—Heat Treated
Gasoline Tank, Location and Capacity	Rear—23 Gallons
Reserve Tank Capacity	3 Gallons
Engine Starter	Delco Electric
Type of Motor	"L" Head

1914 Oldsmobile Chassis
Model 54

1914 Oldsmobile Six
4 or 5-Passenger Phaeton
at Belle Isle

Auxiliary Seats Down

1914 Oldsmobile Limousine

Auxiliary Seats Folded

Fairmount Park, Philadelphia

Oldsmobile a lock embodying the good features of the best locks and eliminating their defects.

RADIATOR—From long experience in building cars, we have found that while the Honeycomb type of radiator is the most expensive it is also the most efficient. One advantage of the Mayo radiator with a German silver casing is that it can be cleaned and polished without the slightest danger of discoloring.

CARPET—Natural horsehair—imported. Can be washed if necessary.

HEADLIGHTS—Special design, nickel plate on brass. The reflector is heavily silver-plated. Patented focusing device. Glass used is pure white, French plate.

STEERING WHEEL—Special Oldsmobile design, Circassian walnut. Probably the most expensive laminated wood steering wheel made, the Circassian walnut being imported from Asia. Spider black enameled to avoid reflection in the driver's eyes.

LEATHER—The best that can be secured, long grained, hand buffed. The water graining which we specify shrinks the leather 14 per cent, removing all possibility of shrinking or stretching when the leather is on the car.

GASOLINE TANKS—Lead tern. The base of this is high-grade steel, which is heavily coated with lead to prevent corrosion by gasoline or water.

WINDSHIELD—Plate glass of silvering quality. Free from bubbles, scratches and imperfections common to ordinary plate glass.

ALUMINUM—Toe boards, heel plates and running boards of cast aluminum. Costly, but it wears a life-time.

IN offering the Oldsmobile Limousine for 1914 we have endeavored to combine Oldsmobile stability with luxury and a refinement that makes its particular appeal to the ladies. The accommodations, quality of finish, and luxurious upholstery are all that Madame could wish for.

The mechanical fitness of this model will satisfy the demands of a man who is entirely familiar with motor-car construction.

The 1914 Limousine accommodates seven passengers—three on the rear seat, two on the auxiliary, and two on the front seat. Unlike some auxiliary seats, the seats in the Oldsmobile are very comfortable and swing back on a pivot when not in use. Open or folded they do not interfere with the knee-room of passengers on the rear seat.

All bodies trimmed in French novelty cloth.

All metal parts are sterling silver finish.

The little refinements such as speaking tube, flower vase, toilet articles, box, umbrella rack, electric lights, and French plate glass windows make the interior as elegant and luxurious as a boudoir designed to meet the most fastidious and exacting requirements.

1914 Oldsmobile
Limousine

1914 Oldsmobile Six
7-Passenger Touring
$1785 Detroit

1914 Oldsmobile
"En Route"

Industrial Railway and Stock

Woodworking Department

Oldsmobile Motor Six-Cylinder, Unit Power Plant Three-Point Suspension

Oldsmobile motors are of the highly efficient L-head type. A compact unit power plant with long stroke and small bore. All valves are enclosed to insure silence and freedom from dirt; this method also retains the oil in its proper place.

In the L-head type we have produced the largest area of cubical contents of compression space with the smallest possible radiating area or heat-absorbing surfaces. This type of motor has a great lugging power at comparatively low speed, which means that its hill-climbing ability is an assured factor. Another advantage possessed by the L type of cylinder is that the intake gases in passing over the valves cool the same, therefore producing an engine which is less susceptible to pre-ignition. There is a preponderance of opinion in favor of this type of motor, including the best-known makes of Europe. Our experience with the six-cylinder motor of this type dates back to 1908, when we produced the first L-head six-cylinder motor on the American market.

1914 Oldsmobile Dash Assembly

Circassian walnut dash, all trimmings nickel. An electric fixture in the top of the dash floods all instruments with light. The instruments are all within easy reach of the driver.

The appointments and finish of the dash assembly on the 1914 Oldsmobile is the most luxurious and complete arrangement to be found on any American-made car at any price.

Equipment 1914 Oldsmobile
Model 54

COMBINATION electric and oil side and tail lamps, special Oldsmobile design; special design Oldsmobile electric head lamps; special design three-way adjustable ventilating windshield; top, boot and patented adjustable side curtains; 60-mile speedometer; adjustable stem setting and winding Waltham clock; rear tire irons, capacity for two tires; demountable rims, one extra; imported horse-hair tonneau mat; motor-driven tire air pump; famous Delco starting, lighting and ignition system; electric light in tonneau; extension electric trouble lamp; tools, jack; patented bow separating top holders; adjustable auxiliary seats in seven-passenger; springs—front, semi-elliptic; rear, ¾ elliptic under-slung; Gabriel snubbers on rear; Klaxon warning signal; (extra, at additional cost — wire wheels, special Oldsmobile touring trunks).

Standard colors—Green, Lake, Gray.

Fifty dollars extra will be charged for color other than standard.

Oldsmobile special touring trunks will be supplied at $45 additional for one, and $80 per pair.

Tires other than standard will be charged for extra, depending upon make.

Wire wheels at additional cost, depending upon make. Seat covers to order, extra, depending upon quality.

Prices

Combination four or five-passenger Phaeton, touring body type, $2975. Seven-passenger touring body, $175 extra. Limousine, $4300.

Fairmount Park Philadelphia

The rear construction on Model 54 is typical of the attention given to details on all Oldsmobile models, the gasoline tank support being integral with the frame. A study of other makes will show that this extremely staunch method of supporting the tank is not common practice with even the highest-priced cars. The tire support is also bolted to the rear frame construction.

The gasoline tank is provided with two splashing partitions to prevent gasoline from splashing when the tank is half full.

The pages that follow show a few views of the exterior and interior departments of Oldsmobile manufacturing facilities. The limited space in this book will not permit the use of views of all departments.

Chicago Branch

St. Louis Branch

Pittsburgh Branch

OLDSMOBILE COMPANY of MO.

Philadelphia Branch

New York Branch

THE OLDSMOBILE COMPANY   BUFFALO BRANCH

Buffalo Branch

1914 Oldsmobile Six
Belle Isle

*J*T IS a wonderful achievement to take a car as good as the PIERCE-ARROW always was and make it as much better as it now is. The Dual Valve Engine increases and intensifies every quality which made the PIERCE-ARROW what it is.

THE PIERCE-ARROW MOTOR CAR COMPANY
BUFFALO, NEW YORK

The Pierce-Arrow was one of America's best known luxury cars.

PEERLESS
Two-Power-Range
EIGHT

The "Loafing" Range

The "Sporting" Range

Modern Lightness—With Stability

PEERLESS leadership in Closed Car construction was established in the early days of the industry.

There is much to be said for newer methods—where they work real improvements.

The Peerless Closed Cars of today embody those fundamental principles developed by the old master coach builders, combined with all that constitutes genuine improvement in modern methods.

The result—modern lightness with stability.

Mounted on the famous Peerless Eight chassis, with its two separate and distinct ranges of power, the Peerless Closed Cars of today maintain their leadership.

The "loafing" range offers the acme of soft, smooth, efficient, economical application of power.

The "sporting" range releases an abundance of power for emergencies and speed.

Let the Peerless dealer show you its remarkable range of performance.

7 passenger Touring $2760   4 passenger Roadster $2760   4 passenger Coupe $3320
7 passenger Sedan $3530   7 passenger Sedan Limousine $3720
f. o. b. Cleveland, subject to change without notice

The Peerless Motor Car Co., Cleveland, Ohio

The Peerless Eight boasted two power ranges, one for "loafing," the other for "sporting."

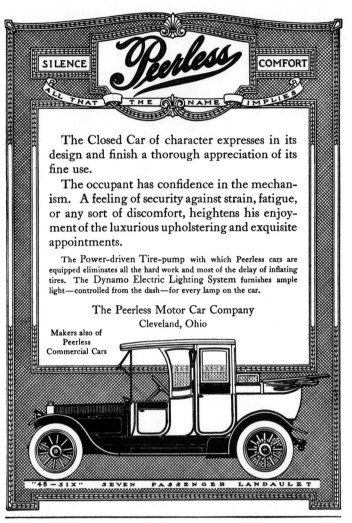

SILENCE *Peerless* **COMFORT**

ALL THAT THE NAME IMPLIES

The Closed Car of character expresses in its design and finish a thorough appreciation of its fine use.

The occupant has confidence in the mechanism. A feeling of security against strain, fatigue, or any sort of discomfort, heightens his enjoyment of the luxurious upholstering and exquisite appointments.

The Power-driven Tire-pump with which Peerless cars are equipped eliminates all the hard work and most of the delay of inflating tires. The Dynamo Electric Lighting System furnishes ample light—controlled from the dash—for every lamp on the car.

The Peerless Motor Car Company
Cleveland, Ohio

Makers also of
Peerless
Commercial Cars

"48—SIX"   SEVEN   PASSENGER   LANDAULET

PREMIER
AMERICA'S GREATEST TOURING CAR
PREMIER MOTOR MFG. CO.
INDIANAPOLIS, INDIANA

Air Free From Oil—At Correct Pressure
FOR EACH SIZE TIRE

SAFE AIR

The CURTIS GARAGE AIR PUMP

Will furnish air free from oil and run 100 working hours on one oiling up. They have unloading device, inspectable valves, fan flywheel, are controlled splash oiled and made in five sizes—stationary or portable.

Curtis Correct Pressure Air Station

Will furnish the air at correct pressure for any size tire—simply turn the pointer to size of your tire—no watching the gauge—no under inflating—no over inflating. Write your jobber or write us.

Curtis Pneumatic Machinery Co., **1546 Kienlen St. St. Louis, Mo.**
New York Office, 133A Church Street

We will exhibit at both New York and Chicago Automobile Shows Booth D 219 at New York and Basement 9 A at Chicago

Pullman AUTOMOBILES

Pullman cars are not sold to dealers because of enormous dealers' commissions—but because Pullman dealers have no trouble in selling Pullman cars at list prices. The purchaser gets the greatest value possible for the money—the dealer gets a good, fair profit. Results—both customer and dealer satisfied.

Four different size motors—3 four cylinder, 1 six cylinder—with a variety of body styles. Self cranking, electric lighting device, full equipment.

PULLMAN MOTOR CAR COMPANY
222 N. George Street   YORK, PA.

The Peerless (top left) featured a power-driven tire pump. Evidently Pullman cars were consigned rather than sold to dealers (lower left).

Packard Increases Power, Not Price

Efficiency Increased by Carburetter and Valve Refinements Without Enlarging Motor—Headlights Redesigned—Closed Body Added to Line.

Only slight changes have been made in the Packard 3-38 and 5-48, the successors of the 2-38 and 4-48, and no changes whatever in the prices. The 7-passenger touring car with the smaller motor costs $3,850 and with the larger motor $4,850; the 5-passenger phaetons $3,750 and $4,750; the roadsters the same as the phaetons; the limousines $5,000 and $6,000, and the 3-passenger coupes $4,450 and $5,450.

Equipment includes top, boot and curtains, windshield, two extra rims, tire holders, trunk rack, pump, tools, etc. Power tire pump and speedometer are

toward the rear to reduce the chance of getting dirt into the carburetter. The hot water jacket and heated intake manifold are continued without change. An increase of power has been effected, without increasing bore or stroke, by slightly increasing the sizes of the valves, changing the timing a little and a few other refinements.

Both cars are exactly alike, so far as design is concerned. The motors are of the L-head type, with cylinders cast in threes; the smaller has a bore and stroke of 4 x 5½ and the larger 4½ x 5½; the S. A. E. ratings are 38.4 and 48.6, re-

FRONT OF 3-38 SHOWING NEW LAMPS

spectively. Ignition is by the Bosch duplex magneto and starting and lighting by Packard-Bijur system. The lubrication system is double in that an extra throttle controlled oil feed is provided for hard service.

Motor and gearset are separate units,

SIX-PASSENGER SALON TOURING BODY AND SALON LIMOUSINE, BOTH ON PACKARD 3-38 CHASSIS

furnished on the 5-48 and are extra on the 3-38.

Of the 20 body styles offered, the three-window salon brougham is the latest, having a low roof and narrow body and a particularly attractive appearance. While the coupe has not been changed much so far as outward appearance is concerned, it has been widened so that three persons can be accommodated on the rear seat and a fourth on the auxiliary seat. A small window in the left rear corner is an added convenience.

So far as the exterior is concerned the most conspicuous change is in the lamp design. The big electric headlights each have an auxiliary electric bulb, each with its individual reflector, for city driving, and the side lights have been reduced in size. All the lamps are controlled by buttons on a control board mounted on the steering column.

The carburetter has been altered to provide a housing for the auxiliary air valve, and the opening has been turned

SALIENT POINTS OF THE TWO LATEST PACKARDS.		
Prices:	3-38	5-48
7-passenger touring ...	$3,850	$4,850
5-passenger phaeton	3,750	4,750
Roadster	3,750	4,750
7-passenger Limousine..	5,000	6,000
3-passenger coupe	4,450	5,450
Make of motor	Packard	Packard
Number of cylinders......	6	6
Shape	L-head	L-head
How cast	Threes	Threes
Bore	4	4½
Stroke	5½	5½
S. A. E. horsepower......	38.4	48.6
Magneto	Bosch duplex	Bosch-duplex
Starting-lighting..	Packard-Bijur	Packard-Bijur
Clutch	Multiple disk	Multiple disk
Gearset	Semi-selective	Semi-selective
Wheelbase	140	144
Tires, front	36 x 4½	37 x 5
Tires, rear	37 x 5	37 x 5
Steering	Left	Left
Control	Center	Center
Rear axle	Floating	Floating

Equipment: Top with envelope and side curtains, windshield, lamps, starting-lighting system, 2 extra rims, tire holders, trunk rack, jack, pump and tools, etc. Power-driven air pump and speedometer on 5-48, extra on 3-38.

the latter being built on the rear axle. The rear axle is of the full floating type. On the 3-38 the tires are 36 x 4½ front and 37 x 5 rear, and on the 5-48 37 x 5. Wheelbases are 140 and 144 inches.

PACKARD TOOL KIT IN DOOR CASE

News about new Packard styles - July, 1914.

AUTO MULTI-HORN PLAYED BY KEY

The latest novelty in automobile horns in England is a 4-note type that is operated by depressing keys, these being fitted on a small board at any convenient position on the car and connecting with the tubes of the horn by battery-charged wires. One key can be pressed down to obtain a single note, or all may be pressed in unison or one after another, as in playing a scale on a

A Novelty in Auto Horns

piano. In fact, with a little practice, a 4-note tune may be played.

"Ask the man who owns one" was the Packard slogan (upper left). Accessory ads on this page include two musical horns.

Packard owners could modernize their cars by adding the Sharrer top.

The Dayton Airless Tire.

SpringfielD
Type Bodies
Lead the World
The New Springfield Four Door Model
The Ultimate Body for Every Use

The Springfield Type body is instantly adaptable for winter or summer—rain or shine—day or night service—combining all the protection, luxury and appearance of the finest limousine as well as the freedom and advantages of the open touring car. Be sure that the next car you buy is equipped with a Springfield Type Body.

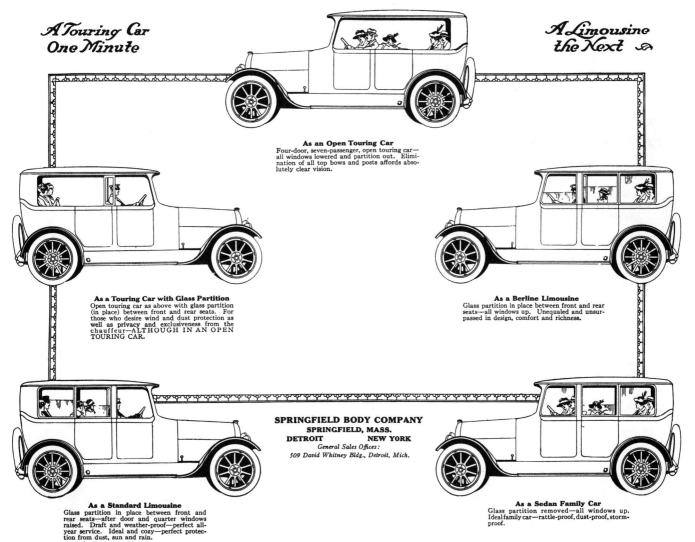

A Touring Car One Minute

A Limousine the Next

As an Open Touring Car
Four-door, seven-passenger, open touring car—all windows lowered and partition out. Elimination of all top bows and posts affords absolutely clear vision.

As a Touring Car with Glass Partition
Open touring car as above with glass partition (in place) between front and rear seats. For those who desire wind and dust protection as well as privacy and exclusiveness from the chauffeur—ALTHOUGH IN AN OPEN TOURING CAR.

As a Berline Limousine
Glass partition in place between front and rear seats—all windows up. Unequaled and unsurpassed in design, comfort and richness.

SPRINGFIELD BODY COMPANY
SPRINGFIELD, MASS.
DETROIT   NEW YORK
General Sales Offices:
509 David Whitney Bldg., Detroit, Mich.

As a Standard Limousine
Glass partition in place between front and rear seats—after door and quarter windows raised. Draft and weather-proof—perfect all-year service. Ideal and cozy—perfect protection from dust, sun and rain.

As a Sedan Family Car
Glass partition removed—all windows up. Ideal family car—rattle-proof, dust-proof, storm-proof.

Springfield furnished auto bodies for many different makes of cars.

PAIGE
The Most Beautiful Car in America

For seven consecutive years, we of the Paige-Detroit Motor Car Company have demonstrated our ability to conceive and produce the type of automobiles that appeal *instantaneously* to the American people.

All of our models have been immediate successes. Our announcements and the endorsement of the public have been almost simultaneous. As a consequence, the history of Paige at the automobile shows has been one long, unbroken series of triumphs.

Such being the case, it must indeed be significant when we say the reception accorded to our new models has far surpassed anything of the kind that we have ever experienced.

At the earlier automobile shows it has amounted to a genuine ovation.

The Paige booths have been thronged with visitors from morning until night. Hundreds of disinterested men and women have personally sought out the officials of our company and congratulated them in the most glowing terms.

Seasoned motor car distributors from all sections of the nation have been equally lavish in their praise, and each day our mails are filled with communications expressing the same enthusiastic approval.

So you can see we have reason to feel proud—and *do* feel proud. We know, too, that every Paige owner will share this feeling with us when he first sees and rides in "The Most Beautiful Car in America."

Stratford "Six-51" 7-passenger $1495 f. o. b. Detroit
Linwood "Six-39" 5-passenger 1175 f. o. b. Detroit

Paige-Detroit Motor Car Company, Detroit

The Paige was advertised as "The Most Beautiful Car in America."

146

The Factory Behind the Car

The Home of the Paige Car covers more than twelve acres of floor space. It is one of the most completely equipped plants in the United States and includes practically every labor saving device known to factory science.

Here the art of precise manufacturing is found in its highest form of development. There is no guess work—no "rule of thumb" measurement. Many of the operations require one one-thousandth of an inch precision and a rigid inspection system sees that these standards are maintained day in and day out.

The Paige Car is superbly built. For that reason it is a glutton for hard work and constant service.

The Paige Car is superbly designed. For that reason it is universally recognized as "the Most Beautiful Car in America."

PAIGE-DETROIT MOTOR CAR COMPANY   DETROIT, *Michigan*

Many of the old-time car ads showed the automobile factory in the background. Above is shown the 12-acre Paige factory.

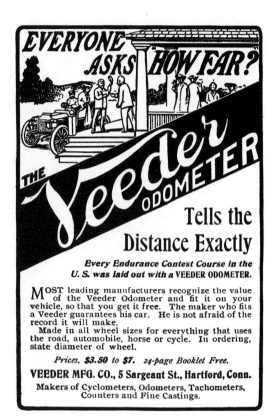

Above, left: 1911 Paige-Detroit $800 25 H.P. car; The Veeder Odometer was a popular accessory; The Dewey Power Tire Pump (lower right) eliminated hand pumping in the day when punctures were all too frequent.

The Rambler Cross Country Has Made Good

The Rambler Cross Country—$1650

We Guarantee Every Rambler
for Ten Thousand Miles

Subject to the conditions of our signed guarantee which we will give with each car

Ten thousand miles! Think what it means!

Step into the Rambler in New York and journey across four states to Chicago. Take your bearings and strike due west across seven states to the Golden Gate.

Run down the Coast to Los Angeles. Turn back over the mountains and on through eight hundred miles of desert to El Paso. Then on to' New Orleans and back, by way of Atlanta, through eight states to the city of New York.

Strike out again cross country for Chicago. Then drive your car straightway across the American continent to San Francisco. Yet you

have not exhausted the ten thousand mile Rambler guarantee backed by a company of known stability.

We give this guarantee to prove to you our unbounded confidence in every single part that goes into every Rambler car.

The first Rambler Cross Country that left the factory made a three thousand mile test trip through nine states, over the mountains of Pennsylvania to New York, Albany, Boston and back to the factory.

Since then the fame of the Cross Country has spread, and its service has extended to every state in the Union, to every province of Canada, to Mexico, to Australia, South America, Europe and the Orient.

Everywhere this Rambler has gone its performance has strengthened our confidence in its ability to fulfill this guarantee. That is why we do not hesitate to give it.

Eleven years of success in motor car building has so established the stability of this company in manufacturing and financial resources as to make definitely known the responsibility back of this guarantee.

Such a car with this guarantee, backed by such a company whose liberal policy is so widely known, are the reasons why you should have a Rambler. A postal card will bring you a catalog at once.

Equipment —Bosch duplex ignition. Fine large, black and nickel headlights with gas tank. Black and nickel side and tail oil lamps; large tool box; tool roll with complete tool outfit. Roomy, folding robe rail; foot rest, jack, pump and tire kit. Top with envelope, $80—wind shield, $35—demountable wheel, less tire, with brackets and tools, $30—gas operated self-starter, $50.

The Thomas B. Jeffery Company
Main Office and Factory, Kenosha, Wisconsin
Branches: Boston, Chicago, Cleveland, Milwaukee, New York,
Philadelphia, Sacramento, San Francisco

The Rambler was one of America's pioneer cars; the first models were built in 1902. During the next several decades Rambler became one of the most popular cars on the road. The above ad appeared about 1913.

Left: 1918 Rambler ad showing the sixty-five limousine. Right: The Almaco piston was said to "make a four run like a six."

The Reeves Sextoauto was one of the more curious automobiles on the road.

1914 cartoon sequence advertising Hyatt bearings.

You don't guess when you buy a Regal "30"—you know it's a good car. The only five-passenger, four-cylinder touring car at the price that can point to a record of three years' success

Licensed under the Selden Patent

Five-Passenger Touring Car; Baby Tonneau or Roadster;

107 inch Wheel Base;

32 x 3½ inch Tires;

Weight 2000 lbs.

"If you can't buy you can boost"

$1250 Regal "30"

We Point to Our Record

THE Regal "30" is the original touring car of its size and power to be sold for $1250. Other makes may *claim* equal simplicity, style, power and strength, but—no other maker of a car at our price can point to a *record of three years' success.*

What does this three years' experience in the hands of the user mean to *you*? It means that when you buy a Regal "30" you get a *finished* product—without an untried, experimental feature. A car that has gone through the most severe and exacting tests in the service of users and come out triumphant for three years.

When you buy a Regal "30" you get a car without the "kinks" that cause trouble, annoyance and expense; a car that, by a series of progressive refinements, has been developed into a harmonious, reliable unit—a machine that is well nigh perfect, with an established reputation for satisfactory service and *low cost* of operation.

In every essential the 1910 Regal "30" is the same car that braved the terrors of Rocky Mountain roads and Western deserts and now holds the touring car record from New York to San Francisco. (Story of this trip mailed on request).

The Best Proof of Value

We claim that the Regal "30" is, without exception, the greatest automobile value in the world for the

Success, May

FILL OUT AND MAIL
REGAL MOTOR CAR COMPANY
Detroit, Mich.

Please send me information and literature about the Regal "30."

Name...

Address ....

money. How do we prove it? Listen to a few letters from those who have bought:

LOUIS WOLF, Wolf Bros. & Co., Bankers, Philadelphia. "While I own a Mercedes, Renault and other high priced cars, I get more pleasure from my Regal '30' than all the others combined."

F. S. GRIFFIN, M. D., Mansfield, Mass. "Since July 2nd, 1909, have averaged over 2,000 miles a month. I consider the Regal one of the sturdiest, quietest and least expensive to maintain of any moderate priced car on the market. My car has given perfect satisfaction." (Dec. 1, 1909).

O. G. FREYERMUTH, M. D., San Francisco. "In six months have covered over 4,000 miles on all types of roads. Up difficult mountain grades, through deep dust and mud. Cost of maintenance is less than that of a horse."

G. A. LEONARD, Sheffield, Ia. "My car has made 5,000 miles with no expense, except for tires, gasoline and oil. Car is in perfect condition. My next will be a Regal '30.'"

ALBERT E. GIBSON, Waterloo, Ia. "Drove my Regal '30' over 7,000 miles. Consider it the best thing made today for the money, bar none."

Now read this boiled-down history: In 1907 we built 175 cars. There are

6500 Regals Building for 1910

The extraordinary value of this extraordinary car has built up this enormous demand simply of itself. The Regal "30" will do anything that any car can do.

Comparison will prove that it is just as roomy, just as comfortable, luxurious and easy-riding as any car at any price; easier riding than any car at an equal price.

It has Power, Style, Strength, Beauty; it is so simple in control and so easy to operate that any woman can

drive it. Silent, smooth and instantly responsive in operation because of its wonderful refinement.

Specifications of 1910 Regal "30"

Motor: Four cylinder, four cycle; cylinders cast in pairs. 4" bore, 4" stroke, three-bearing crank shaft, 30 horse power. **Cooling:** Water. An exceptionally efficient thermo-syphon system of cooling and large sized fan placed on adjustable bracket on motor. **Ignition:** Remy high tension magneto and batteries. **Lubrication:** Splash System. **Carburetor:** Schebler. **Clutch:** Leather face cone with spring inserts. **Transmission:** Sliding gear selective type; three speeds, forward and reverse. Drive, direct shaft. **Brakes:** Two internal and two external operating on rear wheel drums, double acting and compensating. **Wheel Base:** 107". **Tires:** 32x3½. **Tread:** 56". **Springs:** Front semi-elliptical, rear full elliptical scroll. **Speed:** Five to forty-five miles on high gear. **Upholstering:** Genuine leather over curled hair and deep coil steel springs. **Equipment:** Two gas lamps, three oil lamps and gas generator, Remy high tension magneto, horn, set of tools and complete tire repair kit.

Order Your Regal "30" Now

Deliveries are now being made promptly. But it will be wise for you to see the Regal dealer at once or get in touch with us at the factory and we will give name of nearest distributor, through whom you can arrange a demonstration. Better write today.

To Dealers—If you want to sell the most satisfactory car of its type—a business builder and a business holder—get in touch with us QUICK.

Regal Motor Car Company
Detroit, Michigan
Licensed under the Selden Patent

Canadian Trade Supplied by Regal Motor Car Co. of Canada, Ltd., Walkerville, Ont.

The 1910 Regal "30" sold for $1250.00.

$1400

The New Application of an Old Principle
Regal "35" 5-Passenger "Underslung" Touring Car

TO MAKE A BETTER AUTOMOBILE is, or should be, the ambition of every manufacturer. To that end experiments are constantly being conducted, designs created and thoroughly tested, improvements added from time to time often at the expense of thousands of dollars and long months of trial under every possible condition of service before embodied in the car for public appreciation.

THAT IS WHY the automobile in its present form has been brought to such perfection, yet any expert will frankly tell you there are still many and great opportunities for improvements. It is a recognized law that the closer to perfection a thing attains, the clearer do we recognize its imperfections. This is supremely true of the motor car.

BUT SOMETIMES the very simplicity of a problem defeats the skilled engineer. Often do we hear people say, when discussing a great invention, "how simple, why was it not thought of before?" and right here, that is the point we wish to impress upon the reader. Why has the simple, safe, durable, well tried, old "Underslung" principle of construction not been adapted by automobile manufacturers before?

THE ANSWER IS EASY. It was so simple, so old in practice, that its very superiority escaped them. There can be no other answer, because all swift moving, weight carrying vehicles, such as railroad, interurban trolley cars, etc., have been built the "underslung" way. The interior of a Pullman, traveling anywhere from 10 to 50 miles an hour, would be a very uncomfortable, unsafe place if the body of the car rested upon steel springs balanced upon axles, wouldn't it?

WE DO NOT MEAN TO INFER that automobiles built the ordinary way are unsafe or uncomfortable, but we do claim that the underslung construction adds to the safety, the comfort, the riding qualities of a car, and not only adds these elements of pleasure and economy beyond argument (for they can be mathematically and concretely demonstrated) but adds also, an element of beauty that goes deeper than paint—most noticeable.

THE MAN WHO IS ABOUT TO BUY an automobile, naturally desires the "advanced" car. The Regal "35" five-passenger "Underslung" Touring car is at least a year ahead in improved construction. It presents so many advantages for a moderate expenditure, as prices go to-day, that to see this car and to ride in it, is to buy it, because there are no present existing comparisons in competition with it.—

WHY SHOULD THIS CAR BE YOUR CAR? Because the center of gravity is very much lower by reason of the frame being slung below the axles instead of balanced above them. Because this means "safety," practically eliminating the terrible dangers of turning turtle and skidding. Because this means "economy," preventing destructive side lash

on springs and tires, giving also a straight line drive—the maximum power from motor to rear axle—saving gasoline. Because "Underslung" construction makes the springs shock-absorbing, adding to the life of the car.

BECAUSE the motor and transmission are get-at-able, and being level, ensure a perfect lubrication. Because to ride in this beautiful "Underslung" car will give you a demonstration of what comfort really means—no side swaying—no weaving motion—always straight ahead, while the road clearance is as much as the ordinary type. Last and most urgent reason, because in 1912 and 1913 your Regal "Underslung" will be up-to-date.

THE CAR ITSELF will prove to you infinitely more than we can put in words. But recently it was the big surprise of all 1912 announcements. Over a thousand have already been sold and we will gladly refer you to any owner—anywhere. The remarkable advantages of the "Underslung" construction, the roominess, beauty, big power, speed, simplicity, care-free comfort and economy in upkeep, and above all, safety, places the Regal "35" Underslung Touring Car at the pinnacle of automobile values. Just try to equal it at $1400.

SERVICE. Behind the Regal Car is the Regal Service. A chain of Regal Service warehouses, extending from coast to coast, placed at strategic points, is the Regal method of taking immediate and consistent care of buyers and owners of Regal Cars. Any Regal dealer wherever located can supply any model, any part at short notice through the nearest Regal warehouse. So, every Regal car is under direct factory supervision. The thousands of Regal owners are each and every one members of a great organization which exists for the specific purpose of rendering them not only efficient but instant service.

THE REGAL "35" UNDERSLUNG TOURING CAR is furnished with Demountable Rims (one extra Demountable Rim included). It is the complete car.

HERE ARE A FEW SPECIFICATIONS: Wheel Base, 118 inches—Tires, 34 x 4 in. Three speed and Reverse, Selective Sliding Nickel Steel gear transmission. Four cylinders (in pairs) 35 H. P. Motor. Bore $4\frac{1}{4}$ in., stroke $4\frac{1}{2}$ in. Dual ignition—with magneto. Transmission Hyatt Nickel Steel roller bearings. Standard equipment. Gas searchlights, etc.

OTHER REGAL CARS. Regal "20" Underslung Roadster $900 (the car that created a furore). Regal "30" 5-passenger Touring Car (open body), $1000. Fore-door, $1050. Regal Demi-Tonneau, open and fore-door type, $1000 and $1050. Regal "20" Underslung Coupé, $1250 (the most talked-of car in the country). Regal dealers are everywhere. Visit one or write for descriptive booklet.

The Dealers who handle Regal cars are especially chosen for a high standard of service. They are representative of all that tends to upbuild a permanent and highly profitable business upon the foundation of service. Their interest in customers does not end with the sale of a car but begins with the purchase of a car. We are always looking for the **"Regal Standard"** among dealers. Wire or write.

Regal Motor Car Company, Automobile Manufacturers Detroit, Michigan

This 1911 Regal ad invited dealers to become Regal agents. Note (under "Other Regal Cars") that the $900 Roadster "created a furore" and that the $1250 coupe was "the most talked-of car in the country."

R-C-H

"Twenty-Five" Standard Model

$850

5 Passenger Touring Car —110 inch Wheelbase

f. o. b. Detroit

Fully equipped with top, windshield, generator, Jiffy curtains, 5 lamps, horn, tools and tire repair kit; long stroke motor, 3 speeds, enclosed valves, Bosch Magneto.

Model E E Equipment
Equipped with 32x3½ tires, demountable and quick detachable rims, extra rim, Bosch Magneto, gas tank, windshield, lamps, horn, tools and kit; and Jiffy curtains, adjusted in an instant and make the car entirely weather proof. Long stroke motor, 3 speeds, enclosed valves.

Model E E

5 Passenger Touring Car; 100 inch wheelbase.

$900

Detroit f. o. b.

WE WANT 1000 DEALERS

TO SEND IN THE COUPON BELOW

HERE'S good news for the many dealers who wrote us during the early part of the year, but with whom we could not make arrangements because our entire 1912 output of 10,000 cars was already oversold.

Many sections had to go without R-C-H representation simply because we could not manufacture nearly enough cars to fill the demand.

For the coming season, however, things will be different. We shall make 30,000 R-G-H cars, and want an R-C-H dealer covering every county in the United States.

We do not think that a car which so nearly fills the ideal of the average motorist has ever before been offered within a thousand dollars of the R-C-H price. We do not think that greater all around satisfaction can be purchased anywhere for a thousand dollars more.

Your problem, Mr. Dealer, is to give your public the car that best meets their needs. List over in your mind the possible motor car buyers in your locality. Think just what each of them demands in his car. Then note what the R-C-H offers them. We think you'll agree that there's no other car which has so many different selling points.

So send in the coupon below. It won't bind you in any way, and it won't bind us. But it will give us a chance to get in touch, to learn more about each other, and perhaps to form a permanent arrangement.

Permanence—that is our idea. We don't want the one-season man, the vacillating man, the doubtful man. We've got the plant, we've got the car, we've got the price. If you got the ginger, the hustle, the stick-to-itiveness, write quick. For there's a better present and a bigger future for you with the R-C-H than anywhere else in the industry.

GENERAL R-C-H SPECIFICATIONS—Motor—4 cylinders, cast en bloc—3¾ inch bore, 5-inch stroke. Two-bearing crank shaft. Timing gears and valves enclosed. Three-point suspension. **Drive—Left-side.** Irreversible worm gear, 16-inch wheel. **Control—Center** lever operated through H plate, integral with universal joint housing just below. **Springs—**Front, semi-elliptic; rear, full elliptic and mounted on swivel seats. **Frame—**Pressed steel channel. **Axles—**Front, I-Beam, drop-forged; rear, semi-floating type. **Body—**English type, extra wide seats. **Wheelbase—**110 inches. Full equipment quoted above.

R-C-H CORPORATION, 104 LYCASTE STREET Detroit, Michigan

BRANCHES:
Atlanta, 548 Peachtree Street
Boston, 563 Boylston Street
Buffalo, 1225 Main Street
Chicago, 2021 Michigan Avenue
Cleveland, 2122 Euclid Avenue
Denver, 1520 Broadway
Walkerville, Ont. Canada

R-C-H CORPORATION, 104 Lycaste St., Detroit, Mich.

I want to know more about your car and your dealers' proposition.

I am now selling..........cars. My allotment is.......cars.

Name..................... Address...................

Town..................... State...................

SEND THIS COUPON TO-DAY

BRANCHES:
Minneapolis, 1206 Hennepin Avenue
New York, 1989 Broadway
Philadelphia, 330 No. Broad St.
Detroit, Woodward and Warren Avenues
Kansas City, 3501 Main Street
Los Angeles, 1242 So. Flower St.

This ad was aimed at dealers and invited them to sell the R-C-H car. The firm's goal of one dealer in every county in the United States was never realized.

Notice of the R-C-H Corporation's bankruptcy. The company was later re-organized and continued in business.

Bringing Car Balance To Prospects' Notice

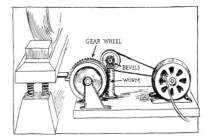

In the window of the Reo branch in New York there is a four-cylinder car balanced on a trestle as shown. Above is shown how a small electric motor is made to tilt the trestle at intervals and permit it to return to balance.

A novel Reo display.

You can have the Reo either way:

>With open front at $1250 (top and windshield extra) or
>With Fore Door and Windshield at $1300, or
>You can get the Fore Door parts separately (fit any 1911 Reo) for $25.

But that isn't the main thing. You get proof with your Reo—real proof in advance. If you could get everything else proved so completely, life would be mighty easy.

New York to San Francisco
in 10 days 15 hours 13 minutes

is the severest test ever made of a car. And yet at the end of nearly 400 miles a day for 10½ days, the Reo was in perfect condition, and broke a world record at hill-climbing.

Your Reo is just as good as that one.

Send for catalogue and "Coast to Coast in Ten Days"

R M Owen & Company Lansing Mich General Sales Agent for Reo Motor Car Company

Canadian Factory St Catharines Ontario

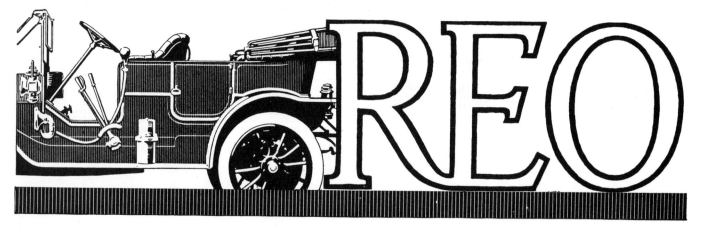

The Reo Motor Car Company was formed by Ransom E. Olds who originally founded the Olds Motor Works. He left the original Olds company in 1903. Within a few years the Reo became a famous car in its own right.

After 10,000 Miles
We Require Reo the Fifth to Stay New

This is why Reo the Fifth has so long held a unique and envied place.

It is built for extremes of service. Built by a man who for 27 years has been learning what cars must stand.

Test cars with this chassis have been subjected to hard usage. They are run at high speed, night and day, on rough roads. After 10,000 miles of this use and abuse we take them apart and inspect them. And we require that vital parts show little evidence of wear.

Must Stay New

Every steel formula, every specification is based on these radical tests. The question is not what will serve for one season. Not what is safe under normal conditions.

We require every gear and bearing, after 10,000 miles of reckless driving, to show up in good condition. Then we know that you won't have troubles. We know that your car will stay new.

Then, to insure this super-strength, we have steel made to formula. And each lot is analyzed twice. We have a four-story laboratory for testing every part and material.

Each must meet the standards that we fix, based on 10,000-mile tests.

Our Radical Tests

Gears are tested in a 50-ton crushing machine. Springs are tested for 100,000 vibrations. Engines get five tests, lasting 48 hours.

All driving parts must stand a test for 50 per cent over-capacity. That is our margin of safety.

We use 15 roller bearings to avoid the risk of ball bearings. We use 190 drop forgings to avoid risk of flaws. In close-fitting parts we require utter exactness.

Our clutch is of a very costly kind. It avoids the clashing of gears which so ruins transmissions. The gears are shifted by a light center rod—by a three-inch movement of the hand. This easy method of gear shifting is exclusive with us.

By slowness and care and costly extremes we add 25 per cent to the necessary cost of each car. But it comes back to users, over and over, in longer service and lessened cost of upkeep.

Now We Save $220

Now all the costly machinery we built for this chassis has been charged against previous output. We enter this year with that item wiped out. This saving, with others, we deduct from our price—$220 in all.

Reo the Fifth, with electric starter, last year sold for $1,395 equipped. This years' model, better equipped, sells for $1,175. Mainly as a result of clinging for years to one perfected chassis. That a car like this can be built at this price is the marvel of the times in Motordom.

This Year's Newness

This year we adopt the beautiful streamline body, now European vogue. We adopt the best type of electric starter and lights. We give you dimming searchlights, a flush-set instrument board, and all you can wish in equipment.

We give you luxurious upholstery, perfect finish, big tires. We have made the beauty of this car match our engineering.

The Car to Keep

Reo the Fifth appeals to men who buy their cars to keep. Men who want cars to stay new. The demand has grown and grown. Last year's sale exceeded all records by 30 per cent. And the evidence is that this year's demand will far exceed our output.

More and more, experienced motorists have come to demand a car like this—the utmost in an honest car—the best that R. E. Olds can do.

Reo the Fifth is sold by a thousand dealers. Name of nearest will be sent with our catalog on request. Go measure up this car.

Reo the Fifth
1914 Model
Now $1,175 Equipped

With Streamline Body—Electric Lights and Starter—Electric Horn—One-Rod Control—35 Horsepower—Demountable Rims—Tires 34x4. Also with Roadster Body.

REO MOTOR CAR COMPANY, Lansing, Michigan

Canadian Factory, St. Catharines, Ont.   Canadian Price, $1,575   (241)

1914 ad for Reo the Fifth.

Above: George B. Selden claimed to be "The Father of Them All." Until his Selden Patent was declared invalid he extracted licensing fees from many other car makers.

Right and below: The Stutz used its racing victories to good advertising advantage.

STUTZ

World's Champion

"By Right of Conquest"

THE SAME engineering ability, the same care in construction, and the same honesty of purpose and knowledge which made the Stutz World's Champion, will effect the stamina and quality of the Stutz stock car, because stamina and worth are inherent in all Stutz cars. Stutz cars now hold these records:

World's Speedway Champion

World's Road-Race Champion

World's Long-Distance Records
250, 300 and 350 miles

World's Record for Consistency
4 consecutive firsts and seconds

Illustrated Literature on Request

Stutz Motor Car Co.

Indianapolis   Indiana

*Prices range from
$2000 to $2550*

Stutz claimed many racing and endurance records.

A Colt in Illinois Mud
and on Kentucky Hills

Good automobiles, like good horses, must be developed.

Like the thoroughbred, the motor car must show its speed, its stamina, its endurance, before it is ready for blue ribbon competition.

The Stephens Six was tested in Southern Illinois, infamous for its rough and muddy roads, and on the legend-haunted hills of Kentucky, where inadequate motor power, defective carburetion, frame and chassis weakness, and lack of riding comfort—due to poor weight distribution and spring suspension are discovered readily if these faults exist.

Before 1917 production was started, the Stephens Six, in these exacting tests, had to satisfy the Stephens Six engineers that its owners would be satisfied. No defect was too trivial to be overlooked.

A Blue Ribbon Winner at the Motor Show

Kentucky is noted for its thoroughbreds.

Among the hills of the Blue Grass State, the Stephens Six was developed into a winner.

At the Chicago Automobile Show the Stephens Six was recognized by thousands as a car of merit. The lines and finish of the handsome streamline body, the depth and comfort-impressive upholstery, the generous equipment, appealed to the crowds that visited our booth.

Even greater Stephens Six enthusiasm was generated in those motorists to whom the power and flexibility of the sturdy motor and the easy-riding qualities of the car were demonstrated on the road.

These demonstrations are most convincing that the Stephens Six represents supreme value and quality at $1150.

Dealers throughout the country realize this and as a consequence we are appointing agents daily. There is still some territory open, perhaps where you are located and where Stephens Six opportunity is knocking.

> TWO MODELS, EACH.........$1150
> FIVE-PASSENGER TOURING CAR
> THREE - PASSENGER ROADSTER

$1150

FREEPORT, ILL.

STEPHENS MOTOR
Branch of Moline Plow Co.
MOLINE, ILLINOIS
Factory: Freeport, Ill.

STEPHENS SIX
"The Car With Punch"

The Stephens Six was tested on the muddy roads of Kentucky and Illinois.

"8" STANDARD

The production of Automobiles by the Standard Steel Car Company is a logical development.

Regularly engaged in designing and building the steel transportation equipment, of all kinds, which has done so much for the safety and comfort of the traveling public—controlling all necessary facilities, in both men and material—and with an organization trained along the lines, primarily, of determining the best thing to do, and then the way of doing that best thing repeatedly and uniformly—the production of Automobiles came nearly as a natural sequence.

About four years ago the Standard Steel Car Company commenced to use its resources and facilities specifically in the designing and manufacturing of Automobiles—its progressive steps being directed by careful study and analysis under laboratory conditions, supplemented and verified by service tests.

One year ago, having foreseen and experimented with the eight-cylinder type of motor, the Standard Steel Car Company brought forward its "Standard Eight"—one of the few of its kind which had been offered to the public.

In now announcing the 1916 Standard Eight, we can state that it has been born of thorough and extensive experience, under all-varying conditions of sufficient severity to detect any defects or oversights in the 1915 product—and with the happy conclusion that no changes have been indicated as necessary in the mechanical features, and only such changes in body construction as are required to meet the latest demands.

It is of the greatest importance that the automobile purchaser should know that he can depend upon the representations and workmanship of the manufacturer, as well as upon the sort of treatment and service he will receive.

The reputation of the Standard Steel Car Company is in itself assurance that the purchaser of its products will not regret his confidence in the people he deals with, nor be deceived or disappointed in what they furnish him.

A 1916 seven-passenger "Standard Eight," at $1,735, is not an experiment with an unknown quantity—but is, rather, the investment of money in an article of proven merit and reliability, produced by people who know what they are doing and have the resources to do what they know should be done.

Among the features of appealing interest and importance of "The Standard Eight" are its light weight, wedge-shaped frame, staggered cylinders, double universal (anti-skid) drive of the Hitchkiss type, the force-feed oiling system, etc.

From all viewpoints the Standard Eight excels. We are exhibiting at the New York and Chicago Automobile Shows.

Cabinet sized photographs, full specifications, and details of our new sales plan will be furnished upon request.

STANDARD STEEL CAR CO.
PITTSBURGH, PA.

The Standard "8" - 1915.

People Generally Are Convinced

That Saxon "Six" Is the Best Car in Its Class

Nor is this belief in Saxon "Six" superiority confined to one part of the country. You'll find it equally as strong in the West as in the East, in the city as in the country.

But what are the specific reasons that have led motor car buyers the country over to this same clear-cut conclusion?

We need only mention the extraordinary gasoline economy of Saxon "Six," its unusual freedom from repairs, its roominess, its comfort, its superlative endurance.

These are too well known and appreciated to call for further comment.

And then we come to what is perhaps the biggest single factor in Saxon "Six" success—namely, the Saxon "Six" motor.

It is understood, of course, that uniform torque—smooth power-flow—is the standard sought by all motor car makers.

With a "less-than-six-cylinder" motor there are naturally intervals between impulses or explosions.

These spell vibration and consequent wear on the motor and parts.

With a six-cylinder motor, however, one explosion merges smoothly into the next.

And this vibrationless power-flow gives rise to several important advantages.

It practically eliminates wear on the motor and parts, gives longer life to the motor, enables higher maximum speed and lower minimum speed, and produces nearly absolute operative quietness.

And best of all it adds perceptibly to the performance of the car.

Just how much it adds can best be grasped, perhaps, through comparison.

Side by side, all conditions equal, a well-known car of less than six cylinders and a Saxon "Six" were tested for acceleration by a group of engineers.

Going from a stand to 45 miles per hour the "less-than-six" required an average time of 30 seconds in six successive trials. Saxon "Six" required only 23 seconds.

In short, Saxon "Six" showed 22% faster "pick-up."

Figured as precisely as possible, the power-flow of Saxon "Six" per foot traveled was 98% smoother than that of the "less-than-six."

This smoother power-flow that helps increase the get-away speed of Saxon "Six" also plays its part in the pulling power of Saxon "Six."

Up a mile-long, winding hill—with a 15 to 18% grade—the "less-than-six" mentioned before was timed at exactly 2 minutes. Once a gear-shift was compelled.

Saxon "Six" made the same hill in 1 minute and 2 seconds—without shifting gears.

You'll most quickly appreciate the importance of these comparative records when you consider that both were stock cars—the same cars you find on salesroom floors the country over.

So you see they are records you can safely accept as justly illustrative of the superiority of Saxon "Six."

(658)

Saxon "Six" is $815 f. o. b. Detroit.

SAXON "SIX"

A BIG TOURING CAR FOR FIVE PEOPLE

SAXON MOTOR CAR CORPORATION, DETROIT

The Saxon Six sold for $815.

SAXON $395

From Coast to Coast

O**N July 4 the Saxon car finally demonstrated its independence of all road conditions. For on that famous day a Saxon reached San Francisco, having traveled 3389 miles overland from New York in 30 days across the Lincoln Highway—the first automobile to make a continuous trip from New York to San Francisco over the Highway and the first car of its size and price to make the journey from coast to coast.

Over the Alleghanies, over the Rockies, over the Sierras went the Saxon without faltering. Through mud, through sand, over the great plains, across the great American Desert, the Saxon held to its schedule and averaged 30 miles to the gallon of gasoline all the way.

8,000 Miles in 60 Days

It went from New York to Canton, Ohio, across the long grades of the Alleghanies through the hottest weather of the year, without needing a drop of fresh water in the radiator. Folks used to say "Cool as a cucumber," now they say "Cool as a Saxon."

The same car from April 8 to May 8, ran 135 miles a day for 30 consecutive days—4050 miles—averaging 30 miles to the gallon of gasoline and 150 miles per quart of oil, covering the entire distance on the original set of tires. In 60 days this transcontinental car has covered almost 8,000 miles—as far as the average owner drives in two years.

34.53 Miles per Gallon

On May 16, 100 regular stock Saxon cars in as many towns all over the country, made non-stop runs of 200 miles each, averaging 34.53 miles per gallon of gasoline—less than half a cent a mile for fuel, less than 1/4 cent a mile per passenger.

Everywhere and under all road and weather conditions the Saxon makes good. Over five thousand Saxon cars have been delivered and orders come faster all the time. This can mean only one thing—that the Saxon has found its market because the Saxon car is pleasing those who use it.

And here are some reasons why the Saxon is making good everywhere:

EXCEPTIONAL ROOMINESS—Plenty of width for two big people to sit comfortably; plenty of length for a tall man to stretch his legs.

COMFORT—Good cushions to sit on; a comfortable back to lean against; springs of cantilever type, same as on high-priced foreign cars.

GOOD LOOKS—Body lines stylish, following most up-to-date French practice; everything in good taste.

EASE OF HANDLING—Nimble footed; turns short; takes up little room; quick to run in and out of traffic. Holds the road at all speeds. Won't skid.

ECONOMY—Low gasoline charge; low oil, low tires, low repairs. 28 to 32 miles per gallon of gasoline; 150 miles per quart of oil.

PERFORMANCE — Stands up under severest usage and keeps running as well as high priced cars; holds many records for durability and reliability.

MOTOR—Four cylinders of special Saxon design; long stroke motor that gives almost the power and flexibility of a "Six."

HONEYCOMB RADIATOR — Finest type known; large cooling surface; keeps motor cool.

WIRE WHEELS—Come as standard equipment; on other cars from $25 to $100 extra. Easy riding, easy on tires.

SLIDING GEAR TRANSMISSION—Proved by engineering practice to be the only really correct type.

DRY PLATE CLUTCH—Same type as $2,000 cars employ.

No other car in the world offers you these features of high grade construction at a price anywhere near the Saxon price of $395. Get in touch with us now. Just ask for catalog.

The 3389-mile run of the coast-to-coast car has again demonstrated to the nation the economy and durability of the sturdy $395 Saxon

Saxon Motor Company, Detroit

Address Dept. N

The $395.00 Saxon model shown above was the first car to travel the new Lincoln Highway from New York to San Francisco - making the trip in 30 days.

The New Speedwell Rotary Six

Series "I"

Is Ready

The Speedwell Rotary Six - 1914.

Studebaker

"FOUR"

$1050

STUDEBAKER dealers have one argument that few, if any, other motor car dealers can rightfully use—and that is the FULL-MANUFACTURED argument.

For the Studebaker FOUR and the Studebaker SIX are manufactured by their maker to a greater extent and in a greater proportion of parts than any other car in the world.

Six thousand distinct and separate manufacturing operations, for instance, are required in the building of the Studebaker FOUR; and each and every one of these operations is performed by Studebaker.

Studebaker does not assemble — in whole or in part—Studebaker MANUFACTURES.

And because Studebaker MANUFACTURES Studebaker cars scientifically and conscientiously—and in huge quantities—they offer both dealer and owner the best motor car values in the world.

Studebaker

Detroit

F. O. B. Detroit

FOUR Touring Car	- - $1050	*SIX Touring Car*	- - $1575
FOUR Delivery Car	- - 1150	*SIX Landau Roadster*	- 1800
	SIX Sedan	- - - - $2250	

In 1914 Studebaker stressed that it made all of the components for its cars - in contrast to the usual industry practice of buying parts from many different suppliers.

165

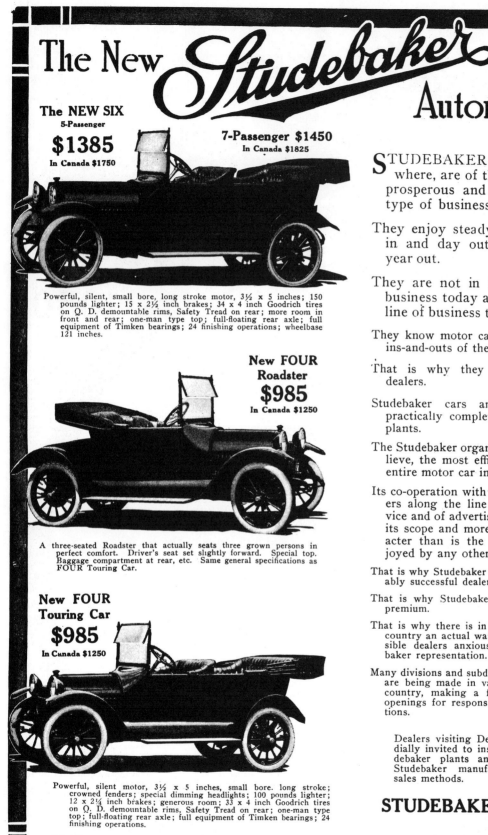

The New *Studebaker* Automobiles

The NEW SIX
5-Passenger

$1385
In Canada $1750

7-Passenger $1450
In Canada $1825

Powerful, silent, small bore, long stroke motor, 3½ x 5 inches; 150 pounds lighter; 15 x 2½ inch brakes; 34 x 4 inch Goodrich tires on Q. D. demountable rims, Safety Tread on rear; more room in front and rear; one-man type top; full-floating rear axle; full equipment of Timken bearings; 24 finishing operations; wheelbase 121 inches.

New FOUR Roadster

$985
In Canada $1250

A three-seated Roadster that actually seats three grown persons in perfect comfort. Driver's seat set slightly forward. Special top. Baggage compartment at rear, etc. Same general specifications as FOUR Touring Car.

New FOUR Touring Car

$985
In Canada $1250

Powerful, silent motor, 3½ x 5 inches, small bore, long stroke; crowned fenders; special dimming headlights; 100 pounds lighter; 12 x 2¼ inch brakes; generous room; 33 x 4 inch Goodrich tires on Q. D. demountable rims, Safety Tread on rear; one-man type top; full-floating rear axle; full equipment of Timken bearings; 24 finishing operations.

STUDEBAKER dealers, everywhere, are of the progressive, prosperous and permanent type of business men.

They enjoy steady business day in and day out, year in and year out.

They are not in the motor car business today and some other line of business tomorrow.

They know motor car values and the ins-and-outs of the business.

That is why they are Studebaker dealers.

Studebaker cars are manufactured practically complete in Studebaker plants.

The Studebaker organization is, we believe, the most efficient unit in the entire motor car industry.

Its co-operation with Studebaker dealers along the line of sales, of service and of advertising is broader in its scope and more helpful in character than is the co-operation enjoyed by any other class of dealers.

That is why Studebaker Dealers are invariably successful dealers.

That is why Studebaker territory is at a premium.

That is why there is in many parts of the country an actual waiting list of responsible dealers anxious to secure Studebaker representation.

Many divisions and subdivisions of territory are being made in various parts of the country, making a few very desirable openings for responsible dealer connections.

Dealers visiting Detroit are cordially invited to inspect the Studebaker plants and investigate Studebaker manufacturing and sales methods.

STUDEBAKER, Detroit

"Quantity Production of Quality Cars"

An invitation for dealers to handle the Studebaker line. Often a local dealer, particularly in a small town, would handle several different makes of cars.

Stages Five 200-Mile Tours to Open Season

Studebaker Dealer in Buffalo Arouses Wide Interest.

Carries Through Whole Plan at Small Expense.

The A. W. Haile Motor Co., which handles the Studebaker in and around Buffalo, N. Y., was selling five fours to one six; Haile wanted to sell more sixes. He conceived a plan, put it into execution and at the end of five weeks was selling six sixes to one four. He had achieved the desired result in a way that surprised even Haile himself.

This is how he did it:

He planned to make five runs of 200 miles each over different routes out of Buffalo, the runs to be held on each of five consecutive Sundays. Data was kept on each run—gasolene and oil consumption, kind of roads, grades, etc. Each run was observed by a reputable newspaper man and the friendship of all the newspapers was secured, valuable publicity being the result.

The results were—15.15 miles to the gallon of gasolene; 421 miles to the gallon of oil; 470 miles to the gallon of water; average cost per mile, $.0103; no punctures; no blow-outs; no added air; no mechanical adjustments during the 1,000-mile test. These and other figures are shown in the reproduction of an ad run by Haile at the end of the test. It was the only ad he ran, and while he values the publicity obtained at more than $1,000 the expense was small.

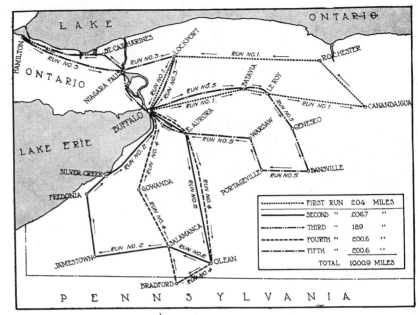

HAILE'S FIVE 200-MILE DEMONSTRATION RUNS OUT OF BUFFALO—HE COVERED HIS TERRITORY WELL

When the 1,000-mile test was started a large banner telling of the runs was stretched across the front of the salesroom at 1015-17 Main street. As each run was concluded a smaller banner was pasted on the window, telling where the car had gone and what it had done. This display drew much comment and caused many passersby to stop and read.

On the Sunday of each run after the first, the newspapers ran a story telling what had been done on the preceding run and stated that another run was being held on the day in question. These stories were a column or a column and a half in extent and were illustrated. The last story in the Buffalo Courier totaled 24 inches, whereas the only paid advertisement Haile used totaled but 15 inches—5 inches, 3 columns.

The cooperation of the newspapers had been assured beforehand, for before starting the test Haile took the matter up with representatives of each paper and took them into the plan. At the end of the test the newspaperman-observer wrote Haile a letter, testifying to the accuracy of the data, and this letter was reproduced and mailed to the prospect list.

"This tour is the best publicity or local advertising I have ever had, and the fact that it was new and that I carried it along for five consecutive Sundays gave me publicity and advertising which I could not possibly have purchased," said Haile.

"In reference to the amount of business obtained from this advertising and publicity, I can only say that we sold 20 Studebaker sixes during the time this run was in progress."

One of the most effective points in connection with the whole plan is that the runs were made over roads familiar to Buffalo prospects.

"Tests in Seattle," said Haile, "mean little to the people of Buffalo. What does mean something to them are tests on roads about Buffalo, the roads they will have to drive over after they buy a car and with which they are familiar." The routes, which are shown in an accompanying illustration, were furnished by the Goodrich Touring Bureau.

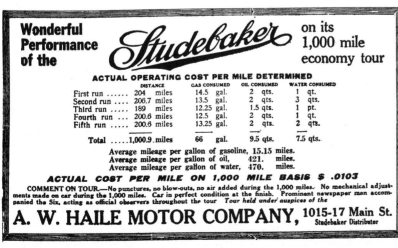
The success of a Buffalo Studebaker dealer.

Eight Cylinders Crown
The Luxury of Light Weight

Here at last are co-ordinated — in the one car of its kind — those elements of ease, elegance and efficiency which, singly, have made a few of the most notable cars successful.

Applying eight cylinders to the luxuries recognized as distinctively Scripps-Booth, intensifies those luxuries, and adds much more than passing interest to the new

Scripps-Booth
Eight

SB

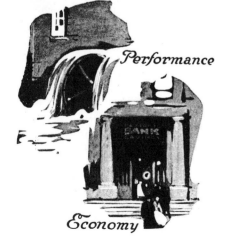

Clientele

Luxury

Beauty

Performance

Economy

Luxury is here, with smooth-flowing power and swiftness.

Beauty is here, in Scripps-Booth individual fashion—a fashion more copied this year, in high-class chassis, than any previous body design in America.

Handiness and economy are here—elements never before marked in a car of Scripps-Booth qualities.

And in the "eight" all of these qualities intensify the luxury of performance for which Scripps-Booth is already famed

An expansion of factory output now comes to match the growing public approval of Scripps-Booth's exclusive luxury-with-lightness origination.

The new Scripps-Booth Eight is displayed at the Chicago Automobile Show, beginning January 27th, in the Coliseum, Space E-4, Main Floor; also by all Scripps-Booth dealers.

Scripps-Booth expansion makes possible the addition of dealers in territories which our former output prohibited.

Eight-Cylinder Four Passenger	.	$1285
Eight-Cylinder Town Car .	.	$2575
Four-Cylinder Roadster	.	$935
Four-Cylinder Coupé	.	$1450

Scripps-Booth Corporation
Detroit, Mich.

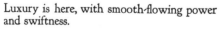

The Scripps-Booth "Eight" offered luxury, beauty and handiness.

168

NORMAN A. PABST, INC., 851 WOODWARD AVENUE, DETROIT, STATES THAT IT
HAS THE FIRST EXCLUSIVE CYCLECAR SALESROOM IN THE UNITED STATES—
IT DISTRIBUTES THE SCRIPPS-BOOTH IN MICHIGAN—THE DISPLAY IS SIMPLE
BUT ATTRACTIVE AND FORCEFUL

Scripps-Booth Cyclecar display.

STODDARD-DAYTON'S PHILADELPHIA SHOWROOM WITH ITS STRIKING SETTING

An elaborate Stoddard-Dayton showroom.

The Sterling-New York Roadster (1916) appealed to the low-price market.

Left: Michelin Tires prevented skidding. Right: The Tobias Glare Eliminator sold for 75¢ per pair.

$3,500
With Complete Equipment

Thomas Flyer Model M 1910
6-40 Touring Car

Every Stroke of This Engine Saves You Money

For in the new Thomas Flyer Model "M" we have incorporated the new "long stroke" motor design that has revolutionized motor construction abroad.

This car does things which other cars cannot do, because, while its six cylinders (4¼-inch bore with 5½-inch stroke) are rated at 40 horse power (43.8 A. L. A. M. rating), it actually develops over 60 horse power on test.

See the New Candidate for Public Favor

We began the design in 1907 and the construction in 1908 to group in this one car all the well-tried improvements of greatest merit that had been evolved in the various popular cars up to date—for the purpose of eclipsing all the high-priced competitors in the 40-50 horse power class in power, silence, flexibility, smooth running, and efficiency.

We have accomplished our purpose by including in the new motor design, "the new long stroke" (which gives in the Model "M" 14 per cent. more horse power for the same piston area), gas valve openings half the diameter of the piston, water jacketed valve stems, extra large bearings, short, rigid transmission, equipped with nickel steel gears and imported ball bearings throughout, and many other mechanical features, insuring strength, durability, and silent running.

Price, $3,500—Completely Equipped

No other car at the price is so superbly equipped as the new Model "M." Included in the price of $3,500 are the following high-grade accessories:—

A specially made top of silk mohair—folding glass front—high-grade speedometer—a complete set of shock absorbers—two acetylene gas headlights—two oil side lamps—tail lamps—robe rail—horn—Presolite gas tank, etc. $500 worth of equipment free, making this car cost but about $3,000 as cars are usually sold.

Other Thomas Flyers

If you wish larger, more powerful cars, we have the great Model "F" 4-60, a duplicate of the New York-to-Paris car which sells for $4,500.00, and the greatest of all stock touring cars, the Thomas Flyer 6-70 Model "K" at $6,000.00. This car this year is equipped with 38-inch wheels and tires and many other improvements. It has the greatest reserve of power and strength of any stock touring car in the world, and every owner will back up the statement that the Thomas Flyer 6-70 is the last word in smooth running, hill-climbing ability, and all that is good in automobiles.

Members of Association Licensed Automobile Manufacturers.

The Thomas Flyer, a car of the luxury class, sold for $3500.00.

Velie MOTOR CARS 1912

Velie Motor Cars for 1912 stand out prominently before their competitors because of their power and detail of refinement. We invite comparisons with any and all manufacturers of automobiles, irrespective of price, and particularly as respects body lines, finish and trimming, in which we have specialized for 1912 and so successfully that we feel assured of receiving merited compliments from buyers of the nicest discernment.

In the four years' progress in developing and perfecting the "**Velie** 40" from the driver's standpoint of efficiency and control, we have

Long Stroke 40 H. P. Motor 4½ x 5¼.
Enclosed Valves—Double Ignition.
Self Starter—Electric Lights.
Hand Buffed Leather—8½-inch Cushions.
Special Body—Nickle Trimmings.
36-inch Tires—Demountable Rims.
Full Floating Axle— Timken Bearings.
Double Drop Frame.   Spoke Bolted Wheels.
Rear Springs 54 Inches Long.
Completely Equipped—Ready for Road.

not lost sight of the equal importance of the passengers' comfort. In completely equipping **Velie** Cars with every essential requirement, including such features as Self Starter and Electric Lighting System, we furnish the buyer with a car ready for the road—with no extras to buy, rather than appeal to him by means of the apparently lower price mark of an incomplete car.

Complete Line of Models will be Exhibited at Grand Central Palace Show, New York City, January 10-17

Competition demands that the dealer who would be successful must connect himself with a manufacturer who is successful.

The Velie Company is one of the few exceptionally strong automobile manufacturing companies in the country, backed by an organization of unlimited capital—whose reputation has been acquired by seventy years' experience in the manufacturing of high grade products—and whose policy of Service—Satisfaction—is being advanced by large Factory Branches in every section of the country and over 500 established dealers.

We offer the dealer a complete line of cars to supply every demand—the popular price "Velie Jr.," the Standard "Velie 40," with complete equipment at $2,200, and the large, luxurious, six-passenger "Special" at $2,750.

Possibly Your Territory Is Open

Why Not Investigate?

Velie Motor Vehicle Co., Moline, Illinois, U.S.A.

THE NAME INSURES THE QUALITY

Velie Motor Cars for 1912.

Left: 1910 White limousine.

Above: Two 1912 Winton ads.

Below: The high-wheeled 1909 Schacht.

The 1914 Woods Mobilette sold for $380.00. In 1914 cyclecars were at their height of popularity.

An early Waverly Electric car.

Pantasote Top Material was used on many of the more expensive cars.

THE four general magazines carrying the most automobile advertising are the **Saturday Evening Post, Collier's, Literary Digest** and **Christian Herald.** Of these The Christian Herald is the only one with 75 per cent of its circulation in rural towns and small communities.

The statement has been made that 72 per cent of the 700,000 automobiles sold last year were sold to farmers. The Christian Herald unquestionably helped to sell a big percentage of that number.

The CHRISTIAN HERALD is not merely a religious newspaper. It is a national home weekly which carries into the home the news of the world, secular as well as religious, in such a plain, straightforward manner that every member of the family is kept abreast of the times.

The Christian Herald
NEW YORK

The Christian Herald solicited automobile advertising.

THE CHRISTIAN HERALD swelled YOUR business last year, and with your support it will repeat for 1916.

If the manufacturers you represent are buying advertising space, they will be interested in having you speak a good word for a magazine that helps you.

Let us send you a copy of The Christian Herald—Free. Send for YOUR copy today.

Why not find out how many automobiles were purchased in your town through Christian Herald influence?

The Christian Herald
NEW YORK

An assortment of miscellaneous ads from
the 1909-1916 years.

Sees the Electric as Ultimate Vehicle

Its Utility Will Cause It to Prevail, Says Dr. Stein-metz—Immense Field for Electric Garage.

There is no doubt in the mind of Dr. Chas. Proteus Steinmetz of the eventual survival of the electric vehicle for both pleasure and commercial purposes. It is his expressed opinion that in the not far distant future the car that can trace its ancestry back to old Ben Franklin and his kite and his key will be the universal car; that the gasolene vehicle, if not a curiosity, at least will be used but little, is his summing up of the situation. Last February he told the members of the Electric Vehicle Association of America practically the same thing and at the annual convention of the National Electric Light Association, which was held in Philadelphia June 1 to 5, he further emphasized his convictions.

Compares Motor Car With Bicycle.

Dr. Steinmetz is probably the greatest of electrical engineers; he is at present consulting engineer to the great General Electric Co., Schenectady, N. Y. Analogizing the development of the motor car with that of the bicycle, he traced the early experimental stage of the power vehicle down to its reduction to commercial perfection, its wonderful growth as a sporting vehicle, the waxing and waning of cross-country touring, and finally the present-day development of the low-priced vehicle.

He stated that heretofore the gasolene vehicle has had the advantage of the electric vehicle because of its greater speed and mileage capacity. This, he asserted, is fast becoming less of an advantage, as the elimination of the sporting use of the motor car will eliminate the demand for either speed or great mileage capacity, but that as the motor car becomes more of a staple, and distance-riding decreases, the demand for a vehicle that can exceed the city speed limits and that can go farther than the average user ever has occasion to travel in a day will also decrease.

At this juncture he stated that the electric vehicle would be turned to, owing to the fact that it was simpler to operate and required less mechanical attention owing to its simplicity.

That the gasolene vehicle had a field, however, was conceded by the doctor, who said that he thought as a stage and for use in reaching points not reached by railroads, it would always be of use. For commercial purposes, however, he stated emphatically that he considered the electric as the sole vehicle of the future.

Next he brought out the fact that as the field for the motor car becomes changed from that of sport to pure utility, its design will also have to change. He stated that its maximum mileage capacity should be about 30 per day, and its highest speed 20 miles per hour. This he stated would require, for economy, a light battery, and to support such a battery a light structure—less than 1,000 pounds, in his opinion. He stated that the construction would be less luxurious, as dealing with a different class of buyers, but would be made more along the lines of the low-priced gasolene vehicle of today. One of the most surprising predictions was that its price would be not to exceed $500. He stated that there was a market for 1,000,000 such vehicles in the passenger field, and as many more in the truck field.

The most formidable menace to the central station, thought the speaker, was the likelihood of the garages installing isolated private generating plants, thus cutting the central stations off from this tremendous market. He stated that this would not only result in loss to the central stations, but also to the owners of the trucks, as it is more expensive to generate in small quantities with only moderately skilled hands than it is in large central plants with trained experts in attendance. For these reasons the doctor urged the representatives of the central stations to get in early.

Plans During Embryonic Stage.

As to how best to seize upon this business in its embryonic stage, the speaker stated that there were several ways. The first plan of operation that would be called feasible was the exchange method, in which the central station kept a supply of fully-charged standard batteries on hand at all times, which, for a nominal fee would be exchanged for exhausted ones. This he stated would not be universally applicable to practical service because of the variation in types, sizes, and capacities of batteries, and the impossibility of standardizing them.

The second method proposed was a fixed charge in which the user turned his vehicle over to the central station each night and received it fully charged in the morning, paying therefor a fixed monthly sum for all battery attention. This charge he thought would vary from $5 to $20, according to conditions. This he thought was the best scheme and the most universally applicable.

He stated that as a matter of fact most users used less than half of the charge in a single day, and that, therefore, the central station would only have to charge the average battery about half its capacity each night. This he thought would cost an average of $7.50 at current rates per month. If the trucks were stored at the plant, $2.50 should pay the interest, depreciation and help for the storage premises. At $10 per month, therefore, the business would be profitable to the central station.

Car Would Be Very Economical.

An arrangement could be made with some local garage, stated the speaker, for the cleaning and repair of the vehicle on a sub-let basis, for which the customer would pay either as part of the fixed sum paid to the central station, or as a separate account with the garage.

This would make the electric very economical and available to a very large class. Especially so, he thought, in view of the fact that one of the things which has retarded its development in the past has been the difficulty in making satisfactory charging arrangements.

The cost to the user with current at 5 cents per kilowatt-hour would be so little that the electric vehicle would be much cheaper than the horse and wagon. The actual cost of the current to the central station would not exceed 1 cent, declared he, so that the proposition is well worth going after.

In conclusion, Dr. Steinmetz made a final appeal to the electric power men to look ahead of the passing sporting stage of the industry and recognize the principle that underlies the growth of all similar industrial developments, and to get the business now.

Whether or not the central station men were convinced or still remained skeptical was difficult to say, as in spite of an earnest request for discussion from the chair the hall rapidly emptied when the doctor had been enthusiastically applauded, there being no discussion except that Mr. Marshall, executive secretary of the Electric Vehicle Association, offered the hearty co-operation of that organization with any central station desirous of entering the field.

ELECTRIC CARS---

Electric cars achieved their greatest popularity from about 1913 to 1917. During that time there were many predictions that the electric cars would make gasoline operated cars obsolete. Charles Proteus Steinmetz's sentiments as reflected in the article on the facing page are typical.

In theory electric cars had many advantages. In practice their speed was limited (the optimum speed was less than 15 MPH) as was their range without recharging. The batteries for these machines sometimes weighed over a thousand pounds.

Electrics found their best use as town cars where speed and distance was'nt important. The interiors of electric cars were often luxurious with heavily padded upholstery, fine rugs and other such appointments.

By the 1920's electric cars were an anachronism, although manufacture of some continued into the 1930's. The idea of electric cars has not died. Even today one commonly reads about the advantages of electric cars - although none are production line items.

Model LB
Century
$3250
f. o. b. Detroit

The "disturbance" created by this latest Century is based on mechanical superiority

This double-drive Century has many advantages that are not shared with any other car. And they are features that appeal to the experienced electric car buyer—especially when he knows that the Century is backed by a strong, financially sound organization that is a guarantee of the permanence of his investment—an assurance that SERVICE will never be lacking.

First in importance among these advantages is the

Century Magnetic Control

The Greatest Improvement Ever Made in Electric Cars

This marvelously simple device is revolutionizing the driving of an electric car. It is seemingly possessed of almost superhuman intelligence. It stops, starts, slows down, and speeds up the car—and does it without any fussing with keys, switches or levers. ONE FOOT PEDAL, MOVING UP AND DOWN WITHIN A RANGE OF THREE INCHES, DOES IT ALL.

There is nothing experimental about the Century Magnetic Control. It is built for us by the Cutler-Hammer Mfg. Co., Milwaukee, who have a world-wide reputation for making the finest electric-controlling devices money can buy. Cutler-Hammer electric controls are used in electric passenger and freight elevators of the most highly perfected types and on magnificent printing presses, whose cost runs into tens of thousands of dollars; they are used to control the movements of the big, heavy gun turrets on U. S. Battleships; to control the locks on the Panama Canal, and everywhere that positive, unfailing reliability is required and demanded.

This Century Magnetic Control is not a new thing awaiting the verdict of the public as to its success or practicability. It is the crowning achievement of an organization which, for twenty-three years, has devoted *all* its resources to the development and building of electric controls. Its application to the Century is exclusive. *You can get this Century Magnetic Control in no other electric car.*

Every person who operates the Century Magnetic Control (and everyone can learn how to do it in a few minutes) marvels at its simplicity. In a very short time every movement becomes automatic—instinctive. One does not have to think what to do next. The right foot does the right thing instinctively. No wonder those who drive the Century—who have threaded through the traffic of a big city without the slightest nervousness or strain —describe the Century as "The Car of Instinctive Control."

This Magnetic Control costs more but *it is the best* and that is why you find it in the Century.

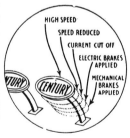

The Century Electric Brakes—Another Big Feature

Closely and intimately connected to the Magnetic Control, are the Electric Brakes, which positively prevent skidding. *The Century Cannot Skid*—even on wet and slippery pavements with the electric brake applied *abruptly* when running at full speed. A demonstration of this feature awaits every prospective dealer and purchaser of a Century electric—and a demonstration is more powerful and convincing than a thousand arguments and reasons why.

This non-skidding feature is the last word in SAFETY.

And it's another reason why there is quick appreciation of the Century wherever the car is demonstrated. Ask us the "why" of this feature if you are interested. We will be glad to answer questions—still better pleased to give demonstrations.

183

The directions for changing the Century drive from front seat to rear or rear to front with utmost safety and dispatch can be given in eleven words

To change from rear to front—"TAKE OUT MASTER KEY AND INSERT IN HOLE AT FRONT SEAT." That's all. To change the other way, reverse the operation. Could anything be simpler? Can you imagine the pleasure in selling or driving an electric where instructions can be so briefly and so plainly given—so easily followed?

The Century has the simplest Duplex Drive in the world. Do you wonder that women who inspect it are "crazy about the Century?"

We submit that this is absolutely the best Duplex Drive obtainable. It had to be, to be adopted by the Century.

Triple Platform Spring Suspension

The spring suspension of the Century is recognized by experts as *ideal*. Users say the Century is the easiest riding electric built. Century springs are made from the finest Silico Manganese steel specially heat treated. The triple platform rear spring is 1¾ inches wide, sides 45⅝ inches long, cross spring 39½ inches long. Front springs are semi-elliptic 1¾ inches wide and 43 inches long. Total spring length is in excess of 216 inches. The best in spring suspension is none too good for the Century.

Low Body Suspension

Low body suspension—bringing the body close to the ground—adds to the feeling of safety—makes the center of gravity low—gives the maximum in "safety first."

Timken Axles, Front and Rear

It is unnecessary to praise Timken axles to dealers and the public. It is known that they cost more because they are *better*. It is likewise known that a car has to be correctly engineered before it can get the co-operation of the Timken organization and the use of Timken Axles.

In building the Century we use the best at every point. Nothing less will do.

Century a Wonderfully Clean Car

Frequent doping and oiling is unnecessary. And yet every bearing and every moving part is perfectly lubricated. The springs work in graphited bushings, self-lubricating and noiseless. The steering columns are mounted on imported self-aligning ball bearings, the steering knuckles on extra large Timken roller bearings and even the brake rods are mounted on ball bearings. These bearings contribute to the remarkable ease of steering that is a feature of the Century and they require lubrication not oftener than once a season.

Those are some of the *big* features of the Century. Throughout you will notice thousands of minor refinements that show the care employed in designing every detail of the finest electric car built.

Ball Bearing Steering Post

Some live thoughts for live dealers—get them!

Do you begin to see why this double-drive Century is creating a disturbance in the electric car market? Why buyers everywhere are asking dealers "What do you know about the Century?"

Do you really and truly appreciate what a big thing it means for any dealer to have a car that includes within itself so many striking points of superiority?

Do you begin to see why big electric car distributors and dealers everywhere are writing for territory? Why, even dealers who have never handled electrics are figuring on making

Fall and Winter profits pushing the Century! Think for a moment of the absolute mechanical supremacy of the Century. Recollect that the Century *organization* is not a new nor an untried one—and this remarkable double-drive model is the unhampered development of three years' specialization and study.

Then get in touch with us immediately—you will want to be the dealer in your locality to have the sales rights for "the car of Instinctive Control." We suggest that you note the financial and manufacturing strength of our organization—and then—*apply at once* for territory.

CENTURY ELECTRIC CAR COMPANY
DETROIT, MICHIGAN

Prices of 1916 Electrics Reduced

Greater Sales Opportunity—Open Types More Popular—Body Work Improved

Speed Increased and Weight Cut—Lubrication Simplified—Battery Rental Increasing

THE dealer in electric passenger cars can offer for this year better value than ever before For although the electrics are refined and improved in many ways, factories, by internal economies and increased production and standardization of chassis offer their cars at much lower cost in most cases. Price lowering is the big feature of the year in the industry.

There is no explanation necessary of the fact that this is a general power for increased sales, for it directly broadens the field. In making reductions on all of its models on an average of $700 per car, one of the largest makers of electrics has planned and is meeting a practically doubled output, which is an illustration of just what the changing of price in the right direction can do. In other cases reductions range from $150 to $200, on the average.

Dealers' Field Broadened

With the coming of electric roadsters and cabriolet types, the dealer does not need to confine his activities in the selling of electrics to the feminine contingent alone. In the past the manufacturers largely overlooked the fact that the electric could be made a vehicle of general utility to the business or professional man who had to have a car of utmost dependability and freedom from troublesome delays. They centered their selling activities, and trained their dealers to think along a narrow path, approaching only those who might require a car for social use or for the lady.

But they have now reached out for the broader field, and for the man of affairs who requires a car to wend in and out of congested city traffic with no stopping and starting delays the open types of masculine appearance and sturdy construction have been especially built. With solid tires the electric of today is built to run very satisfactorily, and thus even the possibility of tire trouble is eliminated where dependability and assurance of getting to a certain point at a prescribed time is of vital importance. Most of the leading makers are supplying such roadster and convertible top models, and the dealer makes a mistake who does not pay as much attention to

---

SPECIAL FEATURES

More Cabriolets and Roadsters

Speed Nearly 30 Miles per Hour

Mileage per Charge About 100

Aluminum for Bodies and Fenders

Steel Forgings Replace Castings

Oiling Simpler; Grease-cups Rare

---

this newer field for the electric as he does to the admittedly large class of people who want an electric for purely social purposes within the city.

Not only can the seller offer the advantages enumerated above when going after the business man, but he can now tell him that such a car is capable of pretty close to 30 miles an hour speed. This is more than the speed limits of any city in the country, so that it seems there is nothing left to criticize from the standpoint of utility and speed. Then, too, many of the cars are now offered with a total mileage per charge that is close to 100, which is as much running as one could possibly do in any one day, even if short trips to suburban points were often necessary.

Weight Reduced

In the past some objection has been encountered by the dealer on the grounds of the weight of the electric car, but the manufacturers are helping him out in this direction also by cutting it down wherever possible by the simplification of the chassis construction and a general combing down process.

For example, there is a widening use of aluminum for the bodies and fenders. This naturally plays a very important part. In the batteries there is also reduced weight, one prominent maker by a change in the form of the battery, cutting out 50 pounds at this point alone. Another point where weight has been re-

---

duced is in the rear axle, several of the new models having lighter rear units due to a few minor changes that do not alter the general design.

Again lightness is fostered by the use of better materials. The Anderson Electric Car Co., for instance, has been able to curtail the weight to a considerable extent by the substitution of pressed steel forged parts for previously-used cast pieces. Thus, not only are these stronger than the old parts, but they weigh less. Light weight is also especially a prominent feature in such cars as the Ward, Milburn and Baker.

Another very important thing that the electric salesman can tell the prospect this year is the improvement in the lubrication of the car. In nearly every case some of the former points of lubrication by grease cups have been eliminated and self-lubricating bushings substituted for them. The advantages of this are many, for they render the car much more fool-proof.

Lubrication Simplified

In the steering mechanism this extensive elimination of points for lubrication care is especially noticeable. One or two of the leading makes, in fact, have so arranged things that there is not a single grease cup under the car. Greater accessibility to those that have not been eliminated is another talking point.

Even more beautiful body work than has been done in the past now characterizes the electrics, if such is possible. As a general thing, the demonstrator can point with pardonable pride to the unity between the battery hoods and the body proper, each blending with a pleasing curve into the other with an effect that is most desirable. This is largely accomplished by making the body panels and the hood sides of the same sheet of aluminum or other material, and not only is it more beautiful but it makes for a more substantial unit. There is no chance for vibration or road jarring to pull the hoods away from the body as might have been the case in older designs where the hoods were separate and simply attached to the main body.

Quietness is most accentuated in the electric, as every dealer knows, and with

---

This 1916 article gives an insight into the electric car market at that time.

the almost general use of either worm or spiral-bevel gearing in the rear axle, there is nothing to be attacked at this point. Either type of drive is most efficient from the standpoint of quiet operation.

Luxurious Interiors

Internally the coach work of the modern electric is second to none. In the average case, it does not seem that the dealer will have to expend any great effort in selling this part of the vehicles. In some instances better upholstery has been fitted, deepening the seats and shaping the backs so as to be even more comfortable than in the past. Arm rests have appeared in profusion, and little fittings, such as toilet cases and handy devices that promote the pleasures of driving are almost universally used in the models designed to appeal to the feminine mind in particular.

The forward and rear drives are holding their own, and every maker who has brought one out is continuing it for the new season. They are of a certain utility value that cannot be gainsaid. Little refinements in the double control mechanism have been made, these seeking to make easier the shift from the front to rear seat drive or vice versa.

During the year the electric vehicle manufacturers have fostered better garaging and maintenance facilities for electrics, and a movement has gained much headway looking to offering free day parking facilities in many of the downtown garages in the big cities. Where the half-hour or hour parking limit on the streets of congested districts of some of the big cities is enforced it becomes necessary to have some place to keep the car while shopping, attending the theater or keeping business appointments.

Most electrics are not intended especially for chauffeur operation, hence it is even more important than with other types of cars where a chauffeur can drive the car away to some unrestricted street while waiting for the return of the lady or gentlemen.

Battery Rental Increasing

Many dealers have taken up the battery rental plan, by which they sell a man a car at a certain price minus the battery. Then they supply him with charged battery service for a certain rate a month. This seems to be very satisfactory and helps sales in many communities, but it is a plan that must be adopted with the utmost caution and foresight if the best interests of all concerned are to be promoted. The dealer must have certain stipulations in his rental contract that will protect him in the event of damage to the car through accident, and at the same time he must render a service that will leave no room for complaints.

Three Baker R and L types

From top to bottom—Woods, Waverley, Ohio

Henry Ford and Thos. A. Edison buy

Henry Ford and His New 1914 Detroit Electric Equipped with Edison Batteries

Thos. A. Edison and His New 1914 Detroit Electric Equipped with Edison Batteries

How Would You Like to Have These Master Minds Help You Choose Your Electric Car?

Think what a great privilege it would be to have the advice of Henry Ford, the world's greatest automobile manufacturer, and Thomas A. Edison, the world's greatest electrical authority, in settling the problem of which electric to buy.

We can offer you the result of their investigation and the benefit of their judgment on electric cars. Mr. Ford has owned three Detroit Electrics; and this is the only make of electric car he has ever owned. Mr. Edison has owned three Detroit Electrics; and these are the only electric cars he has ever owned since we placed our cars on the market.

Why not be guided by these two men in choosing your electric? Their repeated purchases of Detroit Electric cars furnish the strongest endorsement they can give.

Advice Worth Millions

It is equivalent to what their advice would be if you were able to take them with you as you examine electric cars and choose the one you will buy.

Mr. Ford and Mr. Edison are only two of many men of national prominence in the automobile world, who after thorough investigation have purchased Detroit Electric cars. A partial list of these critical owners includes:

Henry B. Joy, President, Packard Motor Car Co.

C. J. Moore, Operating Mgr., Packard Motor Car Co.

C. H. Wills, Factory Mgr., Ford Motor Co.

Lee Counselman, Vice-Pres. and Gen. Mgr., Chalmers Motor Co.

Geo. W. Dunham, Chief Eng., Chalmers Motor Co.

J. Frank Duryea, Vice-Pres. and Factory Mgr., Stevens-Duryea Automobile Co.

Howard Marmon, President, Nordyke & Marmon Co.

S. J. Kuqua, Vice-Pres., Cole Motor Car Co.

J. Walter Drake, President, Hupmobile Motor Car Co.

Gilbert W. Lee, Director, Lozier Motor Co.

Charles J. Butler, President, Morgan & Wright Co.

Never before in the history of the automobile business has any one manufacturer been able to offer such concrete proof of the superior design, material and workmanship of his product as is shown by the choice of such men as these.

These Men Know

These men know the advantages of a manufactured car as compared with an assembled one. They realize the advantage of the Detroit Electric chainless direct shaft drive power plant; the large powerful motor; the patented braking system; the pure aluminum plate in bodies, window sash and fenders; the refined elegance of the upholstery, painting and general appointments of the Detroit Electric.

The Car of the Year

Detroit Electric cars this year—as always—offer you the highest possible perfection in motor car building—utmost elegance and beauty in design and finish, the most modern features of convenience and luxury, the best of electrical engineering practice in power, speed, endurance, economy, safety.

A wide range of choice is offered in our list of models:

With Bevel Gear Axle:
Victoria $2300
4-Passenger Brougham (Rear Seat Drive) 2550
5-Passenger Brougham (Front Seat Drive) 2800

With Worm Gear Axle:
Gentleman's Roadster 2500
4-Passenger Brougham (Rear Seat Drive) 2850
5-Passenger Brougham (Detroit Duplex Drive) 3000
(Prices f. o. b. Detroit)

Be guided by the example of Ford, Edison and these other motor experts. Write for the Detroit Electric catalog and for our Opportunity for dealers.

Anderson Electric Car Company, Detroit, Mich.
Builders of the Detroit Electric
World's Largest Manufacturers of Electric Pleasure Vehicles

Henry Ford and Thomas Edison were Detroit Electric car owners.

Model 47, Worm Gear Axle, $2850

Detroit Electric Success Is Based on a One-Price Policy

The Detroit Electric policy of one price—and that a fair price—has been a large factor in creating the prestige, the vogue and the leadership which the Detroit Electric today enjoys.

The Detroit Electric price is not only one price to all, but absolutely the lowest price at which a car of Detroit Electric quality can be sold. Large production makes possible the lower price.

Price doesn't really mean anything except in relation to value. A few hundred dollars added to the price (and then taken off by a cut in price or an excessive allowance for a used car) doesn't change the quality of the car. You dealers don't gain anything in selling an over-priced car.

Detroit Electric cars are sold at catalog prices. They are known as one-price cars. You never have to apologize for, or defend, Detroit Electric prices; for Detroit Electric cars offer the biggest electric car values on the market. They combine the most modern features of electric car construction with the utmost elegance in design and appointments. And their prices are from $300 to $500 lower than corresponding models of cars not nearly equaling the Detroit Electric in quality.

Detroit Electric cars are easy to sell—and they stay sold. Detroit Electric owners are satisfied owners. Write for our beautiful new catalog. Ask for information about our opportunity to dealers.

THE **Detroit** *ELECTRIC*

Anderson Electric Car Company
DETROIT, MICH.

Builders of The Detroit Electric   *Largest Manufacturers of Electric Pleasure Vehicles*

The Detroit Electric cars were produced until the late 1930's, despite the small market of the 1920's and later.

189

A car of French design of the very latest fashion.

HUPP-YEATS
ELECTRIC

$1750

The things you admire most in this car
also have a most practical purpose

The sloping hood, the curved roof, the low-hung body— all of these features which you so greatly admire in the Hupp-Yeats are much more than mere happy accidents of design.

The rare beauty of the Hupp-Yeats serves a serious and practical purpose by contributing factors of safety and economy which greatly enhance the value of the car.

The sloping hood, the curved roof, the low-hung body— these three charming characteristics were designed to reduce the wind resistance encountered by cars of the old style.

If you have ever operated an electric car, you will realize at once how much this feature contributes to conservation of power and economy of current.

But even this advantage is of secondary importance to the fact that the low-hung body of the Hupp-Yeats and the perfect balance of weight were designed to eliminate, and do eliminate, 75% of the danger of skidding.

The same engineering principle prevents the likelihood of overturning (always possible when the body is high above the ground), and the Hupp-Yeats is less liable to this danger than other electric cars.

The beauty of the Hupp-Yeats alone is sufficiently striking to induce you to give it preference over any other car.

But you are not asked to rest content with this superiority.

It assures you, in addition, 50% less wind resistance; 75% less danger of skidding; no danger of overturning; 400 pounds less weight than the average electric, by reducing the number of constituent parts; 75 to 90 miles on one charge of the batteries; and a speed capacity of 17 to 20 miles per hour.

After reciting these advantages—vital to safety, comfort and economy of operation, which no other electric affords—is it necessary to urge you to write for the literature or have a demonstration of the Hupp-Yeats?

The Hupp-Yeats is guaranteed for life.   Design covered by letters patent.

R. C. H. SALES COMPANY, Dept. P, DETROIT, MICHIGAN

Branches in the following cities: DETROIT—Woodward and Warren Avenues   CHICAGO—1509 Michigan Avenue
KANSAS CITY—34th Street and Broadway   MINNEAPOLIS—1334 Nicollet Avenue

The Hupp-Yeats was "A car of French design of the very latest fashion."

Houk Wire Wheels on Beardsley Electric Cars in front of famous Mission Inn, Riverside, Cal.

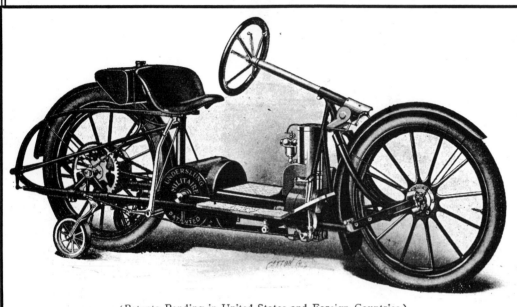
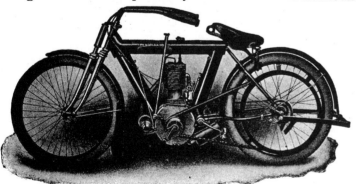
Motorcycling was a popular sport then, as it is today. The above ads (1912) illustrate two of the many models then on the market.

10 Dominant Manufacturers Build Extra Well

Ten big motor truck manufacturers stand out prominently as those whose products find biggest use among the large concerns who buy carefully. The stability of these ten manufacturers is assured—their combined capitalization is $250,000,000: the value of their yearly output runs high into the millions.

Each builds the best truck he can.

Each offers guarantees backed by tremendous resources, tremendous manufacturing facilities; big, strong organizations, established business reputation.

In essential specifications, established practice is closely adhered to.

Eight build trucks in excess of four ton capacity. All build from one to four ton.

Yet with all the tremendous competition, with the tremendous manufacturing efforts to build the best, SERVICE motor trucks stand out among the ten with certain definite marked advantages of big value to purchasers.

Only one of the ten furnishes tires on all types that equal SERVICE in size.

Only one other is built to operate with perfect safety at the same high speed.

SERVICE is the only one of the big ten using the vacuum feed system, assuring maximum fuel economy, steady uniform fuel supply.

Eight use the worm drive: but SERVICE worm drive construction is the strongest that manufacturing ingenuity can devise.

Nine use pressed steel frames, but in the SERVICE motor truck pressed steel frame, greater width of flange, depth of frame, more uniform distribution of load assures maximum resistance to driving stress and strain and clinches SERVICE superiority.

Five use motors of same power as SERVICE, yet SERVICE shows an 11% higher rating than the other four trucks of equal capacity.

In chassis size SERVICE gives greater loading length than any other of ten. This means a larger loading platform—greater carrying capacity—greater even distribution of load. Despite the over-size in construction SERVICE motor trucks, in each model, are notably light in weight. With these points of leadership and with every other feature of construction duplicating even the most expensive of the trucks manufactured by these ten big manufacturers, SERVICE presents a remarkably low initial cost.

67% of Service Motor Trucks Were Re-orders in 1916
60% of Service Motor Trucks Were Re-orders in 1915

Wherever big purchasers, basing their orders on proved mechanical superiority or demonstrated superior service features, are installing motor truck equipment, SERVICE motor trucks are found.

And the big feature that stands out prominently in the history of

SERVICE trucks is the fact that in each year's business 60% of the sales are re-sales to satisfied customers. They are in use by the biggest corporations all over the country, in every line of work, achieving economy results and standards of operating service that make the use of the first SERVICE truck the basis for fleet orders.

6 Sizes of Service Trucks Wait to Do Your Work

SERVICE motor trucks are designed to meet the hardest working conditions—to stay in service day in and day out without time lost for repairs, to operate with minimum mechanical attention, with freedom from necessity for replacement. They are an engineering achievement, particularly built for big practical service.

Each model is built for the especial work it has to do—and range is from the 1-ton model for fast, economical moving of light loads up to the big 5-ton truck for the heaviest hauling. All have been tried out through years of usage. Each is as

individual in design as though it were the sole product of the factory. This is the only way in which proper construction can be achieved. SERVICE trucks are the product of specialists.
Buy now while these startling prices prevail—before the advance in price takes place:

1-ton truck	.	.	$1,375	3½-ton truck	.	$3,000
1½-ton truck	.	.	1,950	3½-ton truck (Special contractor's)		3,250
2-ton truck	.	.	2,250	5-ton truck	.	4,000

13 Point Booklet
Send for our Big Illustrated Thirteen Point Booklet. It is a concise compilation of facts of tremendous importance to you in your selection of Motor Trucks.

Service Motor Truck Company
Main Office and Factory
Wabash, Indiana
Dept. T1

Chicago, Ill.	St. Louis, Mo.	Boston, Mass.	Indianapolis, Ind.	Milwaukee, Wis.	Baltimore, Md.	Canton, Ohio	Washington, D. C.	Hoboken, N. J.	Tulsa, Okla.
New York, N. Y.	Louisville, Ky.	Brooklyn, N. Y.	Buffalo, N. Y.	Bridgeport, Conn.	Columbus, Ohio	Pittsburgh, Pa.	Savannah, Ga.	Philadelphia, Pa.	Detroit, Mich.
Norfolk, Va.	Omaha, Neb.	Newark, N. J.	Salt Lake City, Utah	Des Moines, Iowa	Cincinnati, Ohio	Denver, Colo.	New Orleans, La.	Rochester, N. Y.	Youngstown, O.

The field of trucks and commercial vehicles was intensely competitive. The Service truck shown above was one of the leading makes.

COMMERCIAL VEHICLES
"Recognized as America's Highest Standard"

MODEL R-16, 3-TON BREWERY TRUCK

MODEL M-17, 5-TON FRUIT TRUCK

Perfected through twelve years of practical service in every field of industrial and civic use. Manufactured throughout in the most completely equipped automobile factory in the East. Built in a wide variety of models suitable for every business or civic requirement. Catalogs mailed upon request.

KNOX AUTOMOBILE COMPANY, Springfield, Mass.
Branches—New York; Chicago

MODEL M-3, COMBINATION FIRE CAR

MODEL R-16, 4-TON COAL TRUCK

The Knox Automobile Company of Springfield, Massachusetts was busy in the truck field - as the above ad illustrates.

How Atterbury factory methods conquer bad roads.

A trip through the Atterbury factory would show you three big reasons why the Atterbury gives 100% service, no matter what the condition of road or load:

10 years of truck making experience behind each ATTERBURY

First: No Atterbury workman is ever in a hurry. Every operation must be done right, or not at all.

Second: No piece of material can go into the Atterbury that is not the very best that money can buy.

Third: No Atterbury truck can leave the factory until the general manager himself has approved its road-test card.

Write for the name of the nearest Atterbury dealer.

ATTERBURY MOTOR CAR COMPANY
BUFFALO, N. Y.

ATTERBURY
MOTOR TRUCKS OF   MAXIMUM SERVICE

Atterbury invited would-be truck buyers to tour its factory.

Hauling Mexican dollars—

The Doane Motor Truck Company, San Francisco, used this 5-ton Doane Truck to deliver 350,000 Mexican dollars from the Steamer Jason to The Crocker National Bank of San Francisco. It is completely equipped with

GOODRICH
WIRELESS
TRUCK TIRES

F. H. Doane wrote us March 5, 1914—

"This truck . . . has been operating in our teaming business two years yesterday. Regarding tire equipment — Goodrich Wireless — we are pleased to state that we are still using the original fronts, the rears being replaced last December after twenty-one months' service, which ran far above the guaranteed mileage . . . We therefore highly recommend your equipment."

What Goodrich Wireless Tires are doing for The Doane Motor Truck Company, they will do for you.

The B. F. Goodrich Company

Factories: AKRON, OHIO   Branches in All Principal Cities

Goodrich Wireless Truck Tires - 1914.

196

TWELVE PASSENGER BRAKE WITH CANOPY TOP.

FOR the business man seeking an investment of unquestionable paying value, there is nothing on the market that will compete with our automobiles built for the conveyance of passengers. The points aimed at in their construction — speed, simplicity, wide radius of action, and economy — are recognized as characteristic of the **CHICAGO MOTOR VEHICLES.** The power, speed, and control of our **HOTEL BUSSES, OPEN** and **COVERED EXPRESS WAGONS,** and **AUTO-COACHES** are universally admitted. We also make automobiles for purposes of pleasure. Records of the most convincing kind — buyers invariably pleased. Write us at once, before some one else secures the Auto-Coach line in your city. Write for Catalogue **F.**

CHICAGO MOTOR VEHICLE CO., 370-372 WABASH AVE., CHICAGO, ILL.
Factory: Harvey, Ill.

THIRTY-TWO-PASSENGER FUNERAL COACH WHICH HAS TELEPHONES AND PULLMAN CAR LUXURIES

Two interesting special-purpose vehicles.

On these two facing pages are commercial vehicles from the 1910-1915 era.

"Best Selling Motor Truck on the Market"

THE International Motor Truck is a light-haul, quick-delivery truck that sells. It is ideal in size, capacity, and price for seven out of every ten truck prospects.

Every *International Motor Truck* on the street is a tireless booster for more sales. Remember there are more Internationals in use than any other truck made.

The International Motor Truck is saving money and increasing the trade of thousands of firms in over one hundred lines of business. There are scores of prospects in your neighborhood, just waiting to be shown what this truck will do for them.

Mechanically, the truck is right. It makes good. You need a good light truck to sell. We need good agents.

Write us for information, terms and territory

International Harvester Company of America

(INCORPORATED)

155 Harvester Building   Chicago USA

MANLY TRUCKS—The Biggest Advance in Truck Construction of the Decade, 1½ and 2½-ton Models

DEALERS WRITE

MANLY MOTOR CORPORATION

Factory, Waukegan, Ill.   General Offices, 1432 Michigan Ave., Chicago

---

1000 Lb. Electric Truck

Standard in Every Detail

Sets a new mark in quality, service, efficiency and economy.

| Bare Chassis including Driver's Seat $1450 | Express Body $1500 | Panel Body $1600 |

The first electric truck at a popular price. Write or wire for catalog and proposition.

M & P ELECTRIC VEHICLE COMPANY

Franklin and Dubois Sts., Detroit, Mich.

Automatic Military Band
With Motor Truck

Style No. 1110

18 Music Selections

82 Keys

For Circuses and Advertising Purposes

DESCRIPTION

Body, 13 ft. 8 in. long and 6 ft. 9 in. wide, inside.

Double doors in the rear, and ventilated top.

Ornamented with wood carvings and pillars and carvings on side and rear panels.

The end and side panels are hinged at the bottom, and lean outward 6 in. from the top, in order to allow the music to be heard and to protect the instrument during damp weather.

The side panels are easily removed during fair weather, leaving an opening on each side uncovering the front. To protect the instrument, in case of emergency, canvas roll curtains are placed at the top of the instrument ready to be drawn down in case of sudden rain.

The panels, rear doors and sides and also curtains are ornamented with oil paintings.

Permanent blind work in lower panels to allow ventilation, but exclude dampness.

Top of body is finished with scroll work, among which may be placed hexagon signs which revolve, showing 6 signs one every 30 seconds, on the rear end and both sides and lighted by electric lights.

The signs and the lights in signs are run by an electric motor which receives its power from a storage battery placed in strong boxes situated behind the instrument just inside rear doors, and covered with cushions, making them comfortable seats for attendants.

The chassis is a three-ton truck and has single tires in front and dual tires in the rear.

The chassis is supplied with a cab seat, a mica front curtain and side curtains, and regular standard equipment, including headlight with Presto tank, and is sold under regular guarantee of the motor truck company.

The wheels of the chassis are equipped with sunbursts which are covered with gold leaf, the same as are the carvings and columns on the body.

The body and chassis may be painted any color purchaser desires.

Signs and side panels of body lettered in gold.

The North Tonawanda Musical Instrument Works, a leading manufacture of mechanical musical instruments, outfitted a Mack truck with a military band organ. It was just the thing to head a circus parade.